The European Struggle
to Settle North America

# The European Struggle to Settle North America

*Colonizing Attempts by England, France and Spain, 1521–1608*

Margaret F. Pickett *and*
Dwayne W. Pickett

McFarland & Company, Inc., Publishers
*Jefferson, North Carolina, and London*

Library of Congress Cataloguing-in-Publication Data

Pickett, Margaret F.
The European struggle to settle North America : colonizing
attempts by England, France and Spain, 1521–1608 / Margaret F.
Pickett and Dwayne W. Pickett.
p.     cm.
Includes bibliographical references and index.

ISBN 978-0-7864-5932-2
softcover : 50# alkaline paper ∞

1. Europe — Colonies — America — History.   2. North
America — Discovery and exploration — European.   3. North
America — Colonization.   4. Great Britain — Colonies —
America.   5. France — Colonies — America.   6. Spain —
Colonies — America.   7. Jamestown (Va.) — History.   8. Québec
(Province) — History.   9. Saint Augustine (Fla.) — History.
I. Pickett, Dwayne W., 1966–   II. Title.
E101.P54   2011
970.01— dc22                                            2010049922

British Library cataloguing data are available

Front cover: Map by Baptista Boazio depicting Sir Francis Drake's
attack in 1586 on St. Augustine (State Archives of Florida); (inset)
Pedro Menéndez de Avilés (Library of Congress)

Manufactured in the United States of America

*McFarland & Company, Inc., Publishers*
*Box 611, Jefferson, North Carolina 28640*
*www.mcfarlandpub.com*

In memory of Don,
loving husband to Margaret
and father to Dwayne — we miss you.

To Susan,
loving wife to Dwayne
and daughter-in-law to Margaret.

Don and Susan,
you both gave us much encouragement and support.

# Table of Contents

# Authors' Note

The North American continent encompasses a vast area stretching from Central America and the islands of the Caribbean northward to Greenland. This large area is often, unofficially, divided into subregions. "Northern America," which consists of Bermuda, Canada, Greenland, the islands of Saint Pierre and Miquelon, and the continental United States, is one of these subregions. It is this area that is covered in our book.

By the time the Spanish made their first attempt at settlement in "Northern America" in 1521, they already controlled Mexico and several Caribbean islands. Since we were concerned with colonizing attempts in the unsettled areas of "Northern America," we have not included the settlement of Mexico and the Caribbean islands in this book. Following the example of such scholars as Woodbury Lowery, David Beers Quinn and R. C. Simmons, however, we have used the term North America when referring to "Northern America."

# *Preface and Acknowledgments*

The idea for this book came from a visit to a museum in the old city of St. Augustine some five years ago. The museum chronicled the struggles of the Spanish to establish a foothold in Florida — a land they had discovered in 1513 — and also briefly told the story of French attempts to colonize the area. The information gleaned from this visit was recalled the following year during a discussion of the forthcoming anniversary of the founding of Jamestown. We were talking about the many problems encountered by the English as they tried to establish a colony in Virginia — the failure of the Roanoke and Popham settlements and the tremendous effort required to establish Jamestown. We wondered if the Spanish and French had found it equally difficult to found their permanent settlements. This, of course, brought to mind the visit to the museum in St. Augustine. Obviously, the Spanish and French, like the English, had struggled and been unsuccessful in their colonizing attempts before finally establishing a permanent settlement. We were curious: why were the colonies founded at St. Augustine, Jamestown and Québec successful while the other settlements were not?

Thus began our quest for more information about European settlements in North America, a quest that led us to an enormous amount of information, which we have condensed into this book. While not designed to be an exhaustive study of each settlement, this book will hopefully enlighten readers, contribute to their knowledge of these early settlements and help them understand the people who came to settle the land as well as those who were displaced by their coming.

The book is written from a European viewpoint. The land in North America had been occupied for thousands of years; however, since no Christian nation was dwelling there, the Europeans considered the land uninhabited. The Europeans called the people they found living in North America Indians or natives. For the sake of consistency we refer to the occupants of North America as Indian people, Indians or native people instead of using the more modern term "Native American."

1

New Spain, New France and Virginia were territories composed of vague and overlapping areas, which were not clearly understood in their time and are equally confusing to the modern reader. Therefore, we have used the modern names for most of the places visited or settled by European explorers. The country we know today as Spain was, during part of the time period discussed, composed of two countries: Aragon and Castile. For clarity's sake we refer to these lands collectively as Spain throughout the book.

Spelling of proper names and places is always a challenge when writing about this time period—for there was no standardized spelling. European writers spelled words phonetically and often people spelled their own names differently in the same document. The spelling of Indian words is particularly challenging, as they vary greatly from one European writer to the next. We have had to pick one spelling from among the many and would like our readers to be aware that they may encounter the same word spelled differently in another volume. We have also anglicized the names of some of the Spanish, French and Portuguese rulers.

A project of this size could not have been completed without the support and assistance of many people. First of all, we would like to acknowledge the encouragement and support of Don and Susan, our respective spouses, to whom we have dedicated our book. Their belief in our ability to achieve our goals kept us on track during the many months it took to research, write and rewrite the book. We would also like to thank three good friends at Colonial National Historical Park at Historic Jamestowne for their support: Rangers Bill Warder, Lee Cotton and Kirk Kehrberg, with a special thanks to Bill, whose knowledge and understanding of the past is incredible and who was always willing to read material and discuss ideas.

We would like to thank artist Caroline Taylor for her original drawings and acknowledge our appreciation for the time and effort she put into researching the subjects. We are indebted to Heather Harvey for the excellent maps and want to thank her for finding time in her busy schedule to draw them. The rest of our illustrations were obtained from libraries and state archives, and we are grateful for the time and patience of the employees who helped us locate the images we were seeking. In particular we would like to thank Ann Marie Holland and Gregory Houston of the McGill University Library, Mary Haegert and John Overholt of the Houghton Library at Harvard University, Yuhua Li of the Widener Library at Harvard University, Dana Puga of the Library of Virginia, N. Adam Watson of the State Archives of Florida and Keith Longiotti of the University of North Carolina University Library. Last we would like to thank Wayne Melanson, Interpretation Officer at Port-Royal National Historic Site of Canada, for helping with the translation of the keys to Champlain's drawings.

# Introduction

Around the year 982 Eric Thorvaldson, also known as Eric the Red for the color of his beard, was exiled for three years from his home in Iceland for killing two men. He spent his period of banishment exploring an area he discovered to the west of Iceland and, when his exile was over, returned home with tales of a land that promised a better life. He called the new territory Greenland in hopes of making this ice-covered region sound more appealing and immediately began to recruit setters to colonize it. In 986 he returned to Greenland with several ships filled with settlers and established two promising sites on the west coast. More settlers from Iceland came later and soon the two sites, known as the Western Settlement and the Eastern Settlement, were thriving.

Archeological evidence suggests that there were several agricultural communities clustered around the two settlements. The people had livestock — horses, sheep and cattle; they raised barley, gathered wild plants and berries and fished in the nearby waters. Archeologists found primitive forges, where iron tools were shaped from the bog iron found nearby. Wool from the sheep was spun and woven into warm garments for the long winters. They were a prosperous people, living in large divided houses with central hearths and wearing the latest fashions from Europe, for they had things of value to trade. Ships arrived on a regular basis from Norway, bringing goods and sailing away with walrus ivory and white falcons, which the Emperor Frederick II had made popular with European noblemen. The people were Christian, for archeologists found the remains of a cathedral and ten parish churches in the Eastern Settlement. At one time the population was estimated to be close to five thousand people; but by the middle of the 15th century, they had completely disappeared and Greenland and its settlements were all but forgotten by Europeans.

According to the sagas — ancient Norse stories handed down orally from generation to generation — and historical records, the migration of Norse people to lands outside their country began with a move to Iceland in 874. From there, some went with Eric the Red in 986 to establish settlements in Greenland. Their new home had a drawback, though, for it was lacking in trees, and some of the settlers began to explore the ocean to the west in search of lands where they

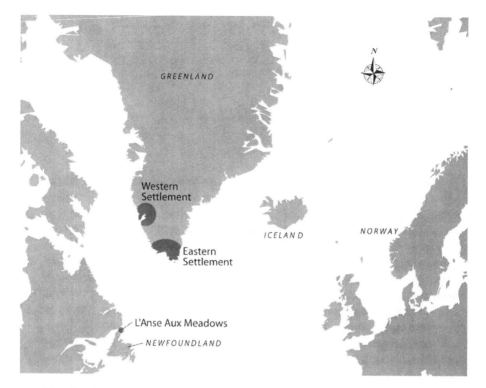

Map showing Norse settlements in Greenland and Newfoundland (Heather Harvey).

could obtain much-needed timber. We have no idea of the places they visited, but about the year 1000 Eric's son Leif Ericsson discovered a promising land with meadows for grazing cattle, a pleasing climate and good fishing — he called it Vinland for the wild grapes he found growing there. Soon settlers came there to live.

In the 1960s archeologists discovered the remains of two large divided houses with central hearths similar to those found earlier in Greenland near Epaves Bay on the Great Northern Peninsula of Newfoundland. They found several smaller houses clustered around the larger ones and the evidence of a primitive forge. Norse artifacts were found indicating that both men and women lived there for a time before abandoning the site. Dr. Helge Ingstad, who with his wife, archeologist Anne Stine Ingstad, directed the excavation, estimated that possibly seventy-five to ninety people were living there at one time. The place is now called L'Anse aux Meadows and it is located in Newfoundland, but in the year 1000 it was part of Vinland.[1]

Greenland and Newfoundland were sites of the earliest attempts by Europeans to plant colonies in the strange new lands in the Atlantic. These lands were discovered and settled without fanfare or publicity and, when the settlements there were abandoned or disappeared, the rest of the world took little notice. The exploits and hardships of the people were recalled only in the sagas—told around the central hearths of the Norse to while away the tedium of the long winter nights.

About a hundred years after the disappearance of the Greenland settlements—in the 16th and early 17th centuries, a new wave of Europeans ventured out into the Atlantic to plant colonies in the newly discovered lands of North America. They faced many of the same problems and hardships that confronted the earlier settlers, and some of their settlements would be abandoned or disappear. However, some would survive and become permanent. They paved the way for others, and North America would be forever changed.

As the first decade of the 17th century came to a close, there were three small European settlements in North America. St. Augustine, started by the Spanish in 1565, was situated in a vulnerable spot on the east coast of present-day Florida. The English settlement at Jamestown, Virginia, had been founded in 1607 and had come very close to being abandoned. And Québec, established by the French in 1608, was maintaining itself by the efforts of a few hardy souls. These colonies would prove to be permanent, successful settlements, but they came only after each of those three European powers had failed in previous attempts to plant colonies in North America.

Why were these early attempts at settlement in North America unsuccessful? And why did St. Augustine, Jamestown and Québec succeed where the others failed? This book examines the factors that contributed to the making of three successful colonies and those that ultimately doomed 13 earlier attempts.

# ONE

# The Beginning

## Setting the Stage

By the beginning of the 15th century Europeans had gained considerable knowledge of the world around them. Educated people knew that the world was a sphere and understood the concept of latitude and longitude. They recognized three large landmasses — Europe, Africa and Asia — although they had no idea of the exact size of any of them. Iceland, they believed, was the most northern inhabited land, although some may have remembered the existence of Greenland. Learned people knew from explorations in Africa that "The Indies," as they collectively called the Far East, could be reached from the east coast of Africa across the Indian Ocean, but they did not realize that the Indian Ocean could be approached from the Atlantic around Africa. Cipangu (Japan) was recognized as a large island off the coast of Cathay (China), but it was not known how far away it was.

During the 15th century improvements in navigation enabled Europeans to extend their knowledge of the world in a manner that had not been possible before. Armed with a compass, quadrant and/or astrolabe and using the North Star as a reference, seafarers were able to measure latitude at sea; they used a system based on compass direction, time and speed — called dead reckoning — to measure longitude. Ships were thus able to sail on the wide expanse of the Atlantic, out of sight of land, and have some reasonable expectation of being able to return to their home port or to find a destination again without difficulty. The Portuguese discovered the clockwise movement of the wind in the northern hemisphere — wind that would allow ships to sail south and then west on the latitude of the Canaries and return east by the Azores.

Many Europeans based their conception of Asia on the writings of Marco Polo, who attributed more land to Asia than is actually there. Europe and Asia, he said, took up so much of the earth's space that only a small part was left to be covered with water. Therefore only a short water passage separated Europe from Asia, and moreover, to sail from one to the other would present no difficulty, as the water passage contained islands that would serve as stopping-off places.

It was the Portuguese who, early in the 15th century, began to actively explore the world and expand their knowledge of it. Under the leadership of Prince Henry the Navigator, the Portuguese sent ships westward out into the Atlantic to search for the mythical island of Antilia, believed to be located somewhere to the west of Portugal. Instead, in 1419 they discovered the Madeira group, and in 1432 three islands of the Azores were found. The islands appeared to be uninhabited, and soon Portugal was sending settlers to live there. The islands proved to be fertile places where crops were easy to grow and cattle flourished, and the discovery led to a heightened interest in finding more such islands. Between 1462 and 1490 there was a concerted effort by the Portuguese to locate these islands—especially since the king might allow the discoverer of an uninhabited island to keep it and reap the rewards of a monopoly of the trade and resources.

Discovering islands did not constitute the sole exploratory aim of the Portuguese. They were also interested in the African trade and the discovery of an eastern sea route to the Indies. With their lateen-rigged caravels, which drew only six feet of water and were the perfect vessel to sail off shore, they began to explore the west coast of Africa. The Portuguese reached Cape Bojador in 1434 and in 1441 brought back the first cargo of gold and slaves from West Africa. They continued to sail down the long coast of Africa — venturing farther with each voyage, hoping that at last they would find a way to enter the Indian Ocean and sail to India.

While the Portuguese were busy discovering islands, sailing the coast of West Africa and establishing trading stations there, the English were exploring the cold waters of the North Atlantic. The seaport of Bristol was interested in finding another mythical island — this one was supposed to be off the west coast of Ireland and was called Hy-Brasil (Gaelic for Isle of the Blest). They were hoping to use it as a base for the new fishing grounds that the city needed and, starting in 1480, ships regularly left Bristol in search of the legendary island.[1]

At the same time a Genoese merchant named Christopher Columbus was busy making plans to seek a western sea route to the Indies. Columbus was greatly influenced by the writings of Marco Polo and others, who were convinced that there was only a narrow passage of water between Europe and Asia. He thought a western water route to the Indies was very practical and, having formulated this plan, he decided to approach John II, king of Portugal, for support. The king was interested, but not enough to sponsor the voyage. The year 1485 saw Columbus in Spain, where he pursued his efforts to obtain royal support for his voyage. In 1486 he had his first audience with King Ferdinand and Queen Isabella of Spain; he was turned down but not totally discouraged. The queen told Columbus to apply again at a more convenient time — when the Moors had been successfully driven from Spain. Columbus then decided to make his offer to John II, again, but by this time it was 1488 and Dias had just rounded the tip of Africa and sailed into the Indian Ocean — John II was no longer interested in a western route to the Indies.

While Columbus waited in Spain for better times, his brother Bartholomew attempted to promote the idea of the western voyage to other European princes. He sailed first to England, where Henry VII turned him down without hesitation. He traveled next to France, where he was received warmly by Charles VIII but never offered any real support. Spain appeared to be the last hope. Finally, in January of 1492, Columbus gained approval for the voyage and in early August set sail.

On October 12, 1492, Columbus landed in the Bahamas and went on to Cuba and Hispaniola (present day Haiti/Dominican Republic). He believed that these were islands off the coast of Asia, and he hurried home to report his success to King Ferdinand and Queen Isabella. He wrote a letter to the Spanish king and queen apprising them of his discovery. The letter, printed in April 1493, was translated into Latin and eventually made its way throughout Europe. His second voyage, in September of 1493, took him to the Lesser Antilles and Puerto Rico, and in January 1494 he founded the first Spanish colony at La Isabela, Hispaniola.

The news of Columbus's discoveries spread throughout Europe, at first in the printed copy of his letter to the Spanish sovereigns and then, for his subsequent voyages, by word of mouth. It caused much excitement and envy and even chagrin on the part of the English and French kings who had turned down the opportunity to sponsor the voyage. It also caused John Cabot, another Genoese mariner, to contemplate a similar western voyage to Asia — but with this difference: he would sail across the Atlantic on a shorter, northern route and reach the coast of northern China in less time than Columbus had taken to reach the islands thought to be off the southern coast of Asia. He tried to gain support in Spain and Portugal but was not successful; then he decided to try England. He and his family moved to Bristol, England, in 1495 — the prosperous seaport whose mariners had been searching for new fishing grounds and the island of Hy-Brasil for 15 years and where his plans were met with enthusiasm.

## The Treaty of Tordesillas

During the 15th century, Spain and Portugal emerged as the two main maritime rivals in Europe. As the Portuguese began to explore the west coast of Africa, they were anxious to keep the Spanish from intruding on their trade and discoveries in the area. They decided to appeal to the Vatican and were able to obtain papal bulls that led to the Treaty of Alcaçoves in 1479. This treaty prohibited the Spanish from exploring or trading below the latitude of Cape Bojador.[2]

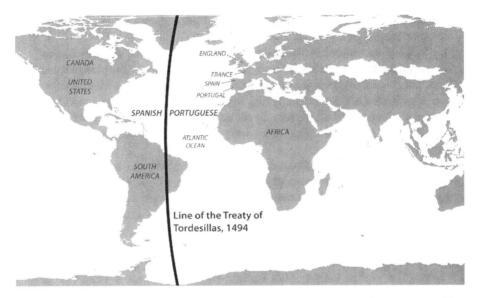

Line of the Treaty of
Tordesillas, 1494

In 1494 Spain and Portugal signed the Treaty of Tordesillas, dividing the world between them. The Spanish claimed all territory west or to the left of the line, which gave them most of the New World. The Portuguese received the land east or to the right of the line, giving them the profitable trading stations on the African coast and control over the trade route to the Far East (Heather Harvey).

On his first voyage, Columbus sailed to lands south of that latitude, and Ferdinand and Isabella could not risk the possibility that the Portuguese would dispute the Spanish claim to this new territory. They, too, approached the Vatican and received a bull of donation on May 4, 1493:

> We, of our own accord, give, grant, and assign to you and your heirs and successors ... all islands and mainlands found and to be found ... towards the west and south, by drawing and establishing a line from the Arctic pole ... to the Antarctic pole ... with this proviso, however, that none of the islands and mainlands ... beyond that said line ... be in actual possession of any Christian King or prince.... We strictly forbid all persons of whatsoever rank ... to dare, without your special permit ... to go for the purpose of trade or any other reason to the islands or mainlands, found or to be found ... said line to be distant one hundred leagues toward the west and south, as aforesaid, from any of the islands commonly known as the Azores and Cape Verdes.[3]

The papal bulls were conflicting, and to settle the matter, the Spanish and Portuguese agreed to reconcile the differences by drawing up the Treaty of Tordesillas. This treaty invalidated the previous competing bulls and redrew the line of demarcation as extending from pole to pole and along the longitude line 370 leagues (approximately 925 miles) west of one of the Cape Verde Islands. The treaty was ratified in 1495.

The treaty consisted of two parts: the Territorial Claim and the Navigation

Law Claim. The Territorial Claim prohibited any exploration or colonization in any of the lands west of the line of Tordesillas by any country except Spain or east of the line by any country other than Portugal. The Navigation Law Claim was aimed at controlling trade in the restricted areas. For example, any country wishing to trade in the Spanish sphere could do so only by following the licensing system in Seville and would have to agree to abide by the Spanish navigation laws, which were very discriminatory.[4] Other countries in Europe considered both parts of the treaty unacceptable, and the Treaty of Tordesillas created friction between Spain and her European rivals for over a century.

The first king to take exception to the Treaty of Tordesillas was King Henry VII of England. John Cabot took his plan of seeking a shorter, northern route to Asia to Henry in late 1495. Henry was not going to let this opportunity slip by; therefore, on March 5, 1496, he gave letters patent to Cabot, granting him full authority to sail to any land in the east, west or north under the English banner. With a crew of 18, Cabot sailed from Bristol about May 20, 1497.

Cabot made landfall on the northeastern coast of Newfoundland on June 24, 1497, and went ashore to take possession of the land for England. He found no native peoples, but he did find items indicating that the land was inhabited. With only 18 crew members, Cabot did not linger long on shore for fear of attack by the natives. He sailed down the entire eastern coast of Newfoundland and, in the waters at the eastern end, found a large number of sizable cod. He reported that the cod were so plentiful that all that was necessary to catch them was to lower a weighted basket into the water and pull it up, teeming with fish. He returned to his original landing point on July 20 and sailed home to Bristol, arriving there on August 6, 1497.

Believing that he had indeed reached an island off the north coast of China, Cabot was anxious to inform Henry VII of his success. Upon landing, he rode quickly to London and had his audience with the king at Westminster on August 10. The king welcomed him warmly and rewarded him generously. Cabot immediately began to plan his next voyage, during which he hoped to sail south and east from his newly discovered island to Japan, where he planned to set up a trading station. On February 3, 1498, he received new letters patent from the king and, with five ships, left Bristol at the beginning of May. One of the ships turned back for repairs shortly after sailing; the other four sailed on and were never seen or heard from again.

Ferdinand and Isabella were not pleased to hear of Henry VII's sponsorship of Cabot's voyage and instructed their ambassador to politely warn Henry that, in approving the voyage, he stood in danger of alienating his good friends the king and queen of Spain. Henry ignored them and the Treaty of Tordesillas, and since Spain and England were allies in a war against France, the Spanish sovereigns did not press him, even when Henry sanctioned Cabot's second voyage. By the time it was clear that Cabot and his fleet of ships were lost at sea, the Spanish realized that the land discovered by Cabot was probably not in their sphere but in that of the Portuguese. Therefore they did not protest the Bristol voyages sponsored by the king from 1501 to 1507. Unfortunately for the English, the voyages were uneventful and nothing new was discovered. There was one more royally sanctioned voyage in 1527 under Henry VIII, but it, too, came to nothing. Thereafter English interest in exploration waned and did not reawaken for a quarter of a century.

The English did not seriously challenge the Treaty of Tordesillas until 1560. During the end of the 15th and the beginning of the 16th centuries, England and Spain were allies in a series of wars against France. As allies, the English were allowed opportunities to trade in the restricted Spanish sphere. These opportunities increased after the marriage of the English King Henry VIII to the Spanish princess Catherine of Aragon. They decreased after their divorce and increased again during the reign of Henry and Catherine's daughter Mary — especially after her marriage to Prince Philip of Spain. As long as they were allowed to trade in the Spanish sphere, the English did not appear to be interested in exploring the New World.

In 1558 Elizabeth I became the queen of England, and two years later the real English challenge to the treaty occurred. Starting in 1560, Elizabethan mariners began to prey on Spanish shipping and to trade in the West Indies without permission. For a time the Spanish were satisfied to deal with these incursions into their territory with diplomacy, but as the number and extent of the raids grew — particularly those led by Sir Francis Drake and John Hawkins — diplomacy proved unsatisfactory. When challenged by the Spanish ambassador, the English replied that their ships had the right to sail where they pleased and trade with whom they pleased and that Spanish laws barring English access to trade in the West Indies were binding only if the Spanish could enforce them.[5]

The English had been slow to explore and colonize in the New World, but during the early years of Elizabeth's reign momentum for settling lands in North America began to grow. The English refused to be intimidated by the Territorial Claim of the Treaty of Tordesillas. Their position was, as the Spanish Ambassador Quadra wrote home on November 23, 1561, "The Pope does not have authority to give nor take away kingdoms."[6]

The most determined challenger to the Treaty of Tordesillas, however, was the French king. Starting in 1494, the French and Spanish were involved in a series of wars. As might be expected during periods of war, French ships frequently attacked and raided Spanish possessions in the Caribbean. When the two countries were at peace, the French were given few if any opportunities to trade in the Spanish territories in the West Indies. The Portuguese also effectively barred them from participation in the African or Brazilian trade. The French therefore decided to take matters into their own hands—first with a challenge to the Portuguese in the North Atlantic.

The Portuguese had not been idle in exploring the cold waters of the North

Atlantic. Starting in 1499, the king of Portugal issued letters patent to several of his Azorean subjects: "to go in search of and discover certain islands of our sphere of influence."[7] Newfoundland, discovered in 1497 by Cabot and claimed for England, was believed to lie on the Portuguese side of the line of Tordesillas, and the king was anxious to settle the land before the English could plant a colony there. The first voyage undertaken found nothing, but the second voyage under Gaspar Corte-Real was more successful. He presumably came upon Newfoundland, which he described as "a land that was very cool and with large trees."[8] He called it Terra Verde and claimed it for Portugal. Unfortunately, Gaspar was lost at sea on his second voyage to the area in 1501, and when his brother Miguel suffered the same fate a year later, interest in exploring the area waned.

The Portuguese had other interests to pursue, for in 1499 Vasco da Gama had rounded the tip of Africa, crossed the Indian Ocean and reached India — the eastern sea route to the Orient had been found. And in 1500 Cabral, on his way down the coast of Africa, was blown off course to the west and discovered a new land in South America, which he claimed for Portugal. Portuguese interest in the North Atlantic was confined to the fishing banks off the coast of Newfoundland. It was there that the first French challenge to the Treaty of Tordesillas was given.

The earliest documented excursion by French fishermen to the cod banks in Newfoundland was 1504. Most probably they encountered fishermen from Portugal there, for by 1506 the volume of fish being brought into Portugal from Newfoundland was so great that the king imposed an import duty on the catch.[9] There is no recorded reaction by the Portuguese to French presence in the area, and Portuguese explorers continued to sail the North Atlantic, discovering and naming various places they visited.

One of these explorers, a man named Fagundes, petitioned the king in 1521 to grant him the right to settle lands he had discovered outside the territory claimed by the Corte-Real brothers. He intended to set up a permanent base in the area so fishermen could cure their catch before shipping it back to Lisbon. He received his grant, recruited settlers from Portugal and the Azores and established a settlement on Cape Breton Island. His colony was successful for over a year, and then the settlers became subject to increasing hostility from the Indians and harassment from French fishermen, who cut their fishing lines and burned their houses. When the settlers received no support from home, they were forced to abandon the colony. There were no further attempts by the Portuguese to settle the area.

The next French challenge came in another part of the New World, namely South America, in the new land discovered by Pedro Alvares Cabral in 1500. Eventually the new land would be called Brazil, for it contained an abundant supply of Brazilwood — a red wood found in several kinds of tropical trees. Brazilwood was good not only for making cabinets but also a source of red and purple dye. Previously dyes had to be imported from India and were very expensive; the textile centers in northern France were especially interested in getting the less costly Brazilwood. Soon French ships began to appear off the coast of Brazil to cut a load of the wood and sail back to France. The voyages increased in number and in 1531 the French decided to establish a trading station on an island off the coast of Brazil. They built a fort and a storehouse for the Brazilwood and left a garrison there to protect it.

The Portuguese might have been willing to overlook French presence off Newfoundland, but they were not willing to have the French cutting Brazilwood and establishing bases near their territory in South America. King John III ordered his men to clear the coast of Brazil of these intruders and destroy any land bases they might have established. This was done in a thoroughly ruthless manner, which so enraged the French that they began to attack Portuguese ships off Europe, Africa or wherever they could find them. They were so successful in these attacks that the Portuguese finally paid them to stop. While the French did not entirely cease from attacking Portuguese ships or occasionally visiting Brazil for a load of the wood, the attacks and voyages lessened considerably and a peace of a sort reigned between the two countries for a while.[10]

In challenging Portugal, the French did not forget Spain and the prohibition against exploring west of the line of Tordesillas. In 1524 Giovanni da Verrazzano sailed along the coast of North America under a French royal commission in flagrant violation of the treaty. Then the French sent Jacques Cartier to North America in 1534 and again in 1535–1536. There is some doubt that the Spanish knew of these voyages, as there appeared to be no formal protest against them.[11] King Francis I of France, seeking to gain recognition of his right to send explorers to the New World, appealed to the pope, and in November 1535 obtained a papal edict stating that the original bulls that divided the new territory in the Americas between the Spanish and Portuguese pertained only to lands actually held by them. As Montmorenci, the constable of France, stated to the Spanish ambassador: "to uninhabited lands, although discovered, anyone may go."[12] To claim the land it must be occupied. This was the French position throughout the century, and it was the basis upon which they established settlements in Brazil, Canada, South Carolina and Florida.

The English and French challenged both parts of the Treaty of Tordesillas—the Territorial Claim and the Navigation Law Claim. Both countries firmly held that "the Popes hold spiritual jurisdiction, but that it does not lie with them to distribute lands among kings..."[13] and "effective occupation"[14] was needed in order to hold claim to a territory—discovered or not. French and English ships sailed in the Caribbean, sometimes trading illegally with Spanish and Portuguese possessions, sometimes raiding them and sometimes attacking the treasure ships from Mexico and South America. They challenged the Spanish and Portuguese to stop them—if they could.

## The World After Columbus

When Columbus reached the islands in the Caribbean, he thought they were merely outlying islands barring the way to Asia and that the continent was but a short distance away. His succeeding voyages were undertaken with the intention of actually landing in Asia. John Cabot, when he discovered New-foundland, thought it was an outpost of China, and during his second voyage intended to sail southeast and find the island of Japan. It would be many years and many voyages and discoveries later before Europeans would be able to gather enough information to come to a better understanding of their discoveries.

In 1513, when the Spaniard Vasco Núñez de Balboa crossed the Isthmus of Panama and discovered the South Sea, as the Pacific Ocean was called, it was seen that the new lands were not Asia after all but a large land mass lying between Europe and Asia. When Magellan circumnavigated the world in 1519–

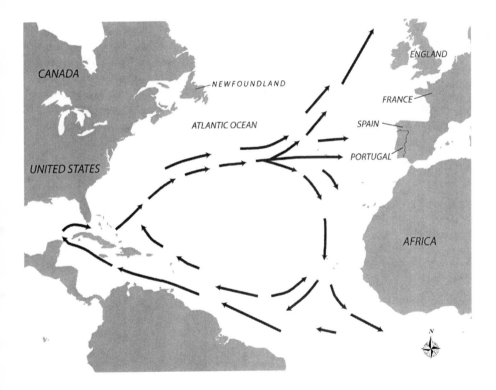

Map showing wind patterns in the Atlantic Ocean. These wind patterns enabled Spanish treasure ships to sail to the New World and return home with their valuable cargoes (Heather Harvey).

1522, Europeans realized that Asia lay on the other side of this large land mass, beyond a vast ocean. So far the only way they had found to reach this ocean and ultimately Asia was to make the long voyage around the southern tip of South America.

But what lay to the north in the area discovered by Cabot? In 1524 Verrazzano sailed up the east coast of North America and Europeans understood that a large land mass lay to the north as well as to the south. Their only hope of a western sea route to Asia lay in finding a way through the northern mass, as Ferdinand Magellan's voyage had shown them there was none in the south. The search for the Northwest Passage through North America would occupy Europeans for the next century.

The Spanish had established colonies in South America, Mexico and the Caribbean Islands, conquered native civilizations and were reaping the rewards of their explorations. Gold, silver, tobacco and pearls were loaded on Spanish ships to make the long voyage back to Spain. Following the Gulf Stream and the clockwise movement of the wind, the treasure ships sailed up the coast of Florida and South Carolina before turning east to catch the winds that would take them to Spain. The French and English cast envious eyes at the riches Spain was reaping from her New World colonies and turned their thoughts to emulating her success. The Spanish and Portuguese controlled the Caribbean and South and Central America, but North America lay unexplored and unsettled. Voyages of discovery were sponsored by the English and French and territory claimed for each country. To claim the land, however, was not enough. In order to hold the territory and defend it from other European powers, a country had to establish a permanent settlement there.

# TWO

# *Spanish Colonization Efforts*

## Juan Ponce de León

By the beginning of the 16th century, the Spanish had established colonies in Hispaniola (present day Haiti/Dominican Republic), Cuba, Puerto Rico, and Jamaica. Spanish explorers sailed the Caribbean looking for other lands and consequently adding to their knowledge of the area. In 1508 Cuba was officially circumnavigated and determined to be an island. Although it is possible at this time that the coast of Florida was seen, it would not be until five years later, in 1513, that Florida was officially discovered and named. The discoverer was Juan Ponce de León, a gentleman volunteer on Columbus's second voyage in 1493, the conqueror of Puerto Rico and at one time its governor.

In 1512 Ponce de León found that he had been replaced as governor of Puerto Rico through no deficiency on his part but through the claims of Diego Columbus, the son of Christopher Columbus, who was entitled by law to the rights of all the lands discovered by his father. In 1509 Spanish authorities had refused to grant Diego these privileges and named Ponce de León governor in his stead. In 1511 Diego took his case to the courts in Madrid and won. Therefore, in 1512, Ponce de León was out of office. He continued living in Puerto Rico with his family; however, he was restless and anxious to add to his large estates and wealth by conquering new lands full of gold and silver and potential slaves. He had heard much of an island to the north of Hispaniola called Bimini, where there was supposed to be a fountain whose waters were said to make old men young again. Whether this was Ponce de León's reason for wanting to discover it or not, he petitioned the king for permission to search for the island, and on February 23, 1512, King Ferdinand gave him a royal grant for a voyage to discover and colonize the island of Bimini.

The terms of the grant gave Ponce de León the authority to take ships at his own "cost and expense"[1] to discover the island and gave him three years from the date of the grant to accomplish the expedition. He had permission to explore and claim any land that he came upon during his voyage provided that the land was not east of the line of Tordesillas—that is, in the Portuguese sphere

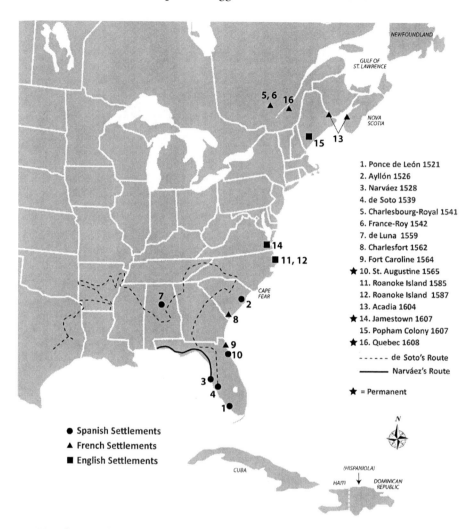

1. Ponce de León 1521
2. Ayllón 1526
3. Narváez 1528
4. de Soto 1539
5. Charlesbourg-Royal 1541
6. France-Roy 1542
7. de Luna 1559
8. Charlesfort 1562
9. Fort Caroline 1564
★ 10. St. Augustine 1565
11. Roanoke Island 1585
12. Roanoke Island 1587
13. Acadia 1604
★ 14. Jamestown 1607
15. Popham Colony 1607
★ 16. Quebec 1608

------ de Soto's Route
——— Narváez's Route

★ = Permanent

● Spanish Settlements
▲ French Settlements
■ English Settlements

Map showing the location of Spanish, French and English settlements in North America. Thirteen of these colonies did not survive. Only three — St. Augustine, Jamestown and Québec — became permanent settlements (Heather Harvey).

of interest. In return for paying for the expedition out of his own pocket, Ponce de León would enjoy a three-year monopoly on exploration in the area and would be given full power and jurisdiction over those lands he discovered for his lifetime. The grant promised him a tenth of all the revenues and profits that belonged to the crown for a period of 12 years and spelled out other favors that were to be given him. The settlers who went with him would be allowed an exemption from tithes and fees for one year — an exemption that would not be given to settlers who came later.[2]

Ponce de León's first voyage was one of discovery. Setting out from Puerto Rico in three ships on March 3, 1513, he intended to search for the island of Bimini off the east coast of present-day Florida. Sailing to the northwest, he encountered bad weather and had to seek a safe harbor — most likely the mouth of the St. John's River near present-day Jacksonville, Florida. Having safely anchored his ships, he went ashore to take possession of the land for Spain. It was early April and Eastertide, and he was so impressed by the beauty of the flowers he found there that he named the land La Florida. At the time he thought the land was an island.

Ponce de León then sailed south along the coast of Florida. He discovered that, although the wind was favorable, his ships were constantly being pushed backward because of the strong current. Europeans would eventually discover that this powerful, warm current began in the Gulf of Mexico, flowed through the Strait of Florida and followed the eastern coastline of North America and Newfoundland before veering across the Atlantic Ocean. We call it the Gulf Stream; the Spanish called it the Bahama Channel, and in the future it would aid Spanish ships laden with treasure from the West Indies as they made their way back to Spain.

Struggling against the current, the three ships continued their voyage south through the Florida Keys and, at last free of the Gulf Stream, made their way up the west coast of Florida, possibly as far as Pensacola Bay. Ponce de León may have been impressed with the land, but he and his men were not impressed with the welcome they received from the natives. Ponce de Léon and his men came ashore twice during their voyage, only to be attacked and driven back to their ships. With this hostility in mind, the Spanish were surprised when they encountered a seemingly friendly Indian on the southwestern coast of Florida. The three ships had been making their way down the coast on the return voyage when Ponce de León decided to drop anchor, take on fresh water and careen one of the ships. While the men were working, they spotted an Indian paddling his canoe in their direction. Warily, they watched as he approached the ships, but much to their astonishment he was not only friendly but also spoke Spanish.

The Indian visitor told Ponce de León and the men clustered around him that he came with a message from the local cacique, or chief. The cacique, he said, had gold in his possession that he was anxious to exchange for Spanish goods. Would the Spanish be willing to wait in the area until the cacique arrived? Ponce de León readily agreed. However, the next day a great number of Indians appeared in canoes and began to attack the Spanish, who managed to drive them off and take four prisoners. Ponce de León sent two of the Indian prisoners back to the cacique to assure him that, in spite of the attack, the Spanish were still anxious to barter with him. The messengers returned with the news that the cacique would come the next day to trade and again the Spanish waited and again the Indians appeared in canoes to attack. However, they were easily driven off, and in a few days the Spanish returned to Puerto Rico with the conviction that the Indians in La Florida were decidedly unfriendly.

As a result of this voyage, on September 27, 1514, King Ferdinand appointed Ponce de León *adelantado* or governor-conqueror of Florida and issued a new grant that confirmed all the terms of the previous grant and added new ones. The king specifically requested that Ponce de León "build houses in the said island [Florida], and villages of habitations of the sort that are made and built in these realms [Spain]."[3] He even stipulated that the foundations should be made of a layer of stone and another of earth. Ponce de León was also instructed to see to the planting of corn, grapes "and fruit-bearing and non-fruit bearing trees"[4] in his colony.

A new condition was laid down for the handling of the Indians, as concern over the manner in which they had been treated in the island colonies had been growing in Spain. Ponce de León was instructed, as soon as he arrived in Florida, to summon the chiefs and all their people together to hear the terms of the Spanish occupation: the Indians were to convert to the Catholic faith and obey and serve the Spanish as they were required. As long as they obeyed and lived in peace with the Spanish, the Indians were not to be enslaved or treated unjustly, but there was a caveat, as the king stipulated that if "they do not wish to obey what is contained in the summons, you [Ponce de León] can make war and seize them and carry them away for slaves."[5]

Seven years would pass before Ponce de León was ready to leave on his colonizing expedition, the purpose of which was to settle Florida, explore the land and, since, it was supposed to be an island, discover the mainland. He was also to look for gold, silver, and other things of value and to convert the Indians to the Catholic faith. On January 25, 1521, Ponce de León appointed deputies to take over his duties in Puerto Rico, and on the 10th of February he wrote to the cardinal of Tortosa:

> I have decided ... to serve His Majesty and go off to the island of Florida, and settle it if I could and discover as much else as I could: I will leave here for there in five or six days with two ships and as many people as I can take: and I shall send an account of whatever happens there to His Majesty and Your Honour.[6]

Ponce de León sailed from Puerto Rico at the end of February 1521 with two ships carrying 200 men. There is no mention of women being aboard the ships, and we do not know the occupations of the men who accompanied him. We can conclude that some were soldiers who more than likely came from the Spanish colonies and that monks and priests were also on board to convert the Indians to the Catholic faith. Queen Juana had specifically written Ponce de León that no heretics, new Christians, ex–Moors or Jews or any foreigners outside the kingdom were to number among the settlers.[7]

There is little documentation for Ponce de León's attempt to colonize Florida; what we do know comes mainly from the historian Gonzalo Fernández de Oviedo y Valdez, who had come to Hispaniola as a colonist in 1514. Upon his return to Spain in 1523 he was appointed historiographer of the Indies and published his first work in 1526. He wrote that in addition to the passengers, the ships carried 50 horses and that Ponce de León "took mares and heifers and swine and sheep and goats and all kinds of domestic animals useful in the service of mankind: and also for the cultivation and tillage of the field[s] he was supplied with all [kinds of] seed."[8]

Details about the voyage are sparse, but the historian Antonio de Herrera y Tordesillas, writing in the early 17th century, related that the ships "suffered many hardships during the voyage."[9] The date of their arrival in Florida is unknown, but as they left Puerto Rico at the end of February and had a difficult voyage, it may have been some time in late March or early April before they reached their destination. The exact location of Ponce de León's attempted settlement is also unknown, but it was somewhere on the southwestern coast of Florida, probably near Charlotte Harbor, possibly Sanibel Island.[10] It was also somewhere near the spot where the Spanish had been tricked by the Indians some eight years before.

The settlement did not last even four months, and we know very little about what happened during those months. Oviedo wrote that Ponce de León thought "the business of colonization consisted of nothing more than to arrive and cultivate the land and pasture his livestock. But the temperature of the region was very unsuitable and different from what he had imagined."[11]

If Ponce de León followed his instructions from the king, he gathered the Indians together and explained to them that they were to convert to the Catholic faith and obey and serve the Spanish in whatever manner they dictated. Whether the Indians were in a position to understand the terms of the summons or not, they evidently chose not to obey and serve the Spanish. Oviedo describes them as being

> a very austere and very savage and belligerous and fierce and untamed people and not accustomed to a peaceful existence nor to lay down their liberty so easily at the discretion of alien volition of other men, or at the determination of those monks and priests by whom he was accompanied.[12]

Since the Indians would not obey, Ponce de León was then authorized to make war on them. Again we are indebted to Oviedo for what happened:

> [W]hen it seemed to him proper, he moved forward with his retinue and attacked by land and entered into a skirmish or battle with the Indians ... and finally they defeated him and killed a number of the Christians ... and he escaped wounded grievously by an arrow and he decided to go to the island of Cuba to be cured, if it were possible, and with a greater retinue and more strength to return to his conquest. And so he embarked and arrived at the island [and] at the port of Havana, where after he had arrived, he lived a short time ... and also died others who were wounded and others of illnesses.[13]

Juan Ponce de León died in Cuba shortly after his arrival in July 1521. Thus ended the first attempt of the Spanish to settle the newly discovered land of La Florida.

## *Breakdown of Ponce de León's Colony*

| | |
|---|---|
| *Nationality of settlement* | Spain |
| *Sponsored by* | Grant given to Juan Ponce de León by King Ferdinand to colonize at his own expense |
| *Physical location* | The southwestern coast of Florida — exact location unknown, but most likely near Charlotte Harbor. Some historians think it was on Sanibel Island. |
| *Why that location* | Unknown |
| *Purpose of settlement* | To settle the land, to explore the area and look for gold, silver, other metals and things of profit and to convert the Indians to the Catholic faith |
| *When settled* | The end of February 1521 |
| *Climatic conditions* | According to Oviedo, the temperature of the region was very unsuitable and different from what he (Ponce de León) had imagined. |
| *Relationship with Indians* | Hostile — according to Oviedo, the Indians were "very bellicose and not willing to lay down their liberty at the discretion of other men nor at the determination of monks and priests." |
| *Internal quarreling* | Unknown |
| *Number of initial settlers* | 200 men |
| *Makeup of initial settlers* | Unknown — except that there were both soldiers and monks and priests among the group |
| *Number of additional settlers* | None — colony did not last long enough for a resupply. |
| *Percentage that survived* | Unknown — many of the 200 men were killed by the Indians; others died later in Cuba of their wounds and others of illnesses. |
| *Initial supplies* | Horses, mares, heifers, swine and sheep and goats and all kinds of domestic animals useful in the service of humankind and also for cultivation and tillage of the fields, he was also supplied with all kinds of seed. |
| *How often supplies arrived* | Unknown |
| *Stability of the mother country* | Spain was involved in a series of wars with France during the early 16th century, but the country was stable. |
| *Fate of settlement* | Abandoned — after being defeated by the Indians, the wounded Ponce de León and his men returned to Cuba, where Ponce de León died a few days later, in July 1521. |

# Lucas Vásquez de Ayllón

The second Spanish attempt to establish a colony in Florida was undertaken not by an explorer but by a judge in the Royal Audiencia in Santo

Domingo, Hispaniola. His name was Lucas Vásquez de Ayllón, a virtuous, well-educated man of considerable wealth who was interested in exploration and particularly fascinated by what might lie to the north of Florida. He decided to pursue his interest in the region by sponsoring a voyage of discovery. In 1521 he outfitted a ship, hired an experienced explorer named Francisco Gordillo as captain and instructed him to sail northward along the east coast of Florida in search of the mainland, for at that time Florida was still considered to be an island. Ayllón also instructed Gordillo to treat any natives he encountered in his expedition cordially and with respect.

During his voyage, Gordillo came upon another vessel from Hispaniola, owned by an official of that island named Juan Ortiz Matienzo. The ship, which had been cruising the area for some time in an unsuccessful attempt to find slaves, was under the command of Pedro de Quexos. After consulting with Gordillo, Quexos decided to join Gordillo's expedition, and the two ships traveled up the coast together, making landfall at the mouth of a large river, probably somewhere in the vicinity of Cape Fear in present-day North Carolina. After landfall, the Spanish were able to make friendly contact with the Indians, who treated them with great hospitality and told them the land was called Chicora.

With Indian guides, the Spanish explored the area, claiming it for Spain and noting the richness and fertility of the land and the waters. The two Spanish captains decided to return home without exploring any more of the coast, and as they were preparing to leave, they invited from sixty to one hundred fifty of the Indians to come aboard the ships.[14] When they were safely on board, the Spanish slipped their anchors and sailed away, taking the Indians with them to be sold into slavery.

When Ayllón discovered the actions of his captain, he immediately set about to free the Indians; but unfortunately many of them had died during the voyage or soon after landing in Hispaniola. The Indians who had survived were to be returned to their country as soon as possible, but until that could be arranged, they remained in the custody of Ayllón and Matienzo, the man who had sponsored the other voyage.

One of the surviving Indians learned to speak Spanish. He converted to Christianity, taking the name Francisco Chicora, and eventually became a servant to Ayllón. When he had mastered the Spanish language well enough, he began to tell Ayllón fascinating stories of his homeland. According to Chicora, the ruler of the area was "of gigantic size,"[15] much larger than any of his subjects, and his extraordinary size was due to having had his bones softened as a baby by application of certain herbs. The bones were then manipulated to make them longer than normal, and this, he said, was a practice that was allowed only in the royal family. Another story was of a race of people who had once lived among them who had tails a meter long, and when they wanted to sit down, they either had to have a chair with no bottom or had to dig deep holes in the ground to hold their tails.[16]

Chicora spoke glowingly about the region, describing the different kinds of trees that grew there — virgin oak, pine and cypress plus a variety of nut and fruit trees. His people had gardens that yielded vegetables in abundance, and the rivers teemed with fish and oysters. It appeared to be a land of plenty, and Ayllón was so intrigued by Chicora's description of his country and his stories about its inhabitants that he determined to go there himself as governor. Therefore he traveled to Spain as soon as he could to secure his discovery by a royal grant and took Francisco Chicora with him.

In Spain, Chicora told the nobles who came to visit Ayllón about his country, the customs of his people and the marvelous things that could be seen there. The Spanish historian Peter Martyr, who on several occasions invited both Ayllón and Chicora to dinner, was captivated by the stories, wrote them down and even used his influence with the king to help Ayllón acquire his governorship. Martyr wrote:

> His Imperial Majesty accepted our advice, and we have sent him [Ayllón] back to New Spain, authorising him to build a fleet to carry him to those countries where he will found a colony. Associates will not fail him, for the entire Spanish nation is in fact so keen about novelties that people go eagerly anywhere they are called by a nod or a whistle, in the hope of bettering their condition, and are ready to sacrifice what they have for what they hope.[17]

In June 1523 Charles V issued a grant to Ayllón, creating him governor and captain general of the new land. The grant was similar to the one given Juan Ponce de León in that Ayllón was to bear the cost of the voyage and settlement with the usual monopoly of exploration and trade in the area for six years. The compensations offered Ayllón were better than those offered Ponce de León. For example, Ayllón was to be paid a salary as governor, be given land and fishing rights and was to keep 15 percent of the income and taxes from the new land.[18]

The grant stipulated that Ayllón be "very careful about the treatment of the Indians."[19] They were not to be divided among the settlers, as was done in the other island colonies in the New World, or enslaved, but encouraged to work for the Spanish as free paid servants. There was no mention of the summons that Ponce de León was required to give the Indians in his colony; instead, Ayllón was instructed to make peace with the Indians and "attract them to our service that they will be protected and not molested ... it has been seen by experience that to keep one's word to the Indians is the principal way to attract them and keep them friendly with the Spanish Christians."[20] To ensure the conversion of the Indians to the Catholic faith, permission was granted to Ayllón to take as many priests as he thought necessary.

The colony was established for the usual purpose of searching the new land for gold, silver and other valuable resources and to convert the Indians to the Catholic faith, but Ayllón and the king had added some new goals. Charles V wanted Ayllón to explore any strait he found to determine if it led to the

Pacific Ocean and to send him an account of it.[21] Soon after the death of Ponce de León in 1521, Francisco de Garay explored the west coast of Florida just as Ponce de León had done, but he continued his exploration to the north and followed the Gulf Coast around to Mexico. Garay proved that Florida was not an island but connected to the mainland; moreover, there was no strait or passage to the Pacific Ocean located in that area. Europeans would have to look elsewhere for a route to the East. Besides looking for the Northwest Passage in his new territory, Ayllón also wanted to start fisheries in the area, as there were reports that the Indians had pearls. He also believed that silk could be easily produced in the region, so he intended to start a silk industry.

After much delay, Ayllón sailed from the Port of Plata on the northern shore of Hispaniola in the middle of July 1526. His fleet consisted of six sailing boats carrying 500 people — soldiers, African slaves, silk producers, priests, some women, a doctor, a surgeon and a pharmacist.[22] Also aboard were Ayllón's Indian servant Francisco Chicora and a number of Indians from the region, who had been recruited as guides and interpreters on a reconnaissance voyage sponsored by Ayllón the previous year. Oviedo wrote that most of the people came from the islands and were experienced in these areas. In addition to people, the ships carried "eighty or ninety excellent horses."[23]

Ayllón's ships were well provisioned with the supplies that he thought would be needed on the expedition — including medical supplies. We know from a court statement made by Ayllón that he bought "three thousand loads of cassava bread, plus a thousand fanegas of maize, as provisions for the men on this expedition, both to eat on the voyage and on land ... and also several beef cattle, etc."[24] His ships also carried artillery, as Ayllón stated that he delayed the start of the expedition because he was awaiting the arrival of a fleet from Spain carrying artillery and other things needed for the settlement.

We know nothing of the voyage or when the fleet reached its destination, which was a river located 33⅔ degrees north of the equator — somewhere in the vicinity of Cape Fear in present-day North Carolina. Gordillo and Quexos had called the river St. John the Baptist, since they discovered it on the feast day of that saint; but Ayllón renamed it, calling it the Jordan after one of his captains. Unfortunately disaster struck as the fleet was entering the mouth of the Jordan — the flagship sank with all its provisions and supplies. Fortunately the passengers were rescued. The other ships, being smaller, had no difficulty entering the river; however, the loss of the provisions was devastating.

Upon landing, Ayllón set about building an open boat to replace the one that had been lost, while some of his captains explored the coast and the interior. Francisco Chicora, during his service with Ayllón, had described the region in glowing terms, naming some 19 provinces with ports and towns, but in their explorations the Spanish found no trace of any of the things Chicora had described. A few days after they landed, Chicora and the other Indians fled inland, leaving the Spanish with no interpreters or guides.

One of the exploring parties returned with news of a better land to the south. With food in short supply and no hope of obtaining any from the Indians in that area after the desertion of the Indian guides, Ayllón decided to move the settlement south. By this time many of the settlers had become ill and others were weak from lack of food. The women and the sick made the journey south by boat and the rest of the men came overland. They followed the coast south and west and came to a large river, which they called Gualdape (possibly the Pedee in South Carolina),[25] and made their main camp upon its banks. They called the settlement San Miguel de Gualdape.

They immediately set to work to build houses. Oviedo tells us:

> [T]he land was all very flat and marshy, but the river was very full, and with lots of good fish.... Since they were running short of food, and did not find any on the land, and it was very cold, since the land where they had stopped was thirty-three degrees north and flat, many of them went ill, and many of those died.[26]

One of those who were taken ill was Ayllón, and on October 18, 1526, he died, leaving the colony in the care of Lieutenant Francisco Gomez.

After the death of Ayllón, dissatisfaction with the conditions in the colony caused two of the men, Doncel and Bazán, to gather a party of like-minded individuals and lead a mutiny. They captured Gomez and the other officials of the colony and imprisoned them in "harsh conditions."[27] Doncel and Bazán then proceeded to rule the colony with such arrogant cruelty that not only did the Indians in the area retaliate by killing some of the rebel soldiers but a party of, as Oviedo calls them, "better soldiers,"[28] rose up against them. Things came to a head one night when the African slaves rebelled and set fire to the building where the prisoners were being held. In the confusion that followed, the prisoners were freed, Bazán was fatally wounded and Doncel and his followers were arrested. The decision was then made to return to Hispaniola.

Ayllón's body was put on the open boat, which he had built at the site of their first landing, to be taken back to Santo Domingo for burial. The voyage home was not without misfortune as the open boat floundered in the ocean and the men were forced to consign Ayllón's body to the sea. Seven men on one of the other ships froze to death. The survivors went to Hispaniola or Puerto Rico, but only 30 percent of those who set out to colonize the country actually returned — 150 out of 500, and most of them were ill and starving.

Oviedo wrote this about the survivors:

> And despite all their sufferings, some of them praise the nature of the area they knew, saying that if the right equipment was taken to settle there, and enough provisions to last them until they understood and got used to the land, it would be bound to be a worthwhile enterprise.... There is a lot to report as regards fish: the fishing in the river Gualdape is something to wonder at for its great abundance of excellent fish, according to the appointed friars and others.... But despite all this, many men died of hunger, for lack of bread, and unable to fish through illness, or to help each other.[29]

The second attempt of the Spanish to plant a colony in the land they called La Florida had ended in failure.

## *Breakdown of Ayllón's Colony at San Miguel de Gualdape*

| | |
|---|---|
| *Nationality of settlement* | Spain |
| *Sponsored by* | A grant given to Lucas Vásquez de Ayllón by Charles V to colonize at his own expense |
| *Physical location* | On the banks of a large river called Gualdape. The land was all very flat and marshy, but the river was very full and with lots of good fish; it was too shallow at the entrance unless the ships came in on the incoming tide. |
| *Why that location* | The first location on the river Jordan was unsatisfactory, as the flagship sank entering the mouth, with the loss of all the equipment but no loss of life. The Indians interpreters and guides they had brought with them deserted and Ayllón sent men to find a better location. |
| *Purpose of settlement* | To explore the land for gold, silver and other valuable resources, to try to find a strait to the Pacific Ocean, to produce silk, to establish fisheries and to convert the Indians to the Catholic faith. |
| *When settled* | Ayllón's fleet left Hispaniola in mid–July 1526. |
| *Climatic conditions* | The settlers speak of it being very cold. |
| *Relationship with Indians* | Not much is known about contact with the Indians. After they settled on the Gualdape, Oviedo says that the Indians killed a few of the soldiers. |
| *Internal quarreling* | After the leader Ayllón died, there was a mutiny against the new leader Francisco Gomez, Gomez and his officers were imprisoned but later rescued by a countermutiny. |
| *Number of initial settlers* | There were six ships carrying 500 people. |
| *Makeup of initial settlers* | Lowery says there were women among the settlers. Most of the colonists were from the islands and experienced in the area, but there were some who Ayllón said came from Spain to join him. There were priests, African slaves, silk producers, a doctor, a surgeon and a pharmacist in the group. |
| *Number of additional settlers* | None |
| *Percentage that survived* | 150 out of the 500 survived — 30 percent. |
| *Initial supplies* | Ayllón testified that he bought 3,000 loads of cassava bread and 1000 bushels of maize as provisions for the voyage and for use at the settlement until provision could be obtained there. He also reported that he brought several beef cattle, etc. He also carried necessary medicines and some artillery. |

| | |
|---|---|
| *How often supplies arrived* | Colony did not survive long enough to be resupplied. |
| *Stability of the mother country* | Conditions were stable in Spain even though the country was involved in a series of wars with France. |
| *Fate of settlement* | It was abandoned in the late fall of 1526. |

# Pánfilo de Narváez

Pánfilo de Narváez had spent many years serving the king of Spain in the New World, and although he had witnessed at first hand the triumph of Cortés in conquering Mexico, he was not able to share in the wealth or glory of that victory. As a result, he became determined to find another such kingdom that he could conquer and where he too could reap such rewards. Narváez decided to search to the east of Mexico in Florida for a suitable native civilization to subdue and was prepared to invest his entire fortune in the endeavor. Upon returning to Spain, he petitioned the king for the grant of a kingdom and so became the third man to try to establish a settlement in Florida.

On December 11, 1526, Charles V issued a royal grant authorizing Narváez to conquer the territory between the Río de Las Palmas (somewhere near Pánuco on the Gulf Coast of Mexico)[30] to the Cape of Florida. The grant contained the usual terms—Narváez was to explore and settle the land at his own cost and expense and receive the usual compensations. He was ordered to establish two settlements and build three fortresses in his new territory and was to receive a salary as governor of the colony and a salary for maintaining each of the fortresses.[31]

Narváez was to recruit his people from Spain itself and not the island colonies, for the islands had been sadly depleted by emigration to Mexico and Peru—where there were more opportunities for a person to become rich. In 1525 a law had been passed prohibiting emigration from Cuba, Hispaniola, Jamaica and Puerto Rico to other islands or the continent.[32] Ponce de León's expedition had started from Puerto Rico and had been made up of inhabitants of the islands, and while Ayllón had started his expedition in Spain, he recruited most of his 500 colonists from Hispaniola. Narváez not only started his expedition from Spain but also drew his colonists from Spain.

The first settlers and explorers were to receive land of their own on the condition that they remain in the territory for four years. They were also admonished not to treat the Indians cruelly, and a lengthy set of instructions as to how the Indians were to be handled was included in the grant. The king was anxious that "the settlements that are to be made from now on, that they should be carried on without offending God and without death or robbery of these Indians and without enslaving them unjustly ... those Indians that may be rebellious, even after being advised and warned, you may take as slaves."[33]

It was the return of the reading of the summons to the assembled Indians that was contained in the grant given to Juan Ponce de León.

The purpose of the colony was to establish two settlements and build three fortresses on the land, to explore the country for gold, silver and other valuable resources and to convert the Indians to the Catholic faith. On June 17, 1527, Narváez sailed from Spain with 600 colonists in five ships. The colonists included settlers, soldiers, priests, Franciscan friars, African slaves and the wives of some of the members of the expedition. The officials of the towns to be established by Narváez were already chosen and were part of the group that sailed from Spain.[34]

From Spain Narváez sailed to Santo Domingo to gather supplies and horses for the colony, and it was while the fleet was in port there that the expedition received its first serious setback — 140 of the 600 colonists deserted. The second setback occurred in Cuba. Narváez had sailed there to gather more men, arms and horses for the expedition, and as he was in the process of obtaining his supplies, the fleet was hit with a devastating hurricane that caused the death of 60 of the men and the loss of two ships. It was now November and the passengers and crew, battered by the storm and not anxious to put to sea again, begged Narváez to winter in Cuba. He agreed, and it was not until almost four months later, on February 20, 1528, that Narváez and his fleet were able to head for the port of Havana, where the expedition was to begin. The fleet now consisted of five ships carrying 400 people and 80 horses.[35]

The fleet had just gotten under way when, as luck would have it, the pilot grounded the ships on some shoals. The fleet remained stranded there for 15 days before the sailors finally managed to free the ships so they could continue on their voyage. They were making for Havana when another disaster occurred — a storm came up and drove the fleet away from its destination in Cuba toward the western coast of Florida. For almost five weeks the ships, helpless in the storm, were blown due north until finally land was sighted on April 12, 1528.

Two days later on April 14, they came ashore near present-day St. Clement's Point on the peninsula west of Tampa Bay, having somehow missed the entrance to the bay itself. An Indian town was located on the shore, but when the Spanish landed and visited the town, they found that the inhabitants had fled during the night. A thorough search of the village turned up one gold ornament. One of the officials for the new colony, Cabeza de Vaca, who wrote about his experiences later when he returned to Spain, reported that 400 men landed in Florida along with only 42 of the horses, the others having died at sea, and that those 42 were so "lean and fatigued that for the time we could have little service from them."[36]

Narváez, as the new governor, took possession of the land in a formal ceremony in the deserted Indian village with the royal standard flapping in the breeze and the monks, officers and officials standing by in their best attire to present their credentials to the new governor. Narváez, as he had been instructed, then read the required summons—to the empty houses in the village.

The landing place on the point offered poor anchorage for the fleet; therefore Narváez sent one of the ships ahead to search for a suitable harbor. If the search was unsuccessful, the commander was instructed to steer for Havana, where he was to take on more supplies and seek the ship belonging to Narváez that was now in Havana taking on provisions for the colony. The two ships could then come back to resupply the expedition.

Meanwhile, Narváez took a small group of men and began to explore the country. They discovered some inhabited Indian villages, which they raided for corn and where they found some traces of gold. Narváez was eager to find the source of the gold and began questioning the Indians. "Having by signs asked the Indians whence these things came, they motioned to us that very far from there, was a province called Apalachen, where was much gold, and so the abundance in Palachen of everything that we at all cared for."[37] Taking some of the Indians for guides they at last returned to the area where the ships were anchored.

Narváez had chosen a man named Diego Miruelo as his main pilot. Miruelo not only had a great deal of experience in the area but was also reputed to have some knowledge of the location of the Río de Las Palmas and Pánuco, where Narváez had intended to make landfall and establish his settlement. The storm had caused them to land in a different place, but the preferred site for the colony was still Pánuco. However, no one, not even Miruelo, was exactly sure where it was located. Narváez called his officers and officials together and told them that the area they were now occupying had no haven for the ships and "no subsistence ... for the maintenance of a colony."[38] He said that he wanted to leave this area and take the people to look for Pánuco, which supposedly had a better port and a more fertile land. He said "that he desired to penetrate the interior, and that the ships ought to go along the coast until they should come to the port which the pilots believe was very near on the way to River Palmas."[39]

Narváez then asked for his men's opinions. Most of the officers were in favor of the plan of traveling overland, for they were not anxious to board the ships again after the hardships of their voyage there. The pilots had told them that the harbor was only a short distance away and that it "was not possible, marching ever by the shore, we should fail to come upon it ... that whichever might first find it should wait for the other."[40]

Cabeza de Vaca, having seen that the pilots were not sure exactly where the expedition was located at present, placed no great dependence on their finding the harbor nearby and viewed the plan to leave the ships and march inland risky at best. He alone of the group spoke out against the plan and in the following passage gave his reasons:

> I said it appeared to me that under no circumstances ought we to leave the vessels until they were in a secure and peopled harbor; that he [Narváez] should observe

the pilots were not confident, and did not agree in any particular, neither did they know where we were. Above all that we were going without being able to communicate with the Indians ... that we were about entering a country of which we had no account ... and besides all this, we had not food to sustain us in wandering we knew not whither ... ration could not be given to each man for such a journey, more than a pound of biscuit and another of bacon; that my opinion was, we should embark and seek a harbor and a soil better than this to occupy.[41]

The men, however, decided to adopt the governor's plan and accordingly he instructed the three remaining ships, which had on board the women who had accompanied the expedition, to sail along the coast until they found the port at Pánuco and wait for him there. The three ships sailed along the coast without finding the port and finally returned to Tampa Bay — the site of the first landing. They eventually met up with the two ships coming from Cuba with supplies. For several months a search was made for Narváez and his party and at last the searchers gave up in desperation and sailed to Mexico.[42]

Meanwhile, on the first of May Narváez and his men, 300 in all, with 40 of them on horseback, started their journey northward. Instead of staying close to the coast, they headed farther inland toward the land of the Apalachee Indians, where they had been told there was much gold and an abundance of "everything they cared for."[43] The journey was made over difficult terrain — low marshy land giving way to dense forests with many rivers to cross. Food was in short supply and they tried to stretch their meager rations with palmettos. At last they encountered a large group of Indians and were able to capture some of them for guides. The men led the Spanish to their village, where their captors raided their corn supply. The exhausted men stayed in the village for a few days while a scouting party went out to look for a harbor. They returned after an unsuccessful search and the long march began again. Finally, they reached the Indian town of Apalachee, near present-day Tallahassee, which held both food and gold, or so they had been led to believe. They remained there for 25 days, searching the countryside and finding food, but neither gold nor a fabulous civilization such as had been found in Mexico. The land was poor and hard to penetrate and the Indians constantly harassed them.

Narváez decided to seek a more hospitable site to the south, closer to the coast, and set out for the Indian town of Aute where, the Apalachee assured them, they would find plenty of food and friendly people. The journey was completed in nine difficult days, but the men were able to rest in the town of Aute and there was a good supply of food. By this time many of the men, including Narváez, had become ill and the expedition that had been sent to find the sea returned to report that it was still far away. There was apparently a plot to abandon Narváez and the others who were sick, but it came to nothing and the whole party eventually made their way to Apalachicola Bay.

They found no supply ships waiting for them and after a time decided that the ships were not coming. The decision was then made to construct boats so they could travel more easily along the coast to Mexico, as the men were too weak from hunger and sickness to walk. They ate the last of their horses and, on September 22, began their journey by water along the coast — a nightmare of thirst, hunger and harassment by Indians. The weakened men began to die, and by November it was cold and the Gulf waters were rough. Narváez, after some of the boats were grounded close to the shore, decided to leave the coast and head out into the open waters of the Gulf, hoping to reach Mexico. He was never seen again. Several rescue missions failed to find him — the last one taking place early in 1529.

The men in the other boats, weak from hunger and cold, slowly began to die. Some of the boats were grounded on islands close to the coast, and the men crawled ashore to die of hunger and thirst. The boat carrying Cabeza de Vaca was grounded on an island off the Texas coast, and he emerged as the only survivor. He eventually met up with three more survivors of the expedition, and these four men then began their incredible journey by foot across Texas, arriving eight years later on Sunday, July 24, 1536, in Mexico City — the only members of the expedition to survive. Vaca's account of his journey gives interesting details about the country through which he traveled and the customs of the Indians whom he met. However, he reported no splendid civilizations, no gold, silver or precious metals. Narváez had not found them in Florida either. The third attempt by the Spanish to settle Florida had ended in disaster.

### *Breakdown of Narváez's Colony*

| | |
|---|---|
| *Nationality of settlement* | Spain |
| *Sponsored by* | Royal grant issued to Narváez to explore and colonize at his own expense |
| *Physical location* | Somewhere in the vicinity of St. Clement's Point on the peninsula west of Tampa Bay |
| *Why that location* | Blown there by a violent storm |
| *Purpose of settlement* | To establish at least two settlements, to make three fortresses on the land, to explore the country for gold, silver and other valuable resources and to convert the Indians to the Catholic faith |
| *When settled* | April 1528 |
| *Climatic conditions* | Not mentioned |
| *Relationship with Indians* | Hostile |
| *Internal quarreling* | There were disagreements in the group as to the advisability of making the overland journey to find a suitable site for settlement and one plot to abandon the sick — but both these situations were peacefully resolved. |
| *Number of initial settlers* | 600 — started out from Spain, but 140 of the men deserted in Santo Domingo. The group was down |

|  |  |
|---|---|
|  | to 400 when they sailed for Florida, but only 300 men were involved in the overland march to find a suitable site for settlement. |
| *Makeup of initial settlers* | The settlers were all from Castile and included colonists, soldiers, the wives of certain members of the company, Franciscan friars, priests and African slaves. |
| *Number of additional settlers* | None |
| *Percentage that survived* | About 1 percent — 4 men out of the 300 who landed in Florida survived. |
| *Initial supplies* | Eighty horses, ship's biscuit and bacon are mentioned as being on board. |
| *How often supplies arrived* | Soon after landing, one of the ships was sent back to Havana to resupply. The ship was to join another ship waiting there and connect with Narvaez in Florida. The ships never made contact with Narvaez's party. |
| *Stability of the mother country* | Conditions were stable in Spain even though the country was involved in a series of wars with France. |
| *Fate of settlement* | The site for the settlement was never found and therefore the settlement was never started. Narvaez and most of his men were lost in the Gulf of Mexico in November 1528. |

# Hernando de Soto

Hernando de Soto was a veteran in the West Indies, having served under Avila in Nicaragua and being one of the 12 conquerors of Peru under Pizarro. He returned to Spain with a vast fortune accumulated from the conquest of Peru and was interested in finding new territories to explore and exploit. By this time the disappointing end to the expedition led by Narváez was well known and de Soto decided to try his luck in those lands and look for a new Peru in Florida and the provinces abandoned by Ayllón in 1526.

On April 20, 1537, Charles V issued a royal grant authorizing de Soto to conquer and settle the lands that had previously been given to Narváez and Ayllón. In order to make it easier for him to provide for the conquest and settlement of the new territory, de Soto was also appointed governor of Cuba. The conquest and settlement was all to be done at his own expense, but he would receive a salary as governor of Cuba and have the usual compensations as conqueror and settler of the new territories. De Soto was to build "three stone fortresses in the harbors and places most proper for them"[44] for the protection and pacification of the country. He was also asked to build a hospital for the poor. Charles V, perhaps remembering the vast treasures found in the temples,

graves and sepulchers of the Incas, stipulated that if any such treasure were discovered, he, the king, would receive half of it and the finder would receive the
other half. De Soto was required, as Narváez had been, to read the summons
to the Indians and agree to treat them kindly as long as they cooperated with
the Spanish.[45]

The purpose of the expedition was to explore, conquer and settle the new
land, to build three fortresses, to establish a hospital for the poor, to search for
gold, silver, precious stones and other natural resources and to convert the
Indians to the Catholic faith. De Soto was to take 500 men with the necessary
arms, horses and military equipment and enough food for 18 months—all at
his own expense. The men were to be drawn from Spain and the Indies and the
first settlers were to receive land and the usual compensations. The king was
to appoint the officers of the exchequer and the religious men for the expedition.[46]

On April 6, 1538, de Soto set sail from Spain for Cuba with 600 soldiers,
several priests and monks and the wives of some of the officers, including his
own wife, Doña Isabel.[47] At the end of May the fleet reached the port of Santiago
in Cuba, where de Soto took up his duties as governor of the island and set
about collecting supplies for his expedition. He visited each of the towns on
the island, acquired 237 horses and provisions of cassava bread, salted meat
and swine for his journey. The governor bought several grazing farms, where
animals were to be raised to provide his new settlements with meat. He also
sent out two reconnaissance voyages to seek a suitable port on the west coast
of Florida and to bring back Indians to be used as guides and interpreters.[48]

At last he was ready and, leaving his wife and the other wives in Cuba, set
sail with 600 men in nine ships on May 18, 1539. The men included soldiers,
priests and Dominican friars, a surgeon, a cooper, a ship's carpenter and caulkers, African slaves, the four Indians who were to serve as guides and one Spanish
woman. The ships carried arms, artillery, portable forges, medicines, horses,
greyhounds to chase fugitives, and swine to provide meat for the expedition.
There was enough food aboard to feed an armada, wrote one of the officers.[49]

As they reached the coast of Florida, they noticed the smoke of many signal
fires rising into the clear blue sky, for the approach of the Spanish fleet had been
noted by the Indians on shore. On May 30, the Spanish fleet entered Tampa
Bay and made landfall a few miles from an Indian town and near the spot where
Narváez had landed. They disembarked the men and horses, leaving only the
sailors on board. On June 3, 1539, de Soto took formal possession of the land.
They found the Indian town and the surrounding countryside deserted, as the
Indians had fled, and immediately upon landing, the Indians who had been
captured to serve as guides ran away. De Soto was obliged to send a scouting
party out to capture new guides.

The Spanish were fortunate. They found a Spanish man, a member of
Narváez's expedition, who had been living among the Indians for many years

as a captive and who was more than happy to join the company as interpreter. Upon being asked if there was gold in the area, he said there was not, but he did know of a land not far away that was more bountiful than the place they now inhabited. A scouting party was sent there immediately and returned not only having found a more fertile land but with news of a province called Cale to the west, where there was much gold.

De Soto decided to go there at once. Before departing, however, he dispatched his ships back to Cuba to gather supplies and to carry a report of his journey and his prospect of finding gold to the officials in Santiago. Leaving one of his officers with a group of 30 horsemen and 50 footmen to form a garrison at Tampa Bay and leaving also provisions for two years, de Soto set forth on his journey into the interior on August 1, 1539.

In his journey to the east and then northwest, de Soto and his men were following almost in the footsteps of Narváez and his company, and they encountered the same harsh conditions that Narváez and his men had faced. The countryside was low and swampy, with dense woods and many small rivers, and food was in short supply. To make matters worse, the Indians constantly harassed them. Those Indians they did make contact with always spoke of a place farther on where there was much food or gold. The men became dispirited and asked the governor to return, as they were afraid they would all die, as had the men in Narváez's expedition. However, the governor refused to go back, saying: "he would not go back till he had seen with his own eyes that which they [the Indians] reported."[50] He was determined to investigate any place that was rumored to be rich in gold, silver and precious gems.

De Soto then put into practice two systems that he was to use for the remainder of his journey. First, to keep up the spirits of the men, he ordered the officer of the scouting party that was sent out to reconnoiter the country to issue two reports upon his return. One was a true account of what had been found, and that report was to be given only to him. The other was a false report giving favorable information, and that one was to be distributed among the men. The other system involved the Indians and was instituted to ensure the safety of the expedition. De Soto, using whatever means he could, kidnapped the chief of the territory through which he and his men were passing and held him hostage. The chief was then forced to provide his kidnappers with food and native bearers, male and female, to carry their possessions. Once the expedition had left the territory of the kidnapped chief, he was released and the process would begin all over again.

The Indians did not submit tamely to this practice and there were many skirmishes in which the Indians tried to rescue their chief, inflicting casualties on the Spanish. At other times there were attempts by the captive carriers to escape. At one point, over a hundred Indian carriers accompanied de Soto's march — all in chains and wearing iron collars about their necks. Those Indians who tried to escape and were caught were either burned to death or thrown to the greyhounds de Soto had brought with him to chase fugitives and to aid in punishing them.

The company spent the winter of 1539–1540 in Apalachee, near present-day Tallahassee. At this time de Soto sent a messenger to Tampa Bay to bring the men garrisoned there to join him at Apalachee. From a captured Indian, de Soto heard of a country to the east ruled by a woman who lived in a large town and whose subjects gave her large amounts of gold in tribute. De Soto turned his company to the northeast on March 3, 1540, in search of this country. Before leaving, he sent one of his officers, Maldonado, to Cuba for supplies, setting a rendezvous with him at Pensacola Bay in the summer.

It was not until the end of April that de Soto reached the town of Cufi-tatchiqui (on the Savannah River), which turned out to be not as large or as grand as had been described. The ruler was a young woman, who greeted the Spanish cordially and gave de Soto a long necklace of pearls that she had worn around her neck. Upon learning that the custom among the Indians was to bury their important men with their chest cavities filled with pearls, the Spanish proceeded to rob the graves of the Indians, coming away with sacks of pearls. However, these proved to be of little value as they had been damaged by many piercings and by being buried in the ground for a long time. It was here that the Spanish found European articles such as rosary beads, a dagger and other metal objects.[51] The Indians told the Spanish they had found the articles at a place within two days' journey of their town where white men had once stayed. The Spanish concluded that they were not far from Ayllón's abandoned settlement.[52] Some of the men wanted to remain in this pleasant land and colonize the area, but de Soto refused to stay, and so the weary journey began again.

The Spanish historian Oviedo wrote an account of de Soto's expedition as it was given to him by one of the survivors, and he wrote that he, Oviedo, had asked

> a very intelligent gentleman who was with this Governor ... why at every place they came to, this Governor and his army asked for ... Indian carriers ... and why after having given them what they had, they held the chiefs and principal men; and why they never tarried nor settled in any region they came to, adding that such a course was not settlement or conquest, but rather disturbing and ravaging the land and depriving the natives of their liberty without converting or making a single Indian either Christian or a friend. He replied and said that they took these carriers to keep them as slaves ... to carry the loads of supplies which they secured by plunder or gift, and that some died, and others ran away ... so that it was necessary to replenish their numbers ... and that if they held the chiefs ... captive, it was because it would keep their subjects quiet, so they would not molest them when foraging or doing what they wished in their country ... and that whither they were going neither the Governor nor the others knew, but that his purpose was to find some land rich enough to satiate his greed.[53]

The remainder of the expedition was spent wandering from place to place, searching either for food or an Indian civilization rich in gold, silver and precious gems comparable to the kingdoms of the Aztec and Incas. When it was time for the rendezvous with Maldonado and the supply ships, de Soto deliberately led his men away from the coast because he did not want it known in Cuba that as yet he had found nothing of value in his travels. The weary men, their numbers depleted by sickness and Indian attacks, marched without most of their clothing or other supplies, as they had lost almost everything, including the pearls, in a fire. The men trudged doggedly along, dressed in rags and animal skins, their feet covered in bits of leather, accompanied by the Indian slaves, their chains rattling as they walked and iron collars chafing their necks. This long train of people was followed by greyhounds and a pack of hogs numbering in the hundreds. Many of the men were sick and dying, but somehow de Soto managed to cross the Mississippi River with them all.

However, the expedition had taken its toll on its leader, who also became ill, and on May 21, 1542, Hernando de Soto died. Upon his death, his personal possessions were auctioned off in camp. They consisted of two men slaves, two women slaves, three horses and 700 hogs. His successor was Luis de Moscoso, who managed to build seven vessels and carry what was left of the expedition to the River Pánuco on the Gulf Coast of Mexico. On September 10, 1543, they reached the Pánuco, with only 322 men out of the 600 who had started out over four years earlier.

What had been accomplished? A vast amount of territory — the southeastern and south-central parts of today's United States— had been explored. Valuable information had been gathered on the topography of the region, and Indian customs had been observed. The Mississippi River had been crossed and the area west of it explored. No elaborate Indian civilization had been discovered, no gold, silver, or precious stones, and as far as enslaving the natives, they proved to be intractable and warlike. No colonies had been established, no fortresses built and no Indians converted. The fourth attempt to settle Florida ended in failure, as had the first three. It would be 17 years before anyone would try again.

## Breakdown of De Soto's Colony

| | |
|---|---|
| *Nationality of settlement* | Spain |
| *Sponsored by* | A royal grant issued to Hernando de Soto by Charles V to conquer and settle the lands claimed by Narvaez in Florida and the lands claimed by Ayllón in South Carolina all at his own expense. |
| *Physical location* | He landed at Tampa Bay but wandered around for over four years looking for a site for his settlement. None was ever established. |
| *Why that location* | It was thought to be a suitable port |
| *Purpose of settlement* | To conquer and settle the land, to build three fortresses, to discover gold, silver, precious stones |

|  | and other natural resources and to convert the Indians to the Catholic faith |
|---|---|
| *When settled* | June 3, 1539 |
| *Climatic conditions* | Not mentioned |
| *Relationship with Indians* | The Indians attacked the Spanish soon after they landed and there was continuing hostility during the entire march. |
| *Internal quarreling* | De Soto refused to establish a settlement in the Savannah Valley, as some of his men wanted, but there was no outright opposition to his leadership, especially as his policy was to issue favorable and misleading reports on the countryside. |
| *Number of initial settlers* | 600 men on nine ships |
| *Makeup of initial settlers* | Most of the settlers were soldiers, but there were also priests and Dominican friars, a surgeon, a cooper, a ship's carpenter, caulkers, African slaves and two Indians who had been captured on a reconnaissance voyage to act as interpreters. |
| *Number of additional settlers* | None |
| *Percentage that survived* | Roughly 54 percent or 322 out of 600 |
| *Initial supplies* | Members of the expedition reported that they sailed with ample provisions, including 25 shoulders of bacon, a large quantity of maize, hogs, 237 horses, greyhounds to chase fugitives, medicines, armaments and portable forges. |
| *How often supplies arrived* | The company was to be resupplied, but de Soto deliberately led his men away from the rendezvous point because he did not want the supply ship to carry the news back to Cuba that he had found nothing of value as yet. |
| *Stability of the mother country* | The country was stable. |
| *Fate of settlement* | The colony was never established. On September 10, 1543, the survivors of de Soto's expedition reached the Panuco. |

## Tristán de Luna

The disappointing result of de Soto's expedition dampened Spanish enthusiasm for settlement in the area north and east of the Gulf of Mexico. In 1544, two men did apply to the king for the right of conquest in that area, but they were turned down, since the king had lost interest in the region. Except for a few unsuccessful attempts by friars to establish missions there, Florida was all but forgotten. But by 1557, almost a decade and a half after the end of Hernando de Soto's expedition, the Spanish crown turned its thoughts once again to Florida. Reports had reached Spain that the French were becoming active on the east coast of Florida near the Punta de Santa Elena — the supposed site of Ayllón's colony.[54] French privateers were stopping there to gather water and wood and to trade with the Indians. The Spanish were afraid that the French would establish a base there and use it to attack Spanish shipping. King Philip II of Spain felt that the French needed to be kept out of the area at any cost; therefore the fifth attempt of the Spanish to settle Florida would be sponsored and paid for, not by an ambitious conqueror, but by the king himself.

The purpose of the expedition was to establish a strong base at the Punta de Santa Elena on the east coast to counteract French activity in the area and to provide a safe haven for Spanish ships. In addition to this base, another strong outpost was to be established on the Gulf Coast, from which Spanish power and religion could spread to the east and west. Philip II ordered Luis de Velasco, his viceroy in Mexico, to begin preparations for the venture. The royal grant of December 29, 1557, authorized Velasco to spend what was necessary from the royal treasury both to provide for the expedition and to pay the workmen and master masons who were needed to provide adequate buildings in the new colony. He was also authorized to choose a suitable person to be the governor and to lead the expedition.[55]

The man chosen by Velasco to command this expedition was Tristán de Luna, a man of over thirty years' experience in the New World. He had been second in command to Coronado on his western expedition; he was a resident of Mexico and had extensive holdings there. De Luna took his oath of office on November 1, 1558, as governor and captain general of Florida and Santa Elena. The royal grant to de Luna instructed him to "defend the natives thereof, that no injuries may be done to them nor any other evil by any persons."[56]

The king also specifically stated:

> And we command all the captains, both of infantry and cavalry, and all the persons who may go with you on the expedition ... to hold you, Don Tristán de Luna y Arellano, as our governor and general of the said people; and they shall obey you and comply with your orders, both written and oral.[57]

In the fall of 1558, Velasco authorized Guido de las Bazares to reconnoiter the coast for "some good and secure port where the people who go to settle the said La Florida may disembark."[58] Bazares a found a suitable harbor in Pensacola Bay, and it was intended that the first town and fort would be built there. From there, the expedition would proceed overland to the Punta de Santa Elena. Velasco, writing to Philip II of the plans for the expedition, explained the reason for the overland travel to Santa Elena:

> For I have understood from sailors, who have experience of the coast and from soldiers who were with Soto and traversed the country, that the surest way is to go by land the eighty leagues [200 miles] which lie between the district opposite La Havana and Santa Elena, rather than by sea.... There is no certainty in what location Santa Elena is, other than what the people say who were with Soto [namely] that they came upon a river which the Indians told them was the River of Pearls,

and that they were three days' journey from the sea. This river is the one which flows into the sea near the Punta de Santa Elena.[59]

The only favorable experience reported by the survivors of de Soto's expedition was the ease with which they had marched from the Gulf Coast of Florida to the land of the lady of Cufitatchiqui. Not only was the journey effortless, but there was also an abundance of food to be found on the way. It was there that relics from Ayllón's settlement had been discovered, and they reasoned that the Punta de Santa Elena would be only a few days' journey down river from that area. Velasco was proposing that de Luna and his people go overland from Pensacola Bay to the southeastern coast of present-day South Carolina, thinking that it was only 200 miles away — although it is actually over 400 miles.

On June 11, 1559, de Luna left for Florida from the port of San Juan de Ulúa near Vera Cruz with 1,500 people. Five hundred of them were soldiers; then there were the wives and children of the married soldiers, 100 artisans and master masons, some with their families, a number of Mexican Indians as servants, some African slaves and Dominican friars. Included in the group was a physician as well as a contingent of Spanish officials who were to look after the crown's interest and serve as administrators in the towns that were to be established. The fleet of 13 vessels also carried 240 horses, along with weapons and armor and the necessary provisions. The colony was to be resupplied from Mexico to the base at Pensacola Bay and then overland, once a road to the east coast had been established, to Santa Elena. There was even talk of driving cattle overland from Mexico to Pensacola Bay at some point in the future, when its feasibility had been ascertained.[60]

The fleet reached Ochuse in Pensacola Bay on August 14, 1559, and proceeded to disembark passengers and supplies; but before all the supplies could be unloaded, disaster in the form of a hurricane struck on August 19. The storm destroyed all but three of the ships, with the loss of all the supplies that were still on board, while heavy rains damaged the supplies that had already been off-loaded. In early September, de Luna wrote to Philip II and Velasco telling them of the loss of their supplies and ships. While the loss of the provisions was bad, the loss of so many ships was devastating. Few replacement vessels were available in the West Indies, and the lack of ships seriously hampered Velasco in his efforts to resupply the colony. The ship that brought the letters to the viceroy in Mexico City needed repairs before she could sail back to Florida with relief supplies, and Velasco could find only one other ship to send with her. In a letter to de Luna he assured him that the two ships would be ready to sail between November 4 and 10.

In desperation, de Luna sent scouting parties out to comb the land for food, but the area around Pensacola Bay proved to be strangely empty and no Indian towns with food supplies were discovered. However, one of the scouting parties returned with some beans and corn and the news that they had discovered an Indian territory inland (on the Alabama River) that appeared promising.

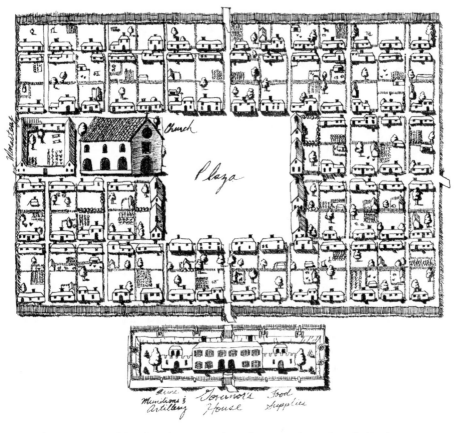

Artist's conception of the plans for a Spanish settlement at Santa Cruz de Nanicapana, based on a written description sent to Philip II by his viceroy in Mexico (see pages 41–42). It is not known how much of the town was actually built (drawing by Caroline S. Taylor).

De Luna realized that the area around Pensacola Bay was not able to sustain the number of people in his expedition, and he began to think of moving the settlement to the more promising inland area. In February he made the decision to move the entire party overland to the northwest in search of a new site for the settlement.

They found a suitable place on a hilltop in an abandoned Indian village in the territory of the Mobile Indians. They called the settlement Santa Cruz de Nanicapana, and de Luna went to work to set up a town according to the instructions he had received from Velasco:

I have intended that the first town to be built and settled in the port shall have no more than one hundred and forty houselots, and that the forty shall be utilized for the plaza, a monastery, a church, and a royal house in which the governor shall dwell and where shall be stored the arms, artillery, munitions, and food supplies. This house is to be large enough for everything and is to be separate and have its defenses and the form of a stronghold. The four gates the town is to have are to be visible from the plaza; it is to be large enough to contain all the people. The hundred houses are to be for one hundred heads of families, which seem enough for the defense of the town.[61]

While the main party had moved to the new site overland, the remainder of the group plus all the provisions received from Mexico came by the surviving ships to Mobile Bay. A post called Polonza was established there on the mouth of the Alabama River and supplies were then sent upriver to the new town.

After the establishment of Nanicapana, de Luna sent one of his officers, Mateo del Sauz, two Dominican friars and 200 soldiers on an expedition to discover the land of the lady of Cufitatchiqui, where de Soto had found the artifacts from Ayllón's colony. From there, the expedition would follow the river down to the Punta de Santa Elena and look around for a suitable place for a settlement. Instead of traveling in a northeasterly direction, however, the party traveled to the north and in 16 days reached the territory of the Coosa Indians, some 200 miles from Nanicapana — in present-day Talledega County in Alabama.

It appears that there were two Indian tribes visited by de Soto with very similar names — Cusabo and Coosa. The former tribe lived north of the Savannah River, in the territory of the lady of Cufitatchiqui. Sauz and his party were supposed to be headed there; instead they went to the town of the Coosa Indians on the Alabama River — 200 miles west of Cufitatchiqui. It is not clear how this mistake was made, but Sauz and his party entered the town thinking that it was Cufitatchiqui. They were welcomed by the Coosa Indians just as de Soto and his men had been welcomed by them. The Coosa helped the Spanish set up quarters a little distance from their town and gave them a daily allotment of food, which was adequate but not overly generous. The Spanish soldiers settled down and the Dominicans went about their business of converting the Indians. There was apparently no attempt to find the Punta de Santa Elena.

Meanwhile, things were not going well at Nanicapana. The food supply sent from Mexico was almost gone and there was no food to be found in the countryside. The Mobile Indians had deserted their villages, burning their houses and fields at the approach of the Spanish, and whatever food they had was taken with them when they left. For 20 miles around Nanicapana there was nothing to eat — even the herbs and wild plants had been picked by the settlers until there were none left. In May, de Luna received a letter from Velasco telling him that two ships with food were due to leave Mexico at the end of the month.

The situation in the town was deteriorating rapidly. On June 17, the married soldiers in Nanicapana petitioned de Luna, expressing their concern over conditions in the settlement. They wrote of the hardships caused by the lack of food and the lack of cooperation from the Indians, who, they said, were in "revolt and cannot be brought by any means to the service of the King nor to the knowledge of our holy faith."[62] They were also concerned because the supply fleet from Mexico was overdue. They contended that even if the ships were to arrive that very day, it would be weeks before the food could reach them at Nanicapana, if it ever did — for there were not enough men left with the strength to row the boats upriver to the town. They finally asked that de Luna have compassion on their wives and children.[63]

It was not just food the colonists were in need of but also clothing and shoes, for the weather was, according to Jorge Cerón, the camp master, ruining them. He wrote: "For every eight or ten days there are hard rains, cold, and great heat, in such intemperate succession that the clothing which the men wear does not last twenty days; that which the soldiers have at present is so scanty that they are nearly naked and barefoot."[64]

The petition of the married soldiers was soon followed by one from the Mexican Indians, who asked that they be sent home. Next, de Luna's officers and the royal officials presented him with their petition. De Luna then proposed that the entire group move farther inland to the town of Cufitatchiqui near the Punta de Santa Elena and join Sauz and the party there — even though he had not heard from them and did not know exactly where they were or even if they had reached their destination. Jorge Cerón, his second in command, all the officers and the soldiers refused to go. They maintained that there were not enough provisions in town for the journey, that the people were too weak from hunger and sickness to travel through marshes, swamps and forests and that the Indians would likely take the opportunity to ambush them.[65]

They suggested, instead, that the whole group move to Polonza on Mobile Bay. It would be an easy journey of only four or five days downriver and, once there, the people could live off the bounty of the sea, the palmettos and the wildlife in the area until the supplies arrived from Mexico.[66] On June 22, de Luna gave in and moved the group to Mobile Bay and later to Ochuse on Pensacola Bay. In July the relief fleet from Mexico arrived, but the food supply was not sufficient to feed the group for very long. It was decided to send the women, children, some of the Mexican Indians and the clergy back to Mexico. The exodus from the colony had begun.

On August 10, de Luna received letters from the viceroy in Mexico urging him to proceed with the settlement at Punta de Santa Elena, as that was the king's preference. De Luna hesitated to send another land expedition to search for Santa Elena, as he had heard nothing from the first expedition he had sent there. He decided, instead, to send one of his captains with 50 men and three ships to sail to the east coast and make a temporary settlement in the vicinity of the Punta de Santa Elena. The mission was hampered by bad weather — the ships were scattered and battered by storms and finally put into port in Mexico, never having rounded the Florida peninsula.

At last, in August, came letters from Sauz and the Dominican friars in

Coosa. One of the friars wrote: "As to making a settlement it appears to me that the country is not so well suited for it as we thought. It seems very densely forested, and inasmuch as the Indians have a good part of it occupied, if a settlement were to be made it would be imperative to take their land from them."[67]

De Luna passed this information on to Velasco in Mexico. Velasco was puzzled, for the reports of de Soto's men spoke of the easy journey to Cufitatchiqui and of the availability of food in the area. He reread the manuscripts and determined that a mistake may have been made and the names of the two tribes confused. He wrote to de Luna to find out if the men had taken the road toward the Río del Espiritu Santo (the Mississippi River). If so, then de Luna and his party should not go there but travel overland to Santa Elena, as the most important thing was to plant a settlement there.

It was too late. De Luna had once again tried to take most of the men inland to the town of the Coosa, which he thought was Cufitatchiqui, leaving a token force at Ochuse to garrison it. He issued his orders, but his officers delayed executing them and finally, in September, the officers, royal officials, friars and soldiers asked de Luna's second in command to take charge. At a meeting in the early part of September, the men voted to send a small party to Coosa to recall the men there. When the people from Coosa arrived, a survey was taken of all the men and it was determined that 100 of them were unfit to stay. Therefore a ship was found to return them to Mexico. There were now only 400 to 450 men left in Ochuse.

In October, de Luna agreed that all the official correspondence between the officers, royal officials, friars and soldiers and all their petitions to him should be sent to Mexico to be reviewed by the viceroy. In their letters to the viceroy, the officers claimed that de Luna was ill and mentally incapable of carrying out his duties; in his letter, de Luna asked the viceroy for permission to return to Spain.

In January 1561, Velasco, the royal Audiencia, the archbishop and the officials of the king decided to grant de Luna his request. Angel de Villafañe was sent to take his place. Villafañe was instructed to leave a small holding party of 50 men at Ochuse who, if they did not receive further orders, were to return to Mexico in six months. Villafañe and another group of men were to leave the Gulf Coast and sail around Florida, find the Punta de Santa Elena and establish a post there. Villafañe arrived in Pensacola Bay in April 1561, and upon his arrival de Luna left for Spain. Leaving 50 men behind as he had been instructed, Villafañe sailed for Cuba with 160 men to prepare for his voyage. While in port, Villafañe chose 90 men to accompany him on his expedition. Two or three months later he sailed with four ships and 70 men — the others having deserted.

The fleet sailed through the Bahama Channel with good weather and reached a point that was thought to be the Punta de Santa Elena. According to depositions given by soldiers serving under Villafañe:

They anchored at the said point three leagues out to sea because of the shoals which are many. Being thus anchored Angel de Villafañe set out in a frigate with twenty men. He went ashore and traveled along the shore of the sea ... looking for the river of the said Punta de Santa Elena until they hit upon it and there on the bank of the river Angel de Villafañe took possession of that land in the name of his Majesty.[68]

The fleet continued sailing up the coast to the River Jordan — the site of Ayllón's first landing — but they did not find any port or river where ships could be anchored. That night a hurricane hit the fleet, sinking two of the ships with all hands on board and blowing another out to sea. Villafañe in the one remaining ship decided to leave the area and make for the nearest port in the West Indies. When he arrived, he wrote to the viceroy in Mexico City that Punta de Santa Elena was a bad place with no suitable port for anchorage. On September 23, 1561, Phillip II of Spain decided that there would be no more attempts to settle or garrison Florida.

## Breakdown of De Luna's Colony

| | |
|---|---|
| *Nationality of settlement* | Spain |
| *Sponsored by* | King Philip II of Spain |
| *Physical location* | Pensacola Bay, Florida |
| *Why that location* | It was a good port. |
| *Purpose of settlement* | To establish a strong post on the Gulf of Mexico from which Spanish settlements could spread east and west; to establish a shore base at the Punta de Santa Elena on the Atlantic coast in order to keep the French from settling the area and to protect and support Spanish shipping; and to convert the Indians to the Catholic faith. |
| *When settled* | June 11, 1559 |
| *Climatic conditions* | The settlers complained "every eight or ten days there are hard rains, cold and great heat in such intemperate succession that the clothing ... does not last twenty days." |
| *Relationship with Indians* | The Indians fled upon the approach of the Spanish, abandoning their villages and taking their food supply with them. They burned their fields so the Spanish would not be able to gather food from them. The Indians at Coosa were friendlier but rationed the food they gave the Spanish. |
| *Internal quarreling* | There were disagreements between de Luna and others in the expedition that led to an outright mutiny, with the officers and the royal officials refusing to obey his orders. De Luna was finally allowed to retire to Spain and was replaced by Angel de Villafañe. |
| *Number of initial settlers* | 1,500 people |

| | |
|---|---|
| *Makeup of initial settlers* | 500 were soldiers; there were also the wives and children of some of the soldiers, civilian families, 100 artisans for building, Mexican Indian servants, African slaves, Dominican friars, and at least one physician. |
| *Number of additional settlers* | None |
| *Percentage that survived* | Not known, as some of the settlers returned home before the expedition was ended. |
| *Initial supplies* | 240 horses and medicines were mentioned as supplies—other than that, the documents state that the expedition was well provisioned. The people and supplies were transported in 13 vessels. |
| *How often supplies arrived* | The colony was resupplied in December 1559, July 1560, late September or October 1560 and April 1561. |
| *Stability of the mother country* | Wars with France were over and the country was stable. |
| *Fate of settlement* | The settlement on the Gulf Coast was abandoned sometime after April 1561 and the planned one on the Punta de Santa Elena was never established. |

# THREE

# French Colonization Efforts

## Prelude to Settlement —
## Early French Explorations

France's first venture into the North Atlantic was to the fishing grounds off Newfoundland in 1504. It is difficult today to imagine how important the discovery of these fishing grounds was to 16th-century Europe. At that time Europe was predominantly Catholic and the church required people to abstain from eating meat during lent and on fast days. As the population of Europe grew, so grew the need for fish and the need to find new fishing grounds. Newfoundland supplied this need, and fish — whether it was smoked, dried or salted — became a staple food for Europeans. Fishermen from Portugal, England and Spain soon joined the French in Newfoundland, but it was the ships from France that were predominant.

For several years the fishing banks off Newfoundland were the sole attraction in North America for the French. However, in 1522, survivors of Ferdinand Magellan's round-the-world voyage sailed into Seville and word quickly spread throughout Europe that a southern route to the east could be achieved only by way of the hazardous Strait of Magellan. Since there was no short, easy southern route to the East, could it be possible that there was a northern one? After all, there was a vast area between Florida and Newfoundland that no one as yet had explored; surely there must be a northwestern passage or strait in that region, leading to the South Sea and the wealth of the Orient. Francis I, King of France, was one of those whose interest was caught by the idea of finding a Northwest Passage. In 1524, encouraged by several Florentine silk merchants in Lyon, he decided to give royal and financial support to a voyage to discover a northern strait to China.

The leader of the expedition was a Florentine named Giovanni da Verrazzano. He began his voyage near the Island of Madeira on January 17, 1524, with one ship, 50 men and "food for eight months, with arms and other articles of war, and naval munitions."[1] Verrazzano sailed on a direct route westward from Madeira, avoiding the West Indies and the Spanish and finally arrived at a "new land which had never been seen before by any man, either ancient or modern."[2] He wanted to discover the relationship of the new land to Florida, so he sailed south and, observing the unbroken coastline, was satisfied that the new territory was connected to Florida. Not wanting to "fall foul of the Spaniards,"[3] he then sailed north along the coast searching for the strait.

As the ship made her way along the North Carolina coast, Verrazzano saw what he thought was the South Sea (it was actually Pamlico Sound in present-day North Carolina) across an "isthmus a mile wide and 200 miles long."[4] He wrote: "We sailed the entire length of this island, in the unyielding hope of finding some strait, or, better still, a promontory terminating this land toward the north, so that we might penetrate to the blessed shores of Cathay."[5]

During his expedition, Verrazzano made landfall several times and sent scouting parties to explore the countryside, which he described in detail in his narrative of the voyage. He and his men had many encounters with the Indians, who were friendly for the most part, and he has left us colorful descriptions of their civilizations. His travels took him to New York harbor, Narragansett Bay, and the New England coast. We are not entirely certain how far north he sailed, but it is believed that he at least reached present-day Maine.

As a result of his voyage, Verrazzano was convinced that this "obstacle of new land"[6] that he had found was not part of Asia, as John Cabot had believed, but a continent lying between "our Western Ocean" and "the Eastern Ocean of India."[7] His voyage was of great importance to the cartographers of the day, for it provided heretofore unknown information about the eastern shoreline of North America. Although he had not found the strait, Verrazzano was convinced of its existence and, when he returned from his expedition on July 8, 1524, was anxious to obtain backing for a follow-up voyage to search for it. However, he arrived in France only to find turmoil.

In his 32 years as king of France, Francis I was involved in five wars with his arch rival Charles I, who was not only king of Spain but, after 1519, also Charles V, emperor of the Holy Roman Empire. In the fall of 1524 Francis I was preparing for his second war with Spain and could not spare ships to Verrazzano for a follow-up voyage. The war took a bad turn for the French, as they lost the battle of Pavia in February 1525 and had the humiliation of seeing their king taken prisoner by the Spanish. Francis I, pining away in a Madrid prison until 1526, was in no position to act on Verrazzano's discoveries. Verrazzano had opened up a vast land with great potential for the French to explore and exploit, but the time for further exploration was not right and they were therefore not able to take advantage of it.

The French based their claim to lands in the New World on the voyage of the next explorer who tried to find the elusive strait — Jacques Cartier. Cartier sailed from the port of St. Malo with two ships and 61 men on April 20, 1534, and "sailing on with fair weather"[8] reached Newfoundland on May 10. Cartier's voyage lasted five months. Besides exploring the western coast of Newfoundland, he sailed into the Gulf of St. Lawrence and explored much of the coastline. On his voyage, Cartier made friendly contact with the Indians, bartering with them for furs. He wrote: "I am more than ever of opinion that these people would be easy to convert to our holy faith."[9]

Cartier and his men spent almost ten days, from July 16 to 25, at a harbor on the Gaspé Peninsula, and it was there that the French met a group of Iroquois Indians led by their chief, Donnaconna. The Indians had set up a seasonal fishing camp in the area and were happy to engage in barter and trade with the French. On July 24, the day before they were to leave the area, Cartier and his men erected a large cross on the point of the harbor. Donnaconna immediately took exception to this act and indicated that all the land around there belonged to him. Eventually the French soothed his feelings by explaining that the cross was a landmark to guide them back to this point of land and that when they returned, they would bring Donnaconna and his people iron wares and other goods.

Cartier then asked that two of the chief's teenage sons, Dom Agaya and Taignoagny, accompany him back to France, assuring the chief that the young men would be returned. Donnaconna agreed, and on July 25, 1534, Cartier and his men sailed into the Gulf of St. Lawrence to continue their exploration with the two Indian teenagers on board. After a week of exploring in unfavorable weather, Cartier decided to head for home, reaching St. Malo on September 5. Cartier had not found the passage to China, but he now thought he knew where to look for it — through a strait, which he called the Strait of St. Peter, between the south coast of the present-day province of Québec and Anticosti Island. On his next voyage, he would explore it and perhaps find the strait to the East.

Cartier's second voyage was undertaken by the command of Francis I for the "completion of the discovery of the western lands."[10] He set sail on May 19, 1535, with three ships and 110 men plus the two young Indian men, Dom Agaya and Taignoagny. By August 15 they had reached the Strait of St. Peter. The two Indians told Cartier that

> this [the Strait of St. Peter] was the way to the mouth of the great river of Hochelaga [now called the St. Lawrence River] and the route towards Canada, and that the river grew narrower as one approached Canada,[11] and also that farther up, the water became fresh, and that one could make one's way so far up the river that they had never heard of anyone reaching the head of it.[12]

Cartier was hoping that the river was an arm of the sea and would lead him to China and the Indies. It was also at this point that the two boys mentioned the kingdom of Saguenay for the first time, indicating that this kingdom was two days' journey from the Strait of St. Peter and that the people there had much copper.

Cartier explored the coast, making sure that he was not overlooking a possible strait, and then headed up the St. Lawrence River. Eventually, the three ships came to the Indian town of Stadacona, the home of Donnaconna and his people, situated at the fork of the St. Lawrence River and the St. Charles River at the foot of a high promontory—the site of present-day Québec City. Donnaconna and his people were pleased to see the Frenchmen again and more than pleased to have Dom Agaya and Taignoagny restored to them.

However, Donnaconna was not pleased when Cartier expressed a wish to travel up the St. Lawrence to the town of Hochelaga and tried to discourage him. Donnaconna and his people had long been dominated by the Indians at Hochelaga and Donnaconna saw an opportunity to reverse the situation by playing the part of middleman in the trade between the people at Hochelaga and the French. Therefore he did not want the French to have any contact with the Indians in the interior.

When Dom Agaya and Taignoagny refused to guide him, Cartier took his smallest ship, two longboats and 50 men and made the journey without guides. He reached the town of Hochelaga at the end of September and was greeted with great hospitality by the inhabitants—an estimated one thousand men, women and children. Hochelaga was a large fortified town built in the shadow of a tall hill, which Cartier called Mont Royal (Montréal).

While he was at Hochelaga, Cartier and his men climbed to the summit of Mont Royal, where they saw the St. Lawrence River "extending beyond the spot where we had left our longboats. At that point there is the most violent rapid it is possible to see, which we were unable to pass."[13] The Indians told Cartier that there were more rapids past those, but that beyond the rapids "one could navigate along that river for more than three moons."[14] Cartier would have to look elsewhere for the strait to the Orient.

The Indians also pointed out a mountain range to the north and told the French that "along the mountains to the north, there is a large river, which comes from the west" [the Ottawa River], which Cartier and his men thought "must be the one that flows past the kingdom and province of the Saguenay"— the land that Dom Agaya and Taignoagny had said contained large amounts of copper.[15] The Indians said the land was inhabited by the Agojuda, or bad people, and "they seized the chain of the Captain's whistle, which was made of silver and a dagger-handle of yellow copper-gilt like gold, that hung at the side of one of the sailors and gave us to understand that these [gold and silver] came from up that river where the Agojuda lived."[16] Saguenay was beginning to take on the aura of a land with great potential for riches.

When Cartier and his men returned to Stadacona, it was October 11 and too late in the season to attempt a voyage back to France. The men "found that the mates and sailors who had stayed behind, had built a fort in front of the ships, enclosed on all sides with large wooden logs, planted upright and joined one to the other, with artillery pointing every way, and in a good state to defend us against the whole country-side."[17]

The men busied themselves gathering wood and salting game and fish for the winter. By the middle of November the ice in the river was over twelve feet thick and the snow was four feet deep on the shore. One of the men wrote "All our beverages froze in their casks, and on board our ships, below hatches as on deck, lay four fingers breadth of ice."[18]

As if the weather did not make life difficult enough, scurvy broke out in the French fort, killing 25 of the 110 men before a cure was given them by the Indians—a tree they called annedda (common arborvitae), the bark of which, when ground and boiled in water, provided a potion that cured the disease.

Donnaconna and his people had often spoken to the Frenchmen about the kingdom of Saguenay, which lay a moon's journey up the Saguenay River. Cartier wrote that the Indians "gave us to understand, that in that country, the natives go clothed and dressed in woolens like ourselves; that there are many towns and tribes composed of honest folk who possess great stores of gold and copper."[19]

When Cartier had arrived at Stadacona the previous fall with Donnaconna's two sons, he indicated that he would be interested in taking another small group of Iroquois back to France with him when he sailed. He said, however, that he would take no adults back to France, only children. During the long, cold winter, Cartier had time to think, and just before departing he changed his mind. He tricked Donnaconna, his two sons and several of his headmen on board his ship and made off with them to France. He had not found the strait, but he thought he had found something better, and he wanted Francis I to hear the story of the fabulous kingdom of Saguenay from Donnaconna himself. When Cartier set sail for France on May 6, 1536, he had ten Iroquois on board his ships.

## Charlesbourg-Royal

Jacques Cartier returned from his second voyage on July 16, 1536, with his Indian captives. He presented Donnaconna and the other captives to the king and his court, but it was Donnaconna who became the center of attention with his stories of the fabulous kingdom of Saguenay — a land filled with gold, silver and great rubies. He peopled the land with creatures that had wings instead of arms or who hopped about on one leg, and when he understood the importance of spices to the French, he added cloves, nutmeg and pepper to the gold, silver and rubies that could be found there. Francis I was delighted with the stories and had them repeated to his nobles. Donnaconna's tales were reminiscent of the ones told by Francisco Chicora to Ayllón and the nobles of Spain. To add even more interest to the new land, Cartier had brought back with him some sparkling rocks, which he thought were diamonds, and some iron pyrites, which were supposedly gold.[20]

The king was intrigued. His wars with Spain and the Holy Roman Empire had been expensive, and he had no wealth from conquered empires in the Americas to fill his coffers, as had his Spanish rival. Was it possible that another kingdom, such as Mexico, with unbounded riches, was waiting to be found in the land above the great river discovered by Cartier? It was certainly worth exploring.

The king had maps and charts drawn up showing the great river and the location of Saguenay and displayed them to members of his court. He even invited a well-known Portuguese navigator named Lagarto to court, spending several days talking with him and showing him the charts and repeating Donnaconna's stories of the spices, gold and silver that could be found there. Donnaconna, the king told Lagarto, had even promised to lead the French to Saguenay and personally show them the clove, nutmeg and pepper plants.

In a letter to the Portuguese King John III, Lagarto wrote that he told the French king, after being asked for his opinion, that he had never known spices to grow at such a northern latitude and that he did not believe gold could be found that far north either — silver perhaps, but not gold. He suggested to Francis I that perhaps Donnaconna was not telling the truth — that he was lying in order to convince the French to return him to his homeland. Francis I assured Lagarto that Donnaconna was an honest man and "would not act other than he had said."[21] Besides, the king told Lagarto, the French had interrogated Donnaconna several times and he always told the same story.

Unfortunately, the king became distracted with the outbreak of his fourth war with Spain and the Holy Roman Empire in 1536. When it ended in 1538, preparations for the expedition to Canada and the search for Saguenay began. Cartier drew up a list of what he needed to establish a settlement and explore the countryside. He thought it would be necessary to have 120 extra mariners to stay in the country for exploring the rivers in the knockdown boats that he would carry on board ship with him; 50 musketeers would provide protection for the colony and 30 carpenters and sawyers with 10 master masons would be required to do the building. His other requirements were tile makers, charcoal burners, blacksmiths, metallurgists, vine dressers, farmers, barbers, apothecaries, jewelers, tailors, cobblers, rope makers, gunners and priests. There would be 274 plus full crews for the six ships it would take to carry all the people, their clothing and provisions to last two years. Also, it would be necessary to take seeds and hogs, poultry, cattle and goats for breeding.[22]

On October 17, 1540, Francis I issued a commission to Cartier to return to the lands that he had discovered and to find Saguenay if he could, and "to mingle with their people and live among them, the better to fulfill our aforesaid intention to do something agreeable to God."[23] The king appointed Cartier captain-general and master pilot of all ships in the expedition. Then, in January 1541, before the expedition could get under way, the king for some inexplicable reason placed Jean-François de la Roque, Sieur de Roberval, a nobleman of Picardy, over Cartier with the title of lieutenant-general, chief, commander and captain of the enterprise.

The commission outlined the objectives of the expedition: they were to discover the kingdom of Saguenay, settle the land and convert the Indians to the Catholic faith. It is curious that this was the first time that conversion of the Indians had been mentioned in connection with a French expedition to North America. On Cartier's first two voyages, he took no priests, monks or friars and made no attempt to convert the Indians. This time conversion of the Indians was a primary goal, equal in importance to the discovery of Saguenay. The commission further stipulated that the profits accrued by the expedition were to be split three ways, one third going to the king, one third to the "adventurers"—that is private investors, and one third to cover the expenses of the enterprise.[24]

The king provided some of the ships and money for provisions and supplies and the rest was supplied by investors—the adventurers who were to share a third of the wealth of the new country. Provisions and supplies along with the domestic animals were gathered and loaded aboard the five ships anchored in the harbor of St. Malo. The colonists were ushered aboard and, in April 1541, Cartier was ready to sail. Roberval, however, was not. He "had not as yet his artillery, powder and munitions, and other things necessary come down ... and he was loath to depart without them."[25] The king had written to Cartier and ordered him to depart immediately, "on pain of incurring his displeasure."[26] Roberval decided that Cartier should "depart with the five ships which he had furnished, and should go before."[27] On May 23, 1541, Cartier sailed out of St. Malo on his third voyage to North America.

There do exist first-hand accounts of the voyages of Cartier and Roberval. The narratives of the first two voyages of Cartier are complete and rich in detail, but unfortunately the accounts of the third and fourth voyages are fragmentary. Therefore we do not know how many people sailed on board the five ships or whether Cartier was able to assemble those skilled persons that, when he was compiling his list in 1536, he thought necessary for the establishment of the settlement. Only gentlemen, soldiers and mariners are mentioned as being aboard, but there must have been priests in the company as well, since converting the Indians was a high priority. Reference was also made later in the account of there being carpenters among the settlers, and there were also male and female convicts aboard, for Francis I gave Cartier and Roberval authority to recruit colonists from among the prisoners being held in the jails. His supplies included seeds, horses, cattle, swine, goats and poultry and enough provisions to last for two years.[28]

The voyage was a difficult one, with

> contrary winds and continual torments ... so that our five ships through these storms, lost company one of another. We stood in great need of water, because of the cattle as well [as] goats, hogs, [and] other beasts which we carried for breed in the country, which we were constrained to water with cider and other drink.[29]

By the end of June the five ships met at the harbor at Quirpon in New-foundland. They remained there for several weeks, taking on water and wood and waiting for Roberval and his ships to arrive. Finally Cartier decided that he could wait no longer and set sail for Stadacona, which he reached on August 23, 1541—exactly three months after he had left St. Malo.

The Indians greeted Cartier and his people with apparent joy, and Agona, who had replaced Donnaconna as chief, came on board to greet Cartier in person. He asked about Donnaconna and the others who had been taken back to France. Cartier told him that Donnaconna had died in France, but he lied about the others, telling Agona that they were alive and well, that they "stayed there as great lords, and were married, and would not return back into their country."[30] In truth, all ten of the Indians brought to France by Cartier had died. Agona, according to the French, showed no anger at hearing the news and the French assumed that he was pleased that Donnaconna was dead, as now he would remain as chief. However, the relationship between the two groups of people was not the same as it had been and soon began to show signs of strain.

Cartier was not anxious to establish his settlement next to Stadacona, so he took two of his longboats and went upriver seven or eight miles to a place he had visited on his previous voyage, which he thought a suitable place to plant his colony. It was on the River Rouge—a small river "which he found better and more commodious to ride in and lay his ships,"[31] and there was good land on both sides of the river. At the mouth of the river, where it emptied into the St. Lawrence, on the east side, there was a high cliff that commanded a good view of the river. At the top of the cliff there was a spring of water, and close by the men found a quantity of stones, which they "esteemed to be diamonds."[32] They also found a mine of iron, "leaves of fine gold as thick as a man's nail,"[33] a forest of fine trees, vines, a meadow where hemp was growing wild, and at the end of the meadow "a kind of slate stone black and thick, wherein are veins of mineral matter, which show like gold and silver."[34]

Cartier had his ships brought up and began the job of unloading his colonists, the animals and all the supplies and provisions. They worked from August 26 to September 2, and when they were finished, Cartier sent two ships back to France with letters for the king, telling him what they had done and found and advising him that as yet Roberval had not arrived. Also on board were samples of the riches they had collected.

Some of the men then started to build a fortified settlement on the shores of the river. Cartier decided to call the settlement Charlesbourg-Royal in honor of the king's son, Charles, duc d'Orléans. While some of the men worked on the fort others carved a "way in manner of a pair of stairs"[35] up the side of the cliff, where another fort was built to protect the lower fort and the ships in the river. They found the land rich for growing food, as the narrator of the account wrote "it is as good a country to plow and manure as a man should find or desire. Here we set twenty men to work, which in one day had labored about an acre and an half of the said ground, and sowed it part with Naveaus or small turnips, which at the end of eight days ... sprang out of the earth."[36]

Having given his orders as to the work that needed to be done, Cartier took two longboats filled with provisions and some of the mariners and gentlemen in order to explore the route to Saguenay. On his last voyage to Canada, the Indians at Stadacona had told Cartier that the easiest, safest and most direct way to way to get to Saguenay was to sail up the St. Lawrence to a point past Hochelaga where a tributary empties into the river. That tributary, they said, flows from the Kingdom of Saguenay. However, past Hochelaga there were falls, or what the French called saults, in the river, and Cartier intended to sail to Hochelaga to "view and understand the fashion of the Saults of water, which are to be passed to goe to Saguenay."[37] Leaving his brother-in-law Vicomte de Beaupré in charge of Charlesbourg-Royal, Cartier left on September 7 with his men to reconnoiter the river passage to the fabulous and rich kingdom of Saguenay.

Along the way Cartier, and his men stopped at a large Indian village where the chief, whose friendship dated from their previous voyage, greeted them with cordiality. On September 11, they reached the outskirts of Hochelaga, passed it and continued upriver to face the first of the falls or rapids—the Sainte-Marie—around which they were forced to portage. The portage led to an Indian village where four young men volunteered to guide them to the next village, situated on the north bank of the Lachine Rapids, which fall 42 feet in two miles. At that village, Cartier learned of the third and greatest of the falls—Long Sault—on the way to Saguenay. It was close to November; the long Canadian winter was beginning to set in and Cartier decided to return to Charlesbourg-Royal. On their way back along the St. Lawrence, the Frenchmen stopped at the Indian village they had visited before, to find it mysteriously empty of the chief and many of his men. In the words of the narrative:

> But in truth he [the chief] was gone to Canada [Stadacona] to conclude with Agona, what they should do against us. And when we were arrived at our fort, we understood by our people, that the savages of the country came not any more about our fort as they were accustomed, to bring us fish, and that they were in a wonderful doubt and fear of us.[38]

To make the French even more uneasy, some of the men had been to Stadacona on a visit and reported that there were a large number of Indian men from around the countryside assembled at the village. Cartier wisely strengthened his defenses and put his men on alert.

Disappointingly that is where the narrative ends—sometime in the late fall of 1541. The next we hear of Cartier and his colonists is in June 1542, when the three ships carrying them sailed into Newfoundland on their way back to France. As luck would have it, they encountered Roberval with three ships full of colonists on his way to join them in Charlesbourg-Royal.

Cartier came to meet with Roberval on board his ship to report on the situation in Canada and give his reasons for returning to France. He told Roberval that they had found gold, silver and diamonds in the countryside and had a large quantity of these treasures aboard the ships. Indeed, the rumor in Newfoundland was that the ships contained "ten barrels of gold ore and seven of silver, and seven quintals of pearls and precious stones,"[39] and that the gold had been tried in a furnace and found to be good. Unfortunately for Cartier, the "riches" he had on broad turned out to be worthless.

Cartier told Roberval that "he could not with his small company withstand the savages, which went about daily to annoy him: and that this was the cause of his return into France."[40]

A Spanish fisherman in Newfoundland at the time of Cartier's arrival met some of Cartier's men aboard his ship. The men told him that some 35 people were dead as the result of Indian attacks — including some carpenters who were out cutting wood.[41] When asked if any men were left at the settlement, they replied "none but the murdered men, and others who died."[42]

According to the narrator of Roberval's voyage,

> Nevertheless, he [Cartier] and his company commended the country to be very rich and fruitful. But when our General being furnished with sufficient forces, commanded him to go back again with him, he and his company, moved as it seemeth with ambition, because they would have all the glory of the discovery of those parts themselves, stole privily away the next night from us, and without taking their leave departed home for Bretaigne.[43]

They reached St. Malo sometime in the middle of October 1542.

Cartier's official reason for abandoning his settlement was the hostility of the Indians, and there seems to be little doubt that the Indians did attack and kill some of the settlers. Roberval, however, seemed to think that Cartier and his people abandoned their fort because they were anxious to return home to enjoy the riches they had gathered and reap the glory of their discovery. Whatever the reason, the settlement at Charlesbourg-Royal was abandoned, and it would be up to Roberval and his colonists to search for the kingdom of Saguenay and establish a permanent settlement in Canada.

## *Breakdown of Cartier's Colony at Charlesbourg-Royal*

| | |
|---|---|
| *Nationality of settlement* | French |
| *Sponsored by* | King Francis I |
| *Physical location* | Near present day Québec City on the River Rouge a tributary of the St. Lawrence River |
| *Why that location* | The river offered a good anchorage for the ships, with good land for farming on both sides. At the mouth of the river toward the east, on a high cliff that commanded a view of the St. Lawrence, a lookout post was built. |

| | |
|---|---|
| *Purpose of settlement* | To discover the kingdom of Saguenay, to establish a settlement and to convert the Indians to the Catholic faith |
| *When settled* | August 23, 1541 |
| *Climatic conditions* | On arrival it was good, as settlers reported that the seeds they planted "sprung out of the ground in eight days." By mid–November there was ice in the river, which did not start to break up until April. |
| *Relationship with Indians* | Cartier had visited the area before and kidnapped the chief and some of his people. All the Indians died in France. When Cartier did not bring the kidnapped Indians back, relations cooled and then turned hostile. |
| *Internal quarreling* | None reported |
| *Number of initial settlers* | The exact number is not known, but they sailed in five ships. |
| *Makeup of initial settlers* | Gentlemen, mariners, carpenters, priests and convicts, both male and female were among the colonists. |
| *Number of additional settlers* | Roberval was supposed to join Cartier with more settlers and supplies but did not arrive until Cartier and his settlers had left. |
| *Percentage that survived* | Unknown; some killed by Indians and some died of disease. |
| *Initial supplies* | It was reported that the fleet sailed with provisions for two years plus seeds for planting, goats, hogs, cattle and "other beasts which we carried for breed in the country." |
| *How often supplies arrived* | They were not resupplied. |
| *Stability of the mother country* | France was involved in a series of wars with Spain and the Holy Roman Empire. There was a war that started in 1542 during the colonizing effort by Cartier. |
| *Fate of settlement* | It was abandoned in June 1542. |

# France-Roy

When Cartier and his five ships left the harbor at St. Malo on May 23, 1541, Roberval had stated that he intended to sail to Rouen "to prepare a ship or two at Honfleur,"[44] where he was expecting his supplies to arrive, and then follow Cartier to Canada. Almost a year passed, however, before he sailed for North America. What had he been doing all that time? According to a Portuguese agent in St. Malo, in October 1541 Roberval:

> came to the entrance of St. Malo, but only landed to buy meat and bread, and then re-embarked and put to sea with four vessels, with which he sails about as a fleet....

He has captured many vessels both Portuguese and English, and so with all others he comes across. He lives on the sea and dares not land, as in all ports watch is kept for him.[45]

It appears that Roberval had taken to piracy and had captured several prizes.

In the spring of 1542, Roberval was finally ready to fulfill the terms of his commission, sailing "with three tall ships, and two hundred persons ... men, women, and children"[46] on board. A Spanish spy in St. Malo reported that there were soldiers, masons, carpenters, priests, physicians and barbers among the passengers, along with gentlemen volunteers and ladies. The ships were well supplied with arms and provisions, which were paid for by the king, and had the usual assortment of domestic animals.[47]

They left La Rochelle on April 16, 1542, and — after experiencing "contrary weather"[48]—finally reached St. John's Harbor in Newfoundland on June 7. A few days later, Roberval was surprised by the arrival in St. John's Harbor of Cartier and his settlers on their way back to France. In spite of Cartier's warning about the Indians at Stadacona, Roberval was firm in his resolution to go there and attempt a settlement. The fleet spent several weeks in St. John's Harbor, taking on fresh water and arbitrating a quarrel between some of the French and Portuguese fishermen. At the end of June they were prepared to sail to the site of Cartier's settlement.

Roberval sailed past Stadacona and made landfall on the banks of the River Rouge, but no mention was made of Charlesbourg-Royal or any of the buildings erected by Cartier. It is possible that the Indians tore them down soon after the French had left. The narrative account of the voyage states,

In this place we found a convenient harbor for our shipping, where we cast anchor, went ashore with our people, and chose out a convenient place to fortify ourselves in, fit to command the main river, and of strong situation against all invasion of enemies. Thus toward the end of July, we brought our victuals and other munitions and provisions on shore, and began to travail in fortifying of ourselves.[49]

Roberval called his settlement France-Roy. He had a fort built,

which was very beautiful to behold, and of great force, situated upon an high mountain, wherein there were two courts of buildings, a great Tower, and another of forty or fifty foot long: wherein there were divers chambers, an hall, a kitchen, houses of office, cellars high and low, and near unto it were an oven and mills, and a stove to warm men in, and a well before the house. And the building was situated upon the great River of Canada, called France Prime, by Monsieur Roberval.[50]

There was also at the foot of the mountain another lodging, part whereof was a great tower of two stories high, two courts of good building, where at the first all our victuals, and whatsoever was brought with us was sent to be kept: and near unto that tower there is another small river.[51]

Roberval had settled in almost the same spot as Cartier, and doubtless his main fort was on top of the promontory where Cartier had his lookout tower.

In the month of August we are told, every person was "occupied in such work as each was able to do."[52] On September 14, Roberval sent two of his ships back to France "to carry news to the king."[53] He also instructed the two captains to return the next year with more provisions and "other things, as it should please the king."[54] Roberval was curious about the diamonds Cartier had brought back to France and asked the captains to "bring news out of France how the king accepted certain diamonds which were sent him, and were found in this country."[55]

After the ships left, the settlers began to prepare for the winter. They took stock of their food supply and found it to be lacking. From now on food would be rationed, so that each mess, (a group of five to eight people[56]) was allowed only two loaves of bread — each weighing one pound — and a half a pound of beef. They had bacon and a half-pound of butter at dinner and beef with two handfuls of beans at supper. Three days a week they fasted and ate dried cod or porpoises and beans. Occasionally the Indians would appear with baskets of fish, which they traded to the French for "knives and other small trifles."[57] There were apparently no fresh vegetables in their diet; therefore, as might be expected, scurvy broke out and killed at least 50 persons. It is not apparent from the narratives whether the people at France-Roy knew of the cure for the disease.

Roberval seems to have been a strict governor, as the narrative account reports that

> Monsieur Roberval used very good justice, and punished every man according to his offence. One whose name was Michael Gaillon, was hanged for his theft. John of Nantes was laid in irons, and kept prisoner for his offense, and others also were put in irons, and divers were whipped, as well men as women: by which means they lived in quiet.[58]

There were no mutinies in France-Roy.

The narrative notes that in April the ice in the river began to break up. The French must have greeted that sight with great pleasure, for it meant that they had survived the winter and could now turn their thoughts to exploration and the kingdom of Saguenay. Roberval began to make his plans, but it was not until June 5, 1543, that he started. With eight barks and 70 men he began the journey. Roberval left 30 people at the fort with instructions to return to France if he had not returned by July 1. Messengers from the exploring party were sent to France-Roy on June 14 with the news that one bark had sunk and eight men drowned. Another group of men arrived at the settlement on June 19 with 60 pounds of Indian corn and letters instructing them to stay there until July 22.

Unfortunately, that is where the narrative ends. Roberval apparently made it to the Lachine rapids and, like Cartier before him, became discouraged and turned back. Evidently he decided not to wait for the resupply from France but rather to abandon the settlement and return home. He reached France on September 11, 1543. Why did Roberval give up? There is no mention in the narratives about Indian attacks or even overt hostility. The only clue comes from an inscription on a map made by Desceliers in 1550. It shows Canada and the St. Lawrence River, and the inscription relates the fact that Francis I sent M. de

Roberval to settle the land. The inscription then states that the settlement was abandoned, the reason being that "It was impossible to trade with the people of that country because of their austerity, the intemperate climate of said country, and the slight profit."[59]

France-Roy, like Charlesbourg-Royal, was abandoned. The gold, silver and diamonds turned out to be as false as the kingdom of Saguenay. The Indians and the long, cold winters discouraged settlement in Canada, and it would be many years before Frenchmen would again venture up the St. Lawrence — the Great River of Canada.

## *Breakdown of Roberval's Colony at France-Roy*

| | |
|---|---|
| *Nationality of settlement* | French |
| *Sponsored by* | King Francis I |
| *Physical location* | On the River Rouge, a tributary of the St. Lawrence River — near the site of present-day Québec City. |
| *Why that location* | It was a good harbor for the ships and was a good defensive site, for there was a high cliff that commanded the main river. It was there that they built their fortified settlement. |
| *Purpose of settlement* | To discover the kingdom of Saguenay, to establish a settlement and to convert the Indians to the Catholic faith |
| *When settled* | July 1542 |
| *Climatic conditions* | Good on arrival, but the winter lasted from mid–November when ice begins to form in the river, until mid–April when it starts to break up. |
| *Relationship with Indians* | Probably strained, but there was no mention of open hostility. The settlers reported that the Indians brought fish to the fort, which they traded for knives and "trifles." |
| *Internal quarreling* | None — Roberval was a stern ruler and punished offenders harshly and swiftly. |
| *Number of initial settlers* | 200 |
| *Makeup of initial settlers* | Gentlemen volunteers, gentlewomen, children, soldiers, masons, carpenters, priests, physicians and barbers |
| *Number of additional settlers* | None |
| *Percentage that survived* | At least 50 died of scurvy and eight men drowned on an exploring expedition. Seventy men went on the expedition and Roberval said he left thirty at the fort. It is possible that some went back with the two ships that returned to France in September 1542. It is also possible that the 30 people left at the fort did not include women and children. |

| | |
|---|---|
| *Initial supplies* | Well supplied with arms and provisions and domestic animals |
| *How often supplies arrived* | Were supposed to be resupplied in the summer of 1543, but the settlers left before the relief ships arrived. |
| *Stability of the mother country* | The last of the five wars fought by Francis I with Spain started in 1542. |
| *Fate of settlement* | It was abandoned at the end of July 1543. |

# Charlesfort

After the failure of Cartier and Roberval to establish a settlement in Canada, French interest in North America seemed to wane. The situation in France might have accounted for the lack of interest, for in 1547 Francis I died, leaving the throne to his son Henri II and leaving the country deeply in debt. Henri carried on with his father's foreign policy, engaged in the bloodiest of the wars with Spain and incurred even more debt. It is no wonder that the French had no time for the frozen world of Canada, especially since the "gold and diamonds" found there proved to be worthless.

By 1559 both France and Spain were tired of fighting and agreed to end the wars by signing a peace treaty, which included the marriage of Philip II of Spain to the daughter of the French King Henri II and his wife, Catherine de Médici. It seemed as though a period of peace and stability was about to begin in France. Unfortunately, at a jousting tournament held to celebrate the marriage of his daughter, Henri II was accidentally killed while participating in one of the events. His throne went to his son, the young and sickly Francis II, whose brief reign ended with his death in 1560. His ten-year-old brother, Charles IX, succeeded him. His reign marked the beginning of 36 years of instability and disorder brought about by religious dissension between Protestants and Catholics and by a struggle for power and influence between two factions at court.

Although, there did not appear to be much official interest in pursuing settlements in North America, the idea had not been forgotten. There were people around the king and his mother, the regent, who had a great deal of interest in the New World. One of these people was Gaspard de Coligny, the admiral of France[60] and a close advisor to Queen Regent Catherine de Médici. Coligny also happened to be a leader of the moderate Huguenots, as the French Protestants were called, and had lands in the seafaring province of Normandy, which had strong Protestant leanings.

There were a number of reasons why the French were interested in North America. They had never accepted the concept that the entire New World belonged to Spain and Portugal and always maintained that anyone had the right to settle uninhabited land. Spain and Portugal were occupying lands in the Caribbean and South America, but North America lay empty of Europeans. France had claimed the vaguely defined lands north of Florida by virtue of the voyage of Verrazzano in 1524, and on most of the maps of the day this area was known as New France. Florida had been claimed by the Spanish, but they had not been successful in settling it. Therefore, since it was uninhabited, the French felt free to try to occupy it themselves. The French crown wanted to share in the prestige and glory of establishing a colonial empire in the New World as the Spanish and Portuguese had done, but they also wanted to find valuable natural resources or even to discover a rich new civilization to exploit. Added to these ambitions was the Northwest Passage, the finding of which was still a major goal.

Coligny would draw the mariners for his voyage to the lands north of Florida from the seafaring Protestant areas of France, but there is no indication that the mission was for the purpose of establishing a colony for Huguenots, although religion may have been part of the reason for it. Coligny had long been a believer in religious tolerance and felt that religious dissenters could at the same time be loyal and patriotic Frenchmen. If the Huguenots could establish a permanent settlement in North America, boosting the power, prestige and wealth of France, they would gain acceptance for themselves and their religion.[61] And as a loyal Frenchman, Coligny hoped that his expedition and the resulting settlement would diminish the power of Spain and perhaps lead to an alliance with Protestant England against their common enemy — Spain.

These issues were in the minds of the queen mother, Coligny and others around the king, but there were those who were moved to participate in the venture for more personal reasons. The wealthy merchants who would give financial backing to the expedition and the mariners who would sign on for the voyage were thinking of the new settlement as a base from which to attack the Spanish treasure fleets. That this was commonly talked of is borne out by the testimony of Guillaume Rouffin, the cabin boy, who was left at Charlesfort when the French abandoned it in 1563 and was captured by the Spanish, who interrogated him very closely. He told them the expedition

> ... came directly to this coast of Florida to settle on the Point and river of St. Helena, and to discover whether it was a good location for going out into the Bahama Channel to capture the fleets from the Indies. This he knows because he heard it said by everyone and it was common knowledge.[62]

Coligny wanted to start the expedition as quickly and quietly as possible so that the Spanish would not know anything about the settlement until it was established. Perhaps he had heard of the failure of Luna's attempt to colonize Florida and wanted to establish his own settlement before the Spanish tried again and were successful. The man he chose to head the expedition was Jean Ribault, a navigator of some renown who had, on previous occasions, worked as a cartographer for the English; he was also a Protestant. The first voyage was intended to be one of discovery, exploration and of formally claiming the land in the name of Charles IX by placing stone markers in the new territory. Subsequent voyages would then bring settlers with adequate supplies to colonize the land, depending, of course, on the situation in France.

Jean Ribault left Havre de Grâce on February 18, 1562, with two ships and 150 men to sail to Florida and explore the coast to the north. The expedition was "made up and sent out at the command and cost of the Queen Mother of France, the Admiral [Gaspard de Coligny] and Monsieur Vendôme [a military adviser to the queen]."[63] The ships were well armed as the larger of the two carried "fifteen large brass cannon and two of smaller size and eight brass falcons, besides other arms and ammunition."[64] The smaller vessel was equally well armed. Accompanying Ribault as his second-in-command was a nobleman from Dieppe named René Laudonnière. Ribault had experienced soldiers with him and gentlemen who may have been officers, and, of course, mariners and pilots.

According to Laudonnière, who wrote an account of the voyage, they navigated "for about two months evading the Spanish route"[65] and on April 30 saw the line of the Florida coast. They turned northward and came to the mouth of a "large and beautiful river"[66] where Ribault decided to anchor his ships so he could explore the area the next day. Taking the "row barges"[67] and a small boat, they entered the harbor and spent the day exploring both sides of the river. They were met by two groups of Indians, one on each bank of the river, who were friendly and anxious to trade. The next day Ribault erected a column of stone with the arms of France carved on it "not far from the mouth of the river and on a little sandy knoll."[68] They called the river the River of May (the St. John's River in Jacksonville, Florida) because it was May 1 when they discovered it.

They spent several days there exploring the river and enjoying the hospitality of the Indians. Then they left to explore along the coast to the north. As they sailed, they found many rivers, which they named after the rivers in France, but they sailed on hoping to reach the land of Chicora (the area of Allyón's first landing), where cities rich in gold, silver and pearls were rumored to be found. But the weather turned bad with "great fogs and heavy seas"[69] and the ships were forced to seek safe harbor in a large river, "exceeding all others in size and beauty,"[70] which they decided to call Port Royal. The next day the weather cleared and they sailed some six or seven miles up the river and went ashore to explore the area, which they found to be beautiful. The Indians they encountered were frightened at first and would not come near the ships, but eventually they overcame their fear and traded gladly with the French.

Two young Indian men were enticed aboard the ship with the idea of taking them back to France, as had been commanded by the queen mother. Laudonnière spent time with them trying to learn their language, and the two Indians invited him to return to their homes with them and said they would introduce him to Chiquola, the great lord of that territory. Chiquola, they said, lived in a large enclosed place with many houses inside it. The inhabitants "had no concern for gold, silver, or pearls because they had them in great abundance."[71] Laudonnière immediately tried to find out from the two Indians where this great city was located. From what he could understand, it was somewhere to the north. He thought it was more than likely to be in the land of Chicora on the Jordan River, which during Ayllón's time was rumored to be rich in pearls. The two young men were anxious to leave the ship, however, and finally managed to escape, leaving the clothing and other things the French had given them behind.

At some point in his exploring, Ribault conceived the idea of leaving some of the men in this pleasant spot to start a fortified settlement. It is ironic that only a year earlier, during the summer of 1561, Villafañe had sailed this coast and been unsuccessful in finding a suitable harbor, declaring the coast to be a bad place with no decent anchorage for ships. Having formulated the idea of starting a settlement on this voyage, Ribault needed volunteers to stay in the country as colonists. Therefore he called all the men together and in a long speech talked of patriotism and duty and the opportunity for ordinary men to advance themselves beyond their greatest dreams. Finally, he asked for volunteers to remain in the country. Twenty-eight[72] men stepped forward. Ribault promised that he would return within six months with "more ships and many people, with cattle and other things, to settle that land."[73] He chose Captain Albert de la Pierria, the first volunteer to step forward, to be in charge of the fort.

The site chosen by Ribault, and approved by the men who were to make it their home, was on an island "which ended on a point toward the mouth of the river."[74] There was a little river flowing from the interior of the island, and Ribault found it deep enough and large enough to accommodate a number of ships. On the brink of the river was an open space suitable for the building of a fortress. Laudonnière and Captain Salles measured out the perimeter, which, considering that 28 men were to live there, measured only "sixteen toises by thirteen in breadth, with flanks in proportion."[75] A toise equals 6.396 U.S. feet. Therefore, the fort measured 102.336 by 83.148 feet. In his account of the voyage, Laudonnière states "We sent to the ships for men and shovels, picks, and other instruments necessary for the work and we worked so hard that in a very short time the fort was made defensible."[76] They decided to call it Charlesfort in honor of the King, Charles IX.

Ribault left the men food for six months and arms and munitions for their defense. In his farewell speech, he asked them to give Captain Albert the obedience a true soldier owes his general and asked them to live as brothers with one another. Then Ribault and the returning men boarded the ships and prepared to sail, leaving the harbor with a fair breeze on June 11, 1562. As they left the harbor, the departing men turned for one last look at the fort and their fellow Frenchmen who were staying. They fired a farewell cannon salute — it was promptly returned by the men in Charlesfort.

The men then set to work to build up their fortifications. According to the testimony that Guillaume Rouffin gave to his Spanish interrogators, the fort consisted of "an enclosed house of wood and earth covered with straw with a moat around it, with four bastions, and on them two brass falcons and six small iron culverins."[77]

That being done, the men made plans to explore the countryside, making contact first with King Audusta and his village and then proceeding to four other villages whose chiefs were allies of Audusta. Everywhere they were greeted with great hospitality, and harmony was established between the Indians and the men in Charlesfort.

In a short time, however, the Frenchmen were obliged to approach their friends for food, as their supply was running low and Ribault had not returned with more provisions. The Indians gave them as much as they could but indicated that in doing so they would be reduced to living off acorns and roots. They advised the settlers to visit a land to the south ruled by Covecxis and his brother Oade. There, they said, the people had corn, beans and flour in abundance. Captain Albert was able to get food from the two brothers, who pledged their everlasting friendship to the French and said they would be happy to supply them with food in the future if they should need it.

Upon their return, the men at Charlesfort stored the food in their wooden house, content in the thought that they had provisions enough to last until Ribault's return. Unfortunately, one night as they slept, tragedy struck. Laudonnière, who got the story from the survivors of the fort, reported that "fire caught up their lodgings with such fury ... that the great room that was built for them before our departure was consumed in an instant. Nothing was saved except a small amount of food."[78]

King Audusta and his people helped the men to rebuild the house. According to Laudonnière, the Indians finished the house in 12 hours. However, King Audusta could not replenish the lost food, and Captain Albert was forced to travel back to the territory belonging to Covecxis and Oade to ask for more corn, beans and flour.

Up to this point the men in Charlesfort had gotten along well, but gradually the situation began to deteriorate. Two men drowned crossing a river in a canoe, and Captain Albert became domineering, using language so rude and harsh that Laudonnière, in his account, would not even repeat it. The captain threatened the men continually in order to make them obey, hanged a drummer at the fort "for a rather minor offense"[79] and banished a solider named LaChere to a distant island, refusing to send him food as he had promised.

The level of discontent among the men rose to such a point that, according to Guillaume Rouffin, when Albert struck one of the soldiers with a club, the soldier retaliated by drawing his sword. In the ensuing struggle, Albert was killed. The men then chose Captain Nicholas Barré to lead them, and being an able and reasonable man, Barré was soon able to restore order in the fort and rescue the banished LaChere.

Peace reigned, but the men were discontented with the dreary little fort, the lack of anything to do and most likely were tired of each other's company. Ribault had not returned, nor had anyone else come to resupply them, and the men longed for home. But how could they return? There were three thousand miles of ocean between them and France, and they not only had no ship but also no means of building one, as there was not a shipwright among them.

Desperate men, however, can often accomplish seemingly impossible tasks. They had the forge Ribault had left them and some iron and tools with which they went to work. They cut the bark from the pine trees in the woods and used the resin to cover the boat. They sewed their shirts and bedding together for sails and caulked the seams of the ship with the long moss that hung from the trees. The only thing lacking was rope, and that difficulty was overcome by Audusta and his men, who upon hearing of the problem, promised to make enough rope to rig the ship.

Soon the ship was ready; the forge, tools, guns, ammunition and food were stored aboard and the men were ready to leave. Guillaume Rouffin, the 15-year-old cabin boy, knowing that there was no navigator among them, decided to stay with the Indians. The French gave what was left of their goods to the Indians, and with a fair breeze set sail for France. Rouffin told his Spanish interrogators in June 1564 that the men had been gone for 14 months, which would put their departure in April 1563.

For several weeks their luck held and steady winds propelled the ship at good speed. Then the winds died and the boat was stuck in the doldrums, traveling only some sixty miles in three weeks. The men had not taken the unpredictability of the wind into consideration and had underestimated the quantity of provisions they would need. Food ran low, and each man was allowed only 12 kernels of maize a day. Soon that was gone, and they ate their leather shoes and leather jerkins. The water barrels were empty, and some of the men began to drink the seawater. The winds picked up and the sea became rough, waves breaking over the top of the boat and threatening to capsize it. The men, weakened from hunger, struggled to bail out the water, and the seams that had been caulked with moss began to leak. Once the wind died down and the seas were calm the boat was no longer in danger of sinking, but the men were desperate for food and there was nothing to eat on board the ship. At last they decided on a human sacrifice, so that while one man would die, the others would live. The lot fell to LaChere — the soldier who had been banished by Captain Albert.

Eventually the men came within sight of the coast of France, but by now their boat was in such bad condition that they had no way of steering it. They were drifting on the water when an English ship came to their rescue. The

English put the weakest of the men ashore and took the others to England, where they were held as prisoners.

But what had happened to Ribault? Why had he not returned with supplies and more settlers as he had promised? When Ribault returned from his voyage to the southeastern coast of North America, he intended to report on his activities to Admiral Coligny and collect colonists and supplies for a return voyage. However, he arrived in France only to find that a religious civil war had broken out in his country. In the midst of the turmoil engulfing France, Ribault had no opportunity to gather either supplies or colonists for Charlesfort.

Eventually Ribault made his way to England, where he tried to enlist the help of Elizabeth I in his venture at Charlesfort. He joined forces with a man named Thomas Stucley — an Englishman who at one time had worked for Henri II of France and who was then heavily in debt and looking for a way to pay off his creditors. Ribault was able to persuade Stucley to carry provisions to the garrison at Charlesfort by telling him of the rich opportunities that awaited him in the area. After obtaining the permission of the queen for his voyage, Stucley began to prepare his fleet, intending to sail in May 1563. Meanwhile Ribault intended to go back to France, where he hoped to outfit other ships with settlers and provisions and return with them to Charlesfort. Unfortunately none of these plans materialized. Ribault was stopped as he was attempting to leave England and held in the Tower of London as a spy for several months.[80] Stucley never crossed the Atlantic with his fleet; he spent his time cruising the waters as a privateer, attacking whatever ships he came across.

The men at Charlesfort were left on their own not from any neglect on the part of Ribault or Coligny but because of events quite outside their control. If Ribault had been able to return as he promised — with new settlers, provisions, domestic animals and seeds for planting — would the settlement have survived? It is hard to say. But because no help came to Charlesfort, its inhabitants, discouraged and neglected, decided to abandon it, and the first attempt by the French to plant a permanent settlement on the southeastern coast of North America ended in failure. They would have to try again.

## Breakdown of the Colony at Charlesfort

| | |
|---|---|
| *Nationality of settlement* | French |
| *Sponsored by* | Queen Mother Catherine de Medici, Admiral Coligny, and Monsieur Vendome |
| *Physical location* | Island in Port Royal Sound — Parris Island, South Carolina |
| *Why that location* | There was a good harbor for the ships and a clear, pleasant site for the fort. |
| *Purpose of settlement* | To lay formal claim to the land by establishing a permanent settlement, to explore the country for valuable resources and rich native civilizations and |

|                                   |                                                                                                                                                                                                                                                                                      |
|-----------------------------------|--------------------------------------------------------------------------------------------------------------------------------------------------------------------------------------------------------------------------------------------------------------------------------------|
|                                   | to search for the Northwest Passage. An underlying motive among the crew and passengers on the voyage was to establish a base from which to attack the Spanish treasure fleets.                                                                                                         |
| *When settled*                    | May 27, 1562                                                                                                                                                                                                                                                                          |
| *Climatic conditions*             | Not mentioned                                                                                                                                                                                                                                                                         |
| *Relationship with Indians*       | Good                                                                                                                                                                                                                                                                                  |
| *Internal quarreling*             | There was discontent with Captain Albert, the leader, who was domineering and unreasonable. The men mutinied and killed him. They chose a new leader who governed with more success.                                                                                                   |
| *Number of initial settlers*      | Twenty-eight men were left at Charlesfort as settlers while the rest went back to France.                                                                                                                                                                                             |
| *Makeup of initial settlers*      | There were soldiers, sailors and gentlemen in the group.                                                                                                                                                                                                                              |
| *Number of additional settlers*   | Charlesfort was supposed to be resupplied with settlers and provisions, but they never arrived.                                                                                                                                                                                       |
| *Percentage that survived*        | 85.7 percent. Of the approximately 28 men left behind, 5 died.                                                                                                                                                                                                                        |
| *Initial supplies*                | The men were left supplies to last them for six months.                                                                                                                                                                                                                               |
| *How often supplies arrived*      | The resupply fleet never arrived.                                                                                                                                                                                                                                                     |
| *Stability of the mother country* | Very unstable. In 1562 the first of the religious civil wars broke out in France. When Ribault returned to France for more settlers and supplies, he found that war had broken out and was not able to gather a fleet to return to Charlesfort. He sought aid in England, but the supply fleet assembled there for the relief of Charlesfort went privateering instead. |
| *Fate of settlement*              | Abandoned. According to the information given the Spanish by Rouffin in June 1564, the men had been gone from the area for 14 months, which would mean they abandoned the fort in April of 1563.                                                                                        |

# Fort Caroline

On September 23, 1561, Philip II of Spain had announced that there would be no more attempts by the Spanish to settle the southeastern coast of North America. In January 1562, barely four months after this announcement, the Spanish ambassador in Paris wrote the king that ships under the command of Jean Ribault were making ready to sail to the west. Ribault's fleet left Havre de Grâce on February 18, 1562, and when news of the French fleet and its probable destination reached Cuba, it caused great concern among the officials there. Fear that the French were about to found a base on the southeastern coast, from which they could attack the Spanish treasure fleet, led them to send a frigate commanded by Hernando Manrique de Rojas to find the French and destroy any settlement they might have established.

Rojas sailed in May 1564 and located Charlesfort in Port Royal Sound, thanks to the information given him by Guillaume Rouffin, whom he found living among the Indians. The French fort was deserted, with no sign of recent habitation; Rojas ordered it burned and returned to Cuba confident that there was no French presence in Florida. He was premature in this assumption, for as he was leaving Port Royal Sound on June 15, Laudonnière's fleet of three ships with settlers and provisions was sailing toward the coast of Florida, making landfall there on June 22.

The idea of starting a colony in New France, as the French called all the land in North America from the southern tip of Florida to Canada, had not been forgotten by Admiral Coligny and others. The religious war that had raged in France was over for the time being and the Treaty of Amboise signed in March 1563. Admiral Coligny was once more in favor at the court of Charles IX and his mother, Catherine de Médici, and he obtained authority to send another expedition to North America to attempt a settlement. Since Ribault was still being detained in England, Coligny asked Laudonnière to head the expedition.

The three ships under Laudonnière's command left Havre-de-Grâce on April 22, 1564. They carried arms, munitions, provisions, sheep, poultry and 200 men — soldiers, mariners, young noblemen who volunteered for the expedition "at their cost and charges,"[81] and artisans such as carpenters, sawyers, smiths, shipwrights and an apothecary. There was one woman in the group who was hired to be Laudonnière's housekeeper and to look after the domestic animals. No farmers were mentioned in the group, and most but not all were Huguenots. Among the settlers was a man named Jacques Le Moyne de Morgues, who had been recruited for the voyage as a recorder of information, "to map the seacoast, and lay down the position of towns, the depth and courses of the rivers and the harbors; and to represent also the dwellings of the natives."[82] His account of the settlement at Fort Caroline presents the history of the settlement from a different viewpoint and adds to the narrative written by Laudonnière.

On June 22, Laudonnière's fleet reached a little river on the coast of Florida. To the delight of the crew and passengers, they found dolphins playing in the water at the mouth of the river; therefore Laudonnière decided to call it the River of Dolphins (today it is called the Matanzas River near St. Augustine). He anchored his ships and went ashore with a small party to reconnoiter the area. Although the Indians they met on shore encouraged them to stay, Laudonnière did not find the harbor there suitable, and the next day the French set sail for the St. John's River (the River of May), which Laudonnière had visited on his voyage with Ribault in 1562.

Upon arrival there, Laudonnière was pleased to be greeted by King Satouriona, who remembered him from the previous voyage. The chief and his followers greeted the Frenchmen with great joy, taking them to view the stone pillar that Ribault had placed on the knoll near the mouth of the river. Le Moyne described the Indians as being adorned with feathers and necklaces of shells and bracelets of fishes' teeth and "having many pearls fastened on their legs. Many of them had also hanging to their legs round flat plates of gold, silver, or brass, so that in walking they tinkled like little bells."[83]

Satouriona presented Laudonnière with a small slab of silver as a welcoming gift. Laudonnière was interested in the source of the gold and silver the Indians were wearing and asked Satouriona where his people had gotten it. The chief answered that his people had taken it by force from the Thimogona, their "most ancient and natural enemies."[84] Observing the interest shown by the French in the gold and silver, he indicated that if Laudonnière would help him make war on the Thimogona,[85] both their goals would be accomplished — he would be revenged on his enemies and Laudonnière would have as much gold and silver as he wished. Laudonnière agreed to do so in order, as he afterwards wrote, "to increase his friendship."[86] The French then left the St. John's River to continue exploring to the north.

They had not traveled far when Laudonnière called all his men together for a consultation on where they should establish their settlement. Port Royal Sound, the site of Charlesfort, was the finest harbor in the West Indies, he told the men, but he felt they would not find it "comfortable or usable,"[87] according to the report of those who had lived there, as food was not readily available in that area. He said,

> In our first year it would be much more important to live in a place with an abundant food supply than to be in a commodious and beautiful port.... We should set ourselves up around the River of May, since on our first voyage we had found it to abound in corn and material for flour, to say nothing of the gold and silver we found there, a thing which gave me hope for some future happy discovery.[88]

It was settled; the men opted to build their settlement on the St. John's River and set sail, arriving there on June 29. In reexploring the area, they decided that the site near a high bluff, which they had visited before, was a suitable location for their fortress. Laudonnière wrote:

> Then, having measured out a piece of ground in the form of a triangle, we went to work, some to dig on all sides, others to cut fagots, and others to raise and give form to the rampart. There was not a man among us who did not have either a shovel, a cutting hook, or a hatchet, either for clearing out the trees or for building the fort.[89]

Le Moyne recorded the fact that all the men, noblemen included, worked hard to build the fort and to build shelters from the weather, and he added that each man, after seeing the gold and silver the Indians possessed, was certain that he would quickly become rich.

With so many willing workers, the fort was quickly completed and, according to Laudonnière,

Drawing of Fort Caroline by Jacques Le Moyne de Morgue, the official recorder of the French expedition sent to establish a settlement on the southeastern coast of North America in 1564 (State Archives of Florida).

Our fort was built in a triangle. The side to the west, the land side, was enclosed by a little moat under turfs turned up into the form of a parapet about nine feet high. The other side, which was toward the river, was enclosed with a palisade of planks of timber in the manner in which dikes are made. It had on the south side a form of bastion where I had a barn built for munitions. All of it was constructed of fagots and earth except for two or three feet of turf from which the parapets were made.... I had an oven built at some distance from the fort because the houses were covered with palmetto leaves and when fire starts in them it is hard to put out.[90]

Laudonnière had a guardhouse built in the center of the south side and a residence on the north side. Chief Satouriona's people, at Laudonnière's request, made a roof of palmetto leaves for the storage building. Laudonnière called it "La Caroline" in honor of Charles IX.

At the beginning the relationship between the French and the Indians was cordial and trading profitable to both sides. At first, Le Moyne wrote, the Indians offered food for trade with the French, but when they saw how much they desired "metals and minerals,"[91] some began to bring them for trade. Laudonnière, seeing how anxiously his men traded for gold and silver, forbade this type of trade unless the goods were put in a common store to be divided equally among them all.

Satouriona was very cooperative, as he believed that the French would help him in his war on the Thimogona. Laudonnière, however, began to regret his rash promise to Satouriona, as it occurred to him that he could obtain the gold and silver from the Thimogona more easily through friendship than through war. Consequently he sent a party of men under the command of his lieutenant M. d'Ottigny to the land of the Thimogona.

Ottigny met with Outina, the chief, and discovered that he was much more powerful than Satouriona; moreover, the Thimogona did not have gold or silver but knew where it could be found. According to the Indians, there were three kings, enemies of the Thimogona, living in the distant land of the Appalachian Mountains, who had many subjects and lived in large fortified enclosures with many buildings inside. Their warriors made arrowheads out of gold and wore gold armor into battle. They had not only gold but also silver and copper in great quantities. Outina and his people lived between the French fort and the Appalachian Mountains; his friendship was therefore extremely important. Ottigny offered to help the Thimogona in the future against their enemies in hopes of gaining access to the gold and silver. When Ottigny returned to Fort Caroline, he brought samples of gold, silver and pearls.

The situation with Satouriona became awkward, as two months after arrival of the French he sent several of his men to the fort to remind Laudonnière of his promise. Satouriona and his men were ready for war, the Indians told Laudonnière, and the chief was counting on his friends at the fort to march with his warriors against the Thimogona. Laudonnière made the excuse that the fort was not as yet complete, saying that he needed his men to stay and finish the work and that he "would not purchase the friendship of one by the hatred of another."[92] The Indians left the fort and repeated the French response to their chief, who was not pleased. The war party left soon afterwards and returned victorious even without the help of the French. Satouriona did not openly display his resentment of Laudonnière's failure to keep his promise, but he allowed the relationship to cool considerably.

On July 28, Laudonnière sent two of his three ships back to France and, in order to preserve his food supply, cut the food ration for the men. Le Moyne wrote:

> M. de Laudonnière proceeded to shorten the allowance of food and drink: so that after three weeks, only one glass of spirit and water, half and half, was given out daily per man; and as for provisions, which it had been hoped would be abundant in this New World, none at all were found; and, unless the natives had furnished us from their own stores from day to day, some of us must assuredly have perished from starvation, especially such as did not know how to use fire-arms in hunting.[93]

Evidently, Fort Caroline was still not complete, for Laudonnière had the men working on it on through the summer. In his account of the settlement, he mentioned sending the men to a nearby Indian village to get clay with which to make bricks for the houses. All the men had worked hard to build the fort, and they were excited by the prospect of becoming rich, for they had seen the amount of gold and silver taken in trade from Satouriona's people and were anxious to find the source of it.

Laudonnière was also very interested in discovering the whereabouts of the gold and silver mines. In early November he sent La Roche Ferrière out to the Appalachian Mountains to explore the region. Ferrière was able to confirm that not only gold but also silver and copper were mined by the Indians living there.[94] Le Moyne recorded that when Ferrière reached the mountains, he

> succeeded by prudence and assiduity in placing himself on a friendly footing with the three chiefs before mentioned.... He was astonished at the civilization and opulence, and sent to M. de Laudonnière at the fort many gifts which they bestowed upon him. Among these were circular plates of gold and silver as large as a moderate-sized platter, such as they are accustomed to wear to protect the back and breast in war; much gold alloyed with brass, and silver not thoroughly smelted. He sent also some quivers covered with very choice skins, with golden heads to all the arrows; and many pieces of a stuff made of feathers, and most skillfully ornamented with rushes of different colors; also green and blue stones, which some thought to be emeralds and sapphires, in the form of wedges, and which they used instead of axes, for cutting wood.[95]

Ferrière's friendship with the three chiefs earned him the hatred of Outina and his people, and from then on he had to use a different route to the fort to avoid the territory of the Thimogona.

Laudonnière was excited by Ferrière's discovery and planned, once the reinforcements came from France, to send men to settle that region. The French at Fort Caroline had discovered an opulent Indian civilization in North America with ample supplies of gold, silver and precious gems—the dream of all the Europeans who had previously tried to establish settlements there and also the dream of those that would come in the future. It is ironic that the events surrounding the destruction of the colony would overshadow this discovery.

The men in the fort began to grumble when they saw the gold, silver and precious gems sent back to the fort by Ferrière and observed that Laudonnière was frequently in closed meetings with certain of the men and did not communicate with the rest of them. Laudonnière, according to Le Moyne, "was a man too easily influenced by others [and] evidently fell into the hands of three or four parasites, and treated with contempt the soldiers, who were just those whom he should have most considered."[96]

Resentment began to build, especially among the young noblemen who had come on the expedition at their own expense; they did not like the fact that they were kept working in the fort and not allowed to explore for riches. And some of the very religious Huguenots began to complain that Laudonnière had not brought a minister to see to their spiritual needs. There was additional disgruntlement over the lack of provisions, for Laudonnière was supposed to have brought enough food to last for a year, which it seemed he had not done. Some of the men began to accuse him of making "wrongful use of the hundred thousand francs given him by the king,"[97] as he had not brought over the required amount of provisions.

When Laudonnière heard the complaints, he tried to convince the men that they could not all go at once to look for the gold mines and that the fort needed to be made secure for those who remained while they were exploring. Moreover, he assured them, all the wealth that was discovered would be shared equally among them. His responses, however, did not satisfy the men. The summer passed and dissatisfaction with the meager rations grew worse, causing the French to become more aggressive in their demands for food from the Indians. In many cases they did not even bother to barter for it but took it by force, burning their houses down if the Indians were reluctant to give it to them. Satouriona took his people far away from the fort, thus depriving the French of his food supply.

The men began to talk among themselves of replacing Laudonnière as governor and even of taking his life. On September 20, on his way back to the fort from the woods, Laudonnière, as he wrote, "overdid myself in some way, fell sick and thought I would die."[98] While he lay ill in bed, the men began to plot. One of the men tried to persuade the apothecary to mix poison in his medicine and another man wanted to blow him up by placing gunpowder under his bed. None of the plans succeeded, and the atmosphere in the fort became very tense.

In early September, Captain Bourdet, a French adventurer who had been cruising in the Caribbean, appeared unexpectedly at the fort. There is evidence that he had spoken with some of the survivors of Charlesfort and had stopped at Fort Caroline to observe the situation there. He and his crew remained at the fort for several weeks, and when he left on November 10, Laudonnière persuaded him to take seven or eight of the troublemakers back to France with him. This he did, leaving behind some of his sailors and two Flemish carpenters to replace the men who were leaving.

The sailors, or perhaps we should call them buccaneers, were not content to remain on land and wanted to resume raiding on the high seas. They persuaded some of the malcontents in the fort to join them, and three days later, on November 13, stealing two of Laudonnière's small sailing ships (called barques), 13 of them left to raid and plunder, cutting the cables of the two small boats in the river so that Laudonnière could not come after them. The Spanish eventually captured the deserters in Cuba after they had attacked a Spanish ship.

Left without his two barques, Laudonnière set his men to work to build two new boats. Some of the men felt it was beneath their dignity to perform such menial labor, especially when there was an opportunity for them to become rich. The number of men who were unhappy with the situation grew, and soon the group of malcontents numbered 66. Through his sergeant, they sent a formal grievance to Laudonnière in which they complained of the shortage of food, the hard work and lack of opportunity to look for gold and silver. They asked Laudonnière to allow them to take the two barques that were being built and cruise around the islands in an attempt to get provisions for the fort.

The queen had commanded Laudonnière "to do no wrong against the subjects of the king of Spain nor anything by which he might conceive any unhappiness."[99] Laudonnière was afraid that if he allowed the men to sail around looking for food, they would inevitably attack Spanish ships or Spanish settlements. Therefore he told them that when the barques were finished, they would be sent along the river to barter with the Indians for food. Besides, there were enough provisions in the fort to last four more months.

Laudonnière then suffered a relapse of his illness, and while he was lying in bed sick, a group of men broke into his chamber, arrested him, put him in fetters and imprisoned him on the ship anchored in the middle of the river. He was kept there for 15 days and forced to sign a document giving the men authority to leave the fort and trade for food in New Spain. The mutineers loaded the two finished barques with artillery, munitions, and food and—forcing one of Laudonnière's pilots on board—sailed off on December 8 to go their separate way and to attack, raid and plunder at will.

After some success in pirating, one of the ships was captured and the men aboard taken prisoner by the Spanish; most of them were hanged. The second ship enjoyed a few triumphs then fell on hard times, and while most of the men were drinking heavily one night, the pilot steered a course for Fort Caroline. On March 25, 1565, they reached the fort. Laudonnière pardoned the men but ordered the four ringleaders hanged. At the last minute Laudonnière, at the request of his men, allowed the four to be shot instead and their bodies hung upon the gibbet. Afterwards, Laudonnière wrote about the mutiny:

> These mutinies could not really be founded upon the lack of food, because ever since our arrival each soldier had received each day, up until the day of their confronting me and even until February 28, one loaf of bread weighing twenty-two ounces. But I recollected how all new conquests made at sea or on land were usually beset by internal rebellions, which are easily started because of the great distances from the homeland and because of the hope soldiers have of profiting from them.[100]

Laudonnière had carefully rationed his food supplies, knowing that during January, February and March the Indians would have little food to spare. There was just enough food left in the fort to last until April, when he was sure that ships from France would arrive with settlers, supplies and provisions. April came and then May, but the ships did not come. Food became very scarce in the fort and Laudonnière mentioned in his writings that because he had given the men the same amount of food each day, some of them ate the whole amount, confident that the next day they would receive more; but others conserved some part of it, and when the food supply ran low, these men actually sold their surpluses to the others.

The men were forced to go out into the woods outside the fort to dig roots and gather acorns to eat. The fields of corn and beans that the Indians planted had not yet ripened, so that the only remaining food source was fish. Some of the men went hunting, for Laudonnière wrote that a few of his men who had been ranging the area hunting had reported that Indian villages they had found to the south had large amounts of food.

The Indians came infrequently to trade with the Frenchmen, who were not so arrogant now in their demands for food. When they did come, they brought just a few fish, for which they demanded more and more trade goods in return. The Indians taunted the French when they complained that the price for the fish was too high by telling them that they would keep their fish and the French could eat their trade goods. When they came to trade, the Indians would not come near the fort for fear of the French guns; instead, they made the settlers come out to them to barter for the fish.

Laudonnière, in his account of the settlement, admitted that he took food by force from several Indian villages. Soon the situation became worse, and the Indians killed two Frenchmen as they tried to steal corn from their cornfields. Outina, the Thimogona chief, offered the French food if they would help him fight his enemies, but when the battle was over, the men received only a meager amount of corn and beans. In their anger at the deception, the men kidnapped Outina and held him for ransom. When the Indians finally paid the ransom of corn and beans, they ambushed the soldiers as they were carrying the food away, killing two of them and wounding 22. As the soldiers were obliged to drop the food they were carrying to fight the Indians, the amount of food salvaged was only enough to feed two men.

The French often climbed the cliff outside the fort and spent many hours looking out to sea, hoping to see sails on the horizon and wondering if some tragedy had taken place at home that prevented ships from coming to aid them, as had happened to the men at Charlesfort. By mid–June the men were completely discouraged and begged Laudonnière to sail for France. Unfortunately they had only one seaworthy ship, the *Breton*, which was not large enough to take them all. According to le Moyne, "It was herein finally concluded to refit as well as possible the third of our ships, and to raise her sides with plank so as to enlarge her capacity; and while the artificers were employed on this work, the soldiers were set to collect provisions along the coast."[101] The men, with the prospect of going home before them, worked tirelessly, even going to the length of tearing up the planks from the palisade around the fort to use on the ship.

On August 3, the lookouts at the fort saw sails in the distance and the men began to dance and shout with joy, thinking that the relief fleet from France had finally arrived. Then frowns took the place of smiles as they began to wonder if the ships were indeed French. The ships anchored in the river in front of the sandbar and sent a long boat ashore. Not knowing if the ships contained friends or foe, Laudonnière put his soldiers on guard and sent his captain and some men out to meet them. The men returned with the news that the fleet was

English and had aboard a Frenchman from Dieppe who had sailed with Ribault in 1562. He was coming to the fort on behalf of their leader, John Hawkins, who asked permission to land and take on fresh water, of which they had great need. The permission was granted and Hawkins came in person to the fort to greet Laudonnière, who entertained the English as best he could by killing some of the sheep and poultry, which, Laudonnière wrote, "to this hour I had carefully guarded in the hope of using them to stock the countryside."[102] Hawkins reciprocated by sending for a large supply of bread and wine to be distributed among the men.

When Hawkins discovered the situation in the fort, he immediately offered to take all the men back to France. Laudonnière, not knowing what relations were at that time between England and France, was reluctant to put himself and his men into English hands. Finally he asked Hawkins if he would sell him one of his ships so they could return on their own. Hawkins agreed and took gunpowder and weapons in payment. The English generously offered to leave food as well, an offer that was greatly appreciated, and barrels of beans, biscuits, flour and one barrel of salt were off-loaded from the English ships and stored in the fort. Seeing that the Frenchmen were, for the most part, without shoes, Hawkins gave them 50 pairs. Laudonnière signed a voucher in payment for them. Having filled his barrels with water, Hawkins and his ships then left for England.

John Sparke, one of the Englishmen with Hawkins, wrote an account of his voyage, including the visit to Fort Caroline. He wrote, with respect to the food supply at the fort, that "maiz [corn] was the greatest lacke they had, because they had no labourers to sowe the same, and therefore to them that should inhabit the land, it were requisit to have labourers to till and sowe the ground."[103]

Laudonnière had brought no farmers with him, and there was never any intention, it seems, of planting gardens to grow food for the settlers. The rivers were full of fish, and Sparke reported that the Indians had given the Frenchmen weirs with which to catch fish, "but when they grew to warres, the Floridians [Indians] tooke away the same againe, and then would not the Frenchmen take the paines to make any more."[104]

The mood in the fort was one of optimism, and the men worked hard both to finish their ship and also to make a large supply of ship's biscuit with the flour they had just received. They thought about destroying what was left of the fort so the Spanish could not occupy it and use it against them and also to keep the Indians from making use of it, but they finally decided against this. By August 28, they were ready to sail. In the afternoon, a favorable wind came up, and just as they were about to board the ships, the lookout sighted sails in the distance. Seven ships, four large and three small, were headed for Fort Caroline, and their identity was unknown.

The ships remained outside the sandbar in the harbor and showed no sign of their identity. Laudonnière sent a barque to find out who they were, but the barque did not return. After a time the anxious watchers in the fort saw that the ships were launching several longboats full of soldiers toward the fort, but still with no indication of their nationality. The fort had only two guns left, the rest having been given to Hawkins in return for the ship, but they were prepared to fire on the longboats when a voice rang out that they were French under the command of Jean Ribault. The relief fleet had come at last, bringing the much-needed provisions and supplies and carrying 500 soldiers and 300 civilians[105] "including several craftsmen and their families."[106]

Ribault had been sent to relieve Laudonnière as commander of the fort with instructions to send him back to France. The men who had returned to France with Captain Bourdet in November 1564 had complained of Laudonnière's behavior as commander of the fort, and Ribault had purposely detained the men sent in the barque to greet him in order to find out what conditions were in the fort. He was satisfied by their answers that the returning men had falsely accused Laudonnière. When he greeted Laudonnière, he handed him a letter from Admiral Coligny in which the admiral kindly requested him to come home to clear his name, indicating that he had full confidence in Laudonnière and knew he would exonerate himself. Ribault encouraged Laudonnière to remain and share command with him, but Laudonnière refused. His recurring illness came upon him again and he took to his bed.

The people aboard Ribault's ships began to land the next day, but it took some time for the ships to be unloaded. The four largest ones could not enter the harbor and had to anchor outside the sandbar while the smaller ships carried the cargo to the fort. Therefore it was not until September 4 that the supplies and provisions were on land. On the afternoon of the fourth, French sailors on board the four ships outside the entrance to St. John's River caught sight of a fleet out to sea, and flying on the mast of the lead ship was the banner of Spain.

The Spanish fleet sailed on seemingly ready to attack the French ships outside the sandbar, but a sudden rainstorm came up and delayed their approach until darkness had fallen. Menéndez, the Spanish commander, ordered his ships to anchor next to the French ships so as to attack at first light. The two fleets were anchored so close that the sailors were able to shout back and forth. Menéndez later wrote to the king that he told the French:

> I, Pedro Menéndez, by command of Your Majesty, had come to this coast to burn and hang the French Lutherans whom I should find there, and that, in the morning I should board their vessels to see if any of that people [Lutherans] were on them, and that, if there were any, I should not fail to execute upon them the justice that Your Majesty commanded.[107]

Just before dawn, the French ships slipped their anchors and sailed out to sea. The Spanish ships followed but could not keep up with them. Menéndez then decided to seek a safe harbor nearby where he could land his soldiers. He traveled some twenty miles and found a harbor through an inlet he had visited on his way to Fort Caroline. He made landfall and took possession of the area, which he decided to call St. Augustine. The French ships followed at a distance to find out what the Spanish were doing and returned to Fort Caroline with the intelligence that the Spanish had entered the River of Dolphins and were landing their troops near an Indian village on the bank of the river.

The French leaders were in disagreement over what action to take. Most, including Laudonnière, favored strengthening their defenses at Fort Caroline to meet the expected Spanish attack. Ribault, however, had another idea. He wanted to take his ships and attack the Spanish where they had landed to the south of the fort. He was afraid that if he did not attack the Spanish now, they might leave and the French would be denied the opportunity of getting rid of "those who are seeking to destroy us."[108] A postscript on his orders from Admiral Coligny had warned him that a Spanish fleet under the command of Menéndez was headed toward Florida. The admiral wrote: "Do not yield a particle to him, and you will do right."[109] Ribault took that as a mandate to destroy Menéndez. Laudonnière warned him "at that time of year a species of whirlwinds or typhoons, which sailors call 'houragans,' from time to time come on suddenly, and inflict terrible damage on the coast."[110] These winds, Laudonnière maintained, could disable his entire fleet and leave Fort Caroline in a very vulnerable position. In spite of the warning, Ribault decided to attack the Spanish at St. Augustine.

On September 8 Ribault took six of the nine ships at Fort Caroline and prepared to sail south in search of the Spanish. He took most of the soldiers with him, along with much of the food that the men at Fort Caroline had loaded on their ships for the voyage home. The newly arrived women, children and artisans were left at the fort guarded by only a small group of soldiers, many of whom had been wounded in the ambush by the Indians some weeks prior. Ribault lingered in the roadstead for two more days, perhaps collecting men and supplies or waiting for a favorable wind, and left on September 10.

The Spanish were busy off-loading their supplies and provisions and trying frantically to build some kind of defense at their landing place when Ribault and his ships appeared at the entrance to the inlet. Across the harbor at St. Augustine there was a sandbar which, at low tide prohibited ships with large drafts from entering. Menéndez, for that reason, had sent two of his largest ships south, out of the way of the French. The Spanish troops had suffered on their voyage to Florida and now found themselves on land without adequate food or the tools necessary to fortify their position. They were extremely vulnerable as Ribault's fleet stood at the entrance to the harbor. Ribault hesitated to attack. His largest ships could not pass the barrier, but he was confident, as he could see that the Spanish were cornered and could not escape. Ribault demanded their surrender and Menéndez refused. Ribault waited, and suddenly the calm, pleasant weather changed. The wind started to blow and kept increasing until the ships were caught in a terrible storm — a hurricane that scattered the fleet and drove it south, away from the River of Dolphins.

Menéndez realized that, with the wind blowing from the north, the French ships could not return to Fort Caroline and also that Ribault must have most of the French soldiers aboard. That left Fort Caroline poorly defended and vulnerable to attack. Menéndez had in his company a Frenchman named François Jean, a member of the first group of mutineers from Fort Caroline, who had been captured by the Spanish in Cuba. He had given them valuable information about the location of the fort and was ready to lead the Spanish there. Local Indians whom Menéndez had contacted told him that the fort could be reached by land in two days, as it was less than thirty miles away. With his French prisoner leading the way and his troops augmented by warriors from the local Indian chief, Menéndez led his weary, hungry and grumbling soldiers thirty miles overland during a driving rain to attack Fort Caroline. It took them four days to make the journey; they arrived in view of the fort on the evening of September 19.

That night there was a torrential downpour and the officer in charge of the sentries at Fort Caroline had taken pity on them and dismissed most of them, leaving only a few token sentries on duty. The morning dawned and the Spanish and their Indian allies, using the scaling ladders they had carried with them, gained easy access to the fort, surprising its occupants completely and killing 130 men. Fifty women and children were spared. Some of the men managed to escape and sought shelter in the woods and marshes around the fort; they were later rescued by the French ships in the harbor. About one hundred Frenchmen eventually made it back to France from Fort Caroline. Le Moyne and Laudonnière were two of those who managed to escape and return to France.[111]

Menéndez left most of his soldiers at Fort Caroline, which he renamed San Mateo, and returned to St. Augustine with a force of 35 men. Part of Ribault's fleet had been wrecked by the hurricane that had arisen and some of the survivors had been stranded on a sandbar a short distance from St. Augustine. The men were weak and unarmed. When the Spanish found them, they asked for transportation back to Fort Caroline, only to be told that the fort was taken and all its defenders dead. The French surrendered to the Spanish and Menéndez separated the Catholics and a few carpenters whose services he needed from the others. These people were sent back to St. Augustine. The rest of the prisoners, with their hands tied behind their backs, were marched ten at a time behind the sand dunes across from the sandbar and executed.

Not long afterwards, on October 10, another group of Frenchmen were found stranded on the same sandbar. Their ships had been wrecked near Cape Canaveral, and the survivors, led by Jean Ribault, had made their way overland to that place. When Menéndez and his soldiers appeared, the French were told that Fort Caroline had been taken. Ribault and 70 of the 150 men surrendered, while the rest fled into the interior. All 70 including Jean Ribault were executed.

Why did Ribault take such a long time to resupply Fort Caroline? Certainly he and Coligny must have know that Laudonnière and his men were expecting ships with fresh provisions and more settlers to arrive in the spring. Le Challeux, one of the civilians on board the relief fleet, wrote that all the settlers intending to go on the voyage were assembled in Dieppe in January, but they did not sail until the middle of May. By then, hundreds of soldiers and more ships loaded with artillery and munitions had been added to the fleet. It is logical to assume that before Ribault was able to sail with his mostly civilian settlers, news reached him of the expedition being sent against Fort Caroline from Spain. The mission changed from one of simple resupply and took on a serious military aspect, which caused a delay in sailing until all the soldiers and munitions were gathered and loaded aboard the ships. To make matters worse, when the ships were ready to sail, they were hampered by adverse winds and were not able to start their voyage until late June, thus putting them in Florida in late August — in the midst of the hurricane season.[112]

The destruction of Fort Caroline by the Spanish led to the establishment of St. Augustine and the first permanent European settlement in North America. On the strength of "effective occupation," the Spanish now had a legitimate claim to Florida. England and France would have to seek their colonial territories farther north.

How did the people in France react to the massacre in Florida? News of the total disaster — that is, both the destruction of the fort and the execution of Ribault and his men — was slow to reach France. It was not until February 18, 1566, that the French ambassador to Spain wrote to his queen telling her of the execution of the Frenchmen under Ribault's command and adding: "this court is rejoicing more than if it had been a victory over the Turk: also they say that Florida is more important to them than Malta."[113] There were loud cries of outrage from the French, especially in the seaport towns of Normandy. There were diplomatic protests, of course, but to the Huguenots these protests seemed very tame. The Spanish took the position that they had taken steps to eliminate Lutheran (which is what the Spanish called all Protestants) heretics from their land, and that while a good many of the heretics were French, there were some of "different nations."[114]

Officially the French let the matter rest, but individuals did not forget what they felt was an insult to the honor of their country. The French settlement at Fort Caroline was gone, replaced by a Spanish fort called San Mateo. In 1568 a company of Frenchmen led by Dominique de Gourgues and assisted by the local Indians attacked it and burned it to the ground. In revenge for the Fort Caroline massacre, Gourgues hanged the captured defenders and hung a sign over their bodies:

> But instead of the writing which Pedro Melendes had hanged over them, importing these wordes into Spanish, I doe not this as unto French men, but as unto Lutherans, Gourgues caused to be imprinted with a swearing iron in a table of Firrewood,

I doe not this as unto Spaniards, nor as unto Mariners, but as unto Traitors, Robbers and Murtherers.[115]

## Breakdown of the Colony at Fort Caroline

| | |
|---|---|
| *Nationality of settlement* | French |
| *Sponsored by* | King Charles IX, the queen mother and Admiral Coligny |
| *Physical location* | Near a bluff in the St. John's River — the site of present-day Jacksonville, Florida |
| *Why that location* | It was a suitable place to build a fortress and had a suitable harbor. The French knew from their previous visit that there was an abundance of food in the area. They also wanted to settle there because the local chief had access to silver and gold. |
| *Purpose of settlement* | To lay a formal claim to the land by establishing a permanent settlement, to explore the land for valuable natural resources and to undermine the power of Spain. |
| *When settled* | June 29, 1564 |
| *Climatic conditions* | Not mentioned |
| *Relationship with Indians* | Good at first but later deteriorated, as the French did not keep their promise to help the local chief against his enemies. Instead, the French made friends with his enemies. As the need for food increased, the French alienated the Indians even more by raiding their villages. They received little help from them. |
| *Internal quarreling* | There were two instances of desertion from Fort Caroline. The men became dissatisfied with Laudonnière's leadership. The first group of 13 stole two barques and left in November 1564 to become privateers. The next group of 66 left in early December after imprisoning Laudonnière and taking two ships, guns, ammunition and food. When one ship returned in March, Laudonnière had the four ringleaders executed. |
| *Number of initial settlers* | 200 |
| *Makeup of initial settlers* | The settlers included soldiers, mariners, gentlemen volunteers who paid their own expenses, carpenters, sawyers, smiths, shipwrights, an apothecary and one woman who was Laudonnière's housekeeper. |
| *Number of additional settlers* | 300, who arrived at Fort Caroline on September 4, 1565 |
| *Percentage that survived* | Not known. A number of them were executed by the Spanish and some were killed in conflicts with the |

|  | Indians. Four mutineers were also executed by Laudonnière. |
|---|---|
| *Initial supplies* | The three ships which sailed from Havre de Grâce carried artillery, guns, munitions, supplies, provisions, sheep and poultry. |
| *How often supplies arrived* | Supplies expected in April did not arrive until the beginning of September. |
| *Stability of the mother country* | France was going through a period of instability due to the conflict between the Huguenots and Catholics and rivalry of two factions of the nobility, which were battling each other for power and influence. |
| *Fate of settlement* | Fort Caroline was captured by the Spanish and most of its defenders killed on September 20, 1565. |

# FOUR

# St. Augustine

Philip II of Spain was alarmed by the reports he received from his ambassador in Paris about French activity in Florida in 1564. He became determined to eliminate the French threat to his interests in the Caribbean and, by establishing a permanent base on the east coast, to prevent any other European power from endangering the safety of the treasure fleet. On March 20, 1565, he issued a royal grant to Pedro Menéndez de Avilés to conquer and settle Florida. Menéndez had considerable naval experience in the Indies, at one time serving as captain-general of the Armada of the Indies charged with the responsibility of protecting the treasure fleet on its journey to Spain — a task that he carried out very successfully.

The grant was reminiscent of those given to previous conquistadors who tried to establish colonies in Florida. He was ordered to take ships "laden with supplies and fully prepared for war" with "five hundred men, one hundred of them farmers and one hundred sailors, and the rest of them naval and military men and officials."[1] Stonecutters, carpenters, sawyers, smiths, barbers, locksmiths and two priests were also to be included among the settlers, and all of this was to be done at his own cost.

Philip's instructions were specific: Menéndez was to proceed to Florida to seek out the best location for a settlement, to discover the presence of any foreign settlement and "cast them out by the best means,"[2] to chart the coast from Florida to Newfoundland so that "the secrets of the said coast and the harbors which may be thereon, shall be known and understood,"[3] and to build and settle "two or three towns of at least one hundred inhabitants each."[4]

Menéndez was also ordered to bring into the country horses and all the cattle and livestock he thought proper. He was to accomplish as much as he could in one year but should complete all of it within three years and it was all to be done with "peace and amity and in a Christian spirit."[5] He was also charged with converting the Indians to the Catholic faith.

In return, Menéndez was appointed governor and captain-general of Florida and all the settlements he established there. Philip also stipulated that "you shall receive from Us each year a salary of two thousand ducats, which are to be paid you from the products and rents which may belong to us in the said country; but if there be none, we shall not be obliged to give and pay you the said salary."[6]

Menéndez was to be given lands, and the title of marquis of those lands was to be bestowed upon him. He was to receive ⅕ part of the income from all the mines of gold and silver that were found there and he was granted two fisheries — one for fish and the other for pearls. There were the usual exemptions from duties on goods brought to the colony, and the king gave Menéndez the use of two ships fully armed for a period of six years. To aid him even further, the king promised to give him 15,000 ducats toward his expenses provided he set sail "in the first fair weather, in the coming month of May of this present year."[7]

Presumably Menéndez was successful in leaving Spain during the month of May, for in the first of a series of letters written by him to Philip II he stated that he left the Canary Islands on July 8, but without the other ships in his fleet, as they had been separated. He continued on his voyage alone and by August 8 reached Puerto Rico to await the arrival of the rest of his ships.

Menéndez clearly understood that he was in a race with the French fleet, which was headed with reinforcements to Fort Caroline, and he was reluctant to wait until the entire fleet had arrived. He felt that if he could reach the harbor where the French fort was located before the reinforcements arrived, he could take the fort and hold it with the number of men who had joined him so far. François Jean, the French mutineer from Fort Caroline, who had been captured by the Spanish, had told him "that they [the French] had built their fort five leagues up the river inland, and that there is an island at the mouth of the river of about a league long within and alongside of the harbor ... which, whoever holds is master of the sea."[8]

Menéndez wrote to Philip II: "I found myself with eight hundred persons, five hundred of them soldiers, who could be landed, with two hundred seamen, the other one hundred being useless people, married men, women and children and officials." He thought that was enough "to sail for this port and take and fortify this island."[9]

On September 4 Menéndez reached the St. John's River, finding that the French reinforcements had arrived and were in control of the island. After a slight confrontation with the four French ships anchored outside the harbor, Menéndez decided to take his ships and seek a landing place near the French. He took his fleet to a small inlet he had reconnoitered on his way north to Fort Caroline. This led to a sheltered bay which offered protection for his ships, and he landed 200 soldiers immediately with instructions to dig trenches to fortify the area — a difficult task, as they had "no shovels or other iron tools ... the ship laden with them not having yet arrived."[10]

On September 8, 1565, Menéndez went ashore and officially took possession in the name of Philip II. He called the settlement St. Augustine, for he had

The Great (or Long) House of the chief of the Seloy tribe of the Timucuan nation could hold 300 people.    The Spanish who arrived in 1565 were invited by the chief of the Seloy to occupy the Great House.    Moat dug by the Spanish. Some traces of such a moat have recently been excavated.

Albert Manucy drew this rendition of the first Spanish settlement at St. Augustine for the *New York Times*. The settlement was a temporary one meant to protect the settlers until they had time to find a permanent location and build a fort. It was located near an Indian village belonging to the Seloy Tribe of the Timucuan Nation. The chief gave the Spanish the Great House, a large, thatched circular building big enough to house several hundred people. The Spanish then added fortifications, possibly a moat, breastworks and a wooden palisade, around the building (State Archives of Florida).

first visited it on St. Augustine's Day. The area where he had chosen to land his men was near a Timucuan Indian village, and when he came ashore Menéndez talked with some of the Indians and gave them little gifts to gain their friendship, which they were quite willing to give, as they had no apparent liking for the French. They told Menéndez that he could get to Fort Caroline by land and so avoid the island guarding the entrance to the harbor. These Indians proved valuable to Menéndez when he launched his attack on Fort Caroline, as they marched and fought with his soldiers.

In a letter to Philip II, Menéndez wrote to ask that the king send maize to feed the domestic animals until he had time to organize the planting of grain and maize in St. Augustine. He must have heard that the French were continually taking food from the Indians, which caused hard feelings between the two groups. He told Philip II:

> for in no manner, will it be well to take it [corn] from the Indians, that they shall not take up enmity against us.... We found great traces of gold, both ordinary and fine, which the Indians wore on them, on their ears, lips and arms. I did not allow any to be taken from them, that they should not suppose that we coveted it.[11]

In a letter to Philip II dated October 15, 1565, Menéndez was able to report that he had successfully accomplished the first two objectives of his mission. He had captured Fort Caroline and killed most of its defenders, sparing the lives of 50 women and children. He had then captured and executed the Frenchmen stranded on the sandbar with the exception of 12 Breton seamen who said they had been kidnapped and four carpenters and caulkers whose services he needed. It must have given him great satisfaction to have been able to report the capture and execution of Jean Ribault and 70 of his men. Menéndez told his king that he only "spared the lives of two young gentlemen of about 18 years old, and three others, drummer, fifer and trumpeter."[12] There were still small bands of Frenchmen left in Florida, but those who escaped capture by the Indians were sure to be found by Menéndez and his soldiers. He had cause to be pleased with what he had accomplished in just five weeks.

According to Gonzalo Solís de Merás, the official recorder of the expedition, opinion was divided in St. Augustine over the execution of the Frenchmen. Merás wrote:

some persons considered him cruel, and others, that he had acted as a very good captain should. It was thought that even if they had been Catholics, and he had not worked justice upon them, both Spaniards and Frenchmen would have died of hunger on account of the Adelantado's [Menéndez's] scarcity of provisions; and the French, because they were more numerous, would have killed us.[13]

Menéndez was able to tell Philip II that they had found muskets, powder, ammunition, flour and wine in Fort Caroline, along with a quantity of cloth and trade goods and domestic animals. He told the king that the French "had news that, a hundred leagues north northeast of Santa Elena they possess the mountain chain that comes down from Zacatecas[14] and that there is much silver there, and Indians have come to them with many pieces."[15] The Spanish found silver in Fort Caroline that was worth five or six thousand ducats.

As far as the second objective of his mission, Menéndez had taken the French fort and renamed it San Mateo, leaving a garrison there to hold it. He had established another fort at St. Augustine. These were just the beginning, as Menéndez intended to establish a series of forts to ensure that "at no time the enemy will be able to attack in the one hundred fifty leagues there are between here and Havana; either fortify themselves, or lie in wait for convoys or ships from the Indias."[16]

Menéndez did not propose to stop there, as he had plans to build a fort at Santa Elena, from which he would establish outposts to the Appalachian Mountains, where he would have access to the gold and silver mines. He planned to travel northward to fortify the Bahía de Santa Maria (Chesapeake Bay); when that was completed, he wanted to explore and settle the Gulf Coast.

Menéndez told Philip II that he envisioned

very excellent gains to be made in this country, for there will be much wine, many sugar plantations, a great number of cattle, since there are extensive pasture grounds, much hemp, tar, pitch and planking, such as Your Majesty has not in all your realms. Many ships can be built here and much salt made.[17]

This was what Menéndez envisioned — a vast and varied colonial empire that would span both coasts of Florida and extend northward to the Chesapeake. In the countryside around the forts, civilians would farm the land, sugar plantations would flourish and tradesmen and craftsmen would settle in the towns that grew up outside the forts. The colonial government in Mexico and the authorities in Spain did not share this vision. What they wanted in Florida was an outpost to guard the fringes of the Spanish empire in the New World and to protect and assist the treasure fleets as they sailed the Bahama Channel and made their way to Spain.[18]

About 20 days after the execution of Jean Ribault and his men, Menéndez learned from the Indians that seventy or eighty Frenchmen were gathered at Cape Canaveral and were building a fort and a ship. On October 26, Menéndez sent 100 men on three ships to sail there while he went over land with 150. When he had dealt with the Frenchmen, he planned to sail to Havana to get supplies and gather the rest of his fleet.

Before he left St. Augustine Menéndez appointed his brother Bartolome Menéndez governor and set down the proper daily rations that should be given from the supplies then on hand and those that should be given when new supplies arrived. He "left the fort traced out and the work of erecting it equally divided among squads of men, and they were to work at the fortifications each day 3 hours in the morning and 3 in the afternoon."[19]

Menéndez dispatched a ship to Spain to give "an account of what had taken place up to that time." When he left,

all the government officials of San Agustín, and the men and women who were there, begged the Adelantado [Menéndez] as a favor that he should not return to that port with the soldiers unless he brought food, as the fewer who remained there, the longer the supplies they had would last.[20]

When Menéndez and his men arrived at Cape Canaveral, the Frenchmen took fright and ran. Menéndez sent a French trumpeter to tell the men that if they surrendered to him, he would spare their lives. All but four or five of the men decided to accept the offer. The Spanish burned the fort and the ship, took the artillery and powder as well as the Frenchmen and journeyed south to the St. Lucie River, which had a suitable harbor and friendly Indians.

Menéndez left a captain and 200 men to fortify the site at St. Lucie, providing them with one of the barques and provisions for 15 days. Later he would go on to establish three more military outposts on the east and west coasts of Florida — at Biscayne Bay, Charlotte Harbor and Tampa. He was intent on keeping any other country from occupying the land to the detriment of the treasure fleet, but he also had another motive. The coast of Florida had proven treacherous to Spanish shipping, and the survivors of many a shipwreck had struggled ashore only to be killed outright by the Indians or enslaved by them. The posts were meant to offer a safe haven for Spanish refugees. Having established his outpost at St. Lucie, Menéndez continued on to Havana.

At the end of December 1565 a ship laden with cassava, meat and cattle arrived at St. Augustine and unloaded part of the supplies, which the people there felt was "but little,"[21] and took the rest to San Mateo. At the beginning of February, another ship arrived at St. Augustine with "maize, wine, oil, cloth, canvas, some ship tackle, rigging and oakum."[22] However, before the ship could be unloaded, 130 of the soldiers at the fort rose in mutiny. They imprisoned the camp master and other officials, seized the ship and made ready to sail away. The ship, however, could not hold all the mutineers, and while they were deciding who should go, the camp master succeeded in freeing not only himself but the other officials as well. These men managed to capture a few of the mutineers, including the ringleader, who was eventually hanged. Those who were already on board the ship were able to escape by cutting the cables and sailing away before the guns in the fort could be used against them.

By March 20, 1566, Menéndez was back at St. Augustine with fresh provisions, but he found the people suffering from lack of food and discontent growing among the soldiers. When he was in Cuba, news had reached Menéndez that a large armada was being sent against him from France. Therefore the king was sending a large relief fleet of 17 ships with 1,500 soldiers aboard, along with a large quantity of supplies and instructions "to injure the armada if it should attack him or his territories."[23] After waiting some time for the ships, Menéndez left St. Augustine as well supplied and protected as he could and, in April, set sail for Port Royal Sound, where he established a fort called San Felipe on the same spot that Charlesfort had stood and garrisoned it with 110 men.[24]

Upon his return to St. Augustine in the middle of May, Menéndez found the situation very serious, as the fort was in great need of supplies and all the Indians between St. Augustine and San Mateo were on the warpath. "He [Menéndez] learned that twice at night they [the Indians] had shot arrows at the sentinels at San Agustín, and had killed two soldiers and set fire to the powderhouse, the roof whereof was thatched with palmetto leaves; in this way the fort was burned."[25]

Menéndez met with the camp master and captains and they decided to move from that vicinity and build a fort at the entrance of the harbor, because there was greater protection there from the Indians and they "could defend themselves better against any vessels of enemies, which might want to enter the harbor."[26] They started to work at once to build the fort. About one hundred seventy men worked on the fort from three o'clock in the morning until nine o'clock and then from two o'clock in the afternoon until six at night. The men were divided into four squads, and they threw dice to see which of the four areas of work "fell to each squad."[27]

At the beginning of June, Menéndez was preparing to sail once again to Havana when a supply ship arrived at St. Augustine. Menéndez ordered it to be unloaded and half the supplies put on a ship in the harbor and sent to San Mateo. Then he ordered the camp master to sink her so that there would be no ship in the harbor in which mutineers could leave the settlement. Mutiny and desertion were a huge problem for the Spanish in their new settlements. Lack of supplies—which included not just food but also clothing, shoes and tools—made life almost unbearable, and then there was the thought in the minds of many of the men that if they were in Mexico or Peru, they would have a good chance of finding gold and silver. It did not appear to most that there was any opportunity to get rich in Florida. Discontent and resentment at the way they were treated by those in charge led to many mutinies. Several of the mutineers were hanged, but the mutinies did not stop.

King Philip II had ordered that any person deserting Florida was to be returned, but there was such dislike of Menéndez in Cuba and the other island colonies that this was not done. In fact, one group of mutineers was given a hearty welcome upon their arrival in Santo Domingo. Desertion from Florida was not the only problem, as some of the people destined for St. Augustine deserted before they even got there. Supply ships always stopped at Havana or Santo Domingo or one of the other island ports before sailing to St. Augustine, and many men jumped ship once they had arrived in the islands. Those who had been in Florida and left spread stories of the hardships and unsuitability of the land, which made it difficult for Menéndez to recruit settlers.

As if the little colony did not have enough problems, the war with the local Indians under their cacique Satouriona added another peril. Despite the good intentions of Menéndez to avoid taking food from the Indians (in order to ensure their goodwill), the untimely manner in which supplies arrived at the fort led groups of soldiers to rove the area foraging for food, taking it mostly from the Indian villages. Even when supplies were plentiful in the fort, small groups of soldiers roamed the countryside robbing the villages. Satouriona and his people retaliated by declaring war on the Spanish forts at San Mateo and St. Augustine and attacked the Spanish whenever they had the opportunity. The soldiers who were forced by lack of food to leave the fort in search of oysters, crawfish and palmettos would do so only in large groups, as men who ventured out alone did not return, and it was impossible to travel the thirty or so miles between the two forts without an armed escort.

The large armada from Spain arrived in July 1566, delivering soldiers and much-needed supplies, to the great relief of the inhabitants of St. Augustine. Menéndez, after consulting his captains, decided to leave half the 1,500 reinforcements just arrived in Florida—dividing them between the three forts of San Felipe, San Mateo and St. Augustine. The rest of the soldiers aboard six vessels would go to "cruise about the islands of Puerto Rico, Santo Domingo and Cuba, in order to chastise the corsairs who might be there."[28] Menéndez would take six ships and sail to San Mateo and San Felipe to learn "the state of things in those parts."[29]

While he was at San Felipe Menéndez decided to send an expedition to the Chesapeake Bay. He chose a captain with 30 soldiers and two Dominican friars to sail there to establish a settlement and "try to make the Indians Christians."[30] The two friars "were from Peru and New Spain ... and had suffered hunger, hardships and dangers in Florida."[31] They were not anxious to remain there, and once the expedition had begun, they were able, with apparent ease, to convince some of the soldiers and the pilot that it would be better to return to Spain than go to the Chesapeake Bay. Arriving in Seville, they explained that because of a storm they had been unable to accomplish their mission. They then went about "defaming the country [Florida] and speaking ill of the King and the Adelanto, because they wanted to conquer it."[32]

In November 1566 Menéndez ordered his captain, Juan Pardo, at San Felipe to take a party of men "to go inland to discover and conquer the land from here to Mexico"[33] [the Appalachian Mountains, which Menéndez mistakenly thought was the mountain range near the city of Zacatecas in northern Mexico]. Captain Pardo was to establish missions on his journey, sketch out the route to Zacatecas and search for the gold and silver mines discovered by the French. Pardo traveled to the northeast, where — about one hundred miles from the fort — he had a log house built to serve as an outpost. He then went west to Cufitatchiqui on the Savannah River and then to an Indian village at the foot of the Appalachians. He built a blockhouse there and left a sergeant and a small party of men to garrison it. He would have gone farther and explored more territory, but a letter from San Felipe reached him during his travels ordering him to come back to the fort. He left a priest and four men at his last stop and returned, having established a series of outposts from Santa Elena to the foot of the Appalachians and advised the Indians in each of the villages he visited that they were to submit to the Spanish king and convert to the Catholic faith.[34]

Sometime in 1567 Menéndez returned to Spain, taking with him six Indians and 32 men. He gave a glorious report to the king of his accomplishments: the destruction not only of the French fort but the French force as well, the exploration of three hundred leagues of the coast with a detailed account of the harbors, the establishment of friendship and peace with the caciques in those three hundred leagues (except for Satouriona), and the establishment of "seven settlements, three forts and four pueblos."[35] He included in his report a description of the fortifications at St. Augustine, San Mateo and San Felipe. He did his best to quell the bad reports that were circulating in Spain about the country and his accomplishments there. Menéndez would not devote much of his time in the future to his settlements in Florida, appointing governors and other officials, usually his relatives, to run the colony for him. The king asked Menéndez to take command of the treasure fleets rather than govern Florida — a post he accepted, as he was the king's loyal servant.

Menéndez's accomplishments in Florida were not quite as rosy as he maintained. In November 1567 an usher of the privy chamber of Charles IX in France reported on the news from Spain. He wrote as follows of the Spanish forts:

> At the fort in Florida called St. Mathieu [San Mateo], which Menéndez seized from the French, there are two hundred men. At San Agustín [Fort St. Augustine], the harbor where he landed, there are two hundred, and at Fort Ste Helene [Santa Elena] there are only sixty. All these men would constitute but a poor defense, since they and their forts are more or less worthless, so I have been told. It is true that they have artillery. Menéndez has gone to Seville to fit out three ships and lade them with flour, wine and other victuals to send to the forts, which are almost without.[36]

It was hardly a glowing account of the situation in Florida. The Spanish force was thinly spread and many of the settlements, forts and pueblos set up by Menéndez in 1565 and 1566 either fell prey to the Indians or were deserted by their inhabitants owing to the lack of supplies. Sometimes the outposts were shut down by order of the governor, who would recall the men if they were needed elsewhere or if a decision had been reached that the post was not necessary.

Soon the number of forts and outposts numbered three. There was San Mateo, with its two blockhouses guarding the entrance to the St. John's River. It had only a garrison force to hold it and would be maintained mostly as a reminder of the Spanish victory over the French. A real attempt was made to settle St. Augustine, but little was actually accomplished. There was a garrison at the fort and a small group of buildings grew up around the administrative offices that were necessary to the settlement. Fort San Felipe at Santa Elena had potential, as a colony of settlers was established outside the fort, and much importance was attached to it as an outpost against the return of the French and as a post from which expeditions to the Outer Banks could be launched. Life for the settlers was hard there, and the Indians were very hostile. In 1577 it fell as the result of an Indian uprising, and in 1586 it was abandoned completely.[37]

In 1572 an unidentified official in Cuba wrote a report on Florida. By this time the fort at St. Augustine had been moved and rebuilt several times. According to this report, the land on which the present fort was constructed was almost an island, being surrounded by water with one open stretch over which the mainland could be reached. The land was wooded and low, "full of roots, and cannot be cultivated except in one part where it is sandy, and here they sow corn, and of this land, most of it belongs to the governor, who makes the soldiers sow for him there."[38]

Apparently there were married soldiers at the fort and a small number of married men, settlers who were not soldiers, living there also. One must assume that there were also children, although the person writing the report did not mention them. Each settler was given land for a vegetable garden in which he would grow "12, 15 or even 20 pounds of corn, no more"[39] as well as some pumpkins. Other vegetable seeds apparently did not do well there. Much of the settlers' time was taken up with grinding the corn each day, as it could not be "kept from one day to the next,"[40] and since there was a lack of domestic animals to provide meat, fishing became an important task for them.

There were about fifty cows grazing on one of the islands, but they were not for the use of the soldiers or settlers, being killed for food only when the governor wished it. The cows were thin and undernourished and rarely gave birth; those few calves that were born generally died from lack of food. There was no fresh water on the island, so the herd was able to get water to drink only when it rained. In 1572 it was reported that there were 50 pigs, but they were killed only for the governor's table and suffered from lack of food and water and the attacks of predators. The few chickens that were in St. Augustine were fed on fish, since the people had no corn to spare and the report stated that the chickens when cooked tasted like fish.

The fort, according to the report, was made of "planks and thick beams for pillars: it lasts four or five years, since the wood rots with the dampness of the land, and because the land is salty, and the soldiers repair it, and they work all year in this fort, and in the houses for the Governors."[41]

The soldiers and settlers worked hard and had to wait for months to receive their pay and rations, which were shipped to St. Augustine from Spain or Mexico and were always late in coming.

After seven years, the level of discontent and frustration within the settlement of St. Augustine was still very high. Soldiers and settlers both wanted to mutiny, but there was no place for them to go on land and the officials were careful to see that there were no ships available for them to steal. The only way to leave was to pay a "ransom" to the governor. Lucky was the soldier or settler who had some money left from what he brought with him from Spain and was able to "collect it together"[42] with his pay and give it to the governor in return for permission to leave.

The most outrageous abuse had to do with the system of giving out rations. The governor paid the rations to the people in the form of money rather than food and supplies, and it was expected that the people would use the money to buy the food and other things they needed. Unfortunately for them, they had to buy these things from the governor, who was in charge of all the provisions that were brought into the colony. And the governor, so the people said, charged exorbitant prices for the items.

The unidentified writer of the report recommended that the forts in Florida be abandoned, as they were costing the Spanish government a great deal of money to maintain and he felt that they served no useful purpose. He criticized the ability of the fort at St. Augustine to defend against an attack and remarked that the colony was not increasing the Spanish empire because funds that could be used to expand in other more promising areas were diverted to maintaining the Florida colony, which was stagnant as far as expansion was concerned. The Indians were not being converted to the Catholic faith, as there were no friars or monks in the colony, and the Christians in St. Augustine had been for a long time without a priest to conduct services for them. Furthermore, it was his opinion that if St. Augustine were abandoned, they need have no fear that the French or English would try to settle it as a base to attack the treasure fleet, for they would not wish the expense of maintaining it.[43]

In spite of the criticism, the fort continued, but only as a frontier outpost with very few new settlers arriving. However, many of the soldiers brought their wives with them or married Indian women, and St. Augustine became a small but stable community with about three hundred inhabitants. After Menéndez died in 1574, the colony was governed by his heirs until 1576, when it became a crown colony with a governor appointed by and responsible to the king. The first governor appointed by the king was Pedro Menéndez Marqués, nephew to Pedro Menéndez de Avilés, who arrived at St. Augustine in July 1577. He brought extra troops with him, restored morale at both San Mateo and St. Augustine and rebuilt San Felipe, which had been abandoned after an Indian attack.

He had no sooner accomplished this than he received news that the French were once again active in the area. They had built a fort north of Santa Elena, but it had been overrun by the Indians and abandoned. However, the Frenchmen had not left the area; they were living scattered among the Indians waiting for the right opportunity to attack the Spanish. In 1579, Marqués— through cajolery, bribery and threats— managed to force the Indians to hand over the Frenchmen, whom he promptly executed. In 1580 a French ship was captured in the St. John's River and those on board killed. In spite of these setbacks for the French, rumors of their encroachment in the area continued from 1580 to 1584.

However, it was not the French who posed a threat to the Spanish in 1584; it was the English. News of the English voyage to Roanoke circulated in the Caribbean, and the next year another English expedition was sent to the North Carolina coast. Because this expedition, under the leadership of Sir Richard Grenville, chose to spend some time visiting in the islands, alarming thoughts of an English attack on Spanish territories occurred to officials in the area. Marqués was warned to be aware of a possible English attack on St. Augustine.

Marqués knew that the English were going to colonize on the east coast, but he did not know where. In late December 1585 he sent an expedition to try to discover where they were. The expedition did not get as far as Cape Fear, so the whereabouts of the English remained a mystery. Marqués began to gather men and ships to mount another expedition to find the English, attack them and drive them out of the area.

Meanwhile the islands of the Caribbean had become the victims of an onslaught of raids by Sir Francis Drake, who arrived there late in 1585. For five months he raided and plundered. Then, in May 1586, he arrived in the harbor of St. Augustine. Perhaps he had heard of the intended expedition to Roanoke planned by Marqués during his time in the region. At any rate, he attacked and destroyed St. Augustine, both the fort and the little town that had grown up next to it. Marqués was forced to move his soldiers and civilians farther inland to a place of safety.

With the help of officials in Cuba, Marqués was able to partially restore St. Augustine, but it resembled a camp rather than a fort and an attendant town. Marqués was still intent on finding the English colony, but he looked for it in the Chesapeake Bay instead of the Outer Banks of present-day North Carolina and so did not find it. Then Spanish attention was drawn from affairs in North America to events in Europe. Spain had declared war on England and was about to launch the great "Enterprise of England"—sending an armada to invade the country in 1588.

By 1589 Marqués knew that the Roanoke settlement was gone, and he was determined to take several hundred men north to the Chesapeake Bay and build a fort there that would effectively end the English threat in the area. Meanwhile, the king was forming other plans—he wanted Marqués to organize the treasure fleets that sailed from Havana to Spain every year. Marqués left as governor of Florida in 1589 and no expedition to the Chesapeake Bay was mounted. When he finished organizing the treasure fleet, Marqués declined to return to St. Augustine as governor.

In 1590, with the English threat gone, life at St. Augustine became stable and relatively quiet. Shipwrecks were very rare, and France and England seemed to have lost interest in the southeastern coast of North America. People began to question the feasibility of continuing the settlement. The debate on the future of St. Augustine lasted a decade—from 1595 to 1605—with many people arguing that Mexico and Spain were spending a large amount of money to maintain the fort and its garrison. So far the fort had proved to be of no use, and it had spawned no colony—just a little town that housed the governor and his officials, the necessary administrative buildings and a church.

In 1597 a new governor came to St. Augustine. His name was Gonzáles Méndez de Canzo, and he was interested in expanding the colony with a new settlement on the Chesapeake Bay. However, Philip III, the new king of Spain, was not interested in expansion; in fact, just the reverse—he was thinking of reducing his territories, not enlarging them. Canzo was told that there was to be no new settlements established in North America. The question was, instead, whether the settlement at St. Augustine should be continued.

In 1602 a commission was appointed to study the situation in Florida. They arrived in St. Augustine to interview the people there and get their opinions. A number of people, including soldiers, officials and friars, surprisingly felt that the fort served a useful purpose and should be maintained. The discussion on the fate of the fort continued until 1606, when the Council of the Indies decided in favor of keeping it.

In 1606 news reached Florida that the English were once again attempting to plant a settlement in the area north of Florida. This news caused a problem for the Spanish. Should they send a fleet to the area to attack the English, as many in Spain were suggesting, or should they wait and see if the colony was successful? After all, the colony the English tried to establish at Roanoke was a failure, and this one might be also. Indecision on what to do resulted in no action, although reconnaissance voyages were sent to the Chesapeake — one from Florida and the other from Spain. The news out of Virginia was not encouraging as far as the settlement was concerned. The English settlers were apparently suffering great hardships, and the death rate was very high. Many in Spain thought that the colony would fail on its own and save them the trouble and expense of destroying it.

By 1612 the English colony was still alive and the French had planted a settlement in Canada on the St. Lawrence River. Spain decided to tacitly accept the existence of French and English colonies to the north of them and to admit secretly that their claim to all of North America was unrealistic. However, the existence of French and English colonies made the settlement at St. Augustine even more important to the Spanish. They needed a foothold in Florida, as they did not wish to publicly relinquish their claim to North America.

St. Augustine never became a place that attracted settlers looking for a chance for a better life or investors looking to make a profit. Better opportunities existed for them in Mexico, Peru and the island colonies. It did, however, perform a necessary service — it kept other countries from setting up a base in the area from which to attack the treasure fleets, thereby guarding the passage of ships carrying things of value back to the mother country.

### *Breakdown of the Colony at St. Augustine*

| | |
|---|---|
| *Nationality of settlement* | Spanish |
| *Sponsored by* | Pedro Menéndez and King Philip II of Spain |
| *Physical location* | First settlement was on Anastasia Island on the east coast of Florida, but was later moved to the mainland across from the island. |
| *Why that location* | Menéndez was looking for a suitable place to land his men that was near the French Fort Caroline. He wanted to be near the coast to protect and assist Spanish shipping. |
| *Purpose of settlement* | To establish a permanent settlement in Florida, to discover the presence of any foreign settlement and destroy it, to chart the coast from Florida to Newfoundland and to convert the Indians to the Catholic faith. |
| *When settled* | September 8, 1565 |
| *Climatic conditions* | There was a violent hurricane soon after Menéndez landed on Anastasia Island. |

| | |
|---|---|
| *Relationship with Indians* | At first the relationship was good and the Indians helped the Spanish attack the French. However, the situation deteriorated quickly; the Indians then became hostile and attacked the settlement. |
| *Internal quarreling* | Mutiny and desertions were a big problem in St. Augustine. Some were caught and hanged, but the mutinies and desertions did not stop. Men deserting from Florida to the island colonies were supposed to be returned, but colonial officials did make sure that it was done. |
| *Number of initial settlers* | 800 |
| *Makeup of initial settlers* | 500 soldiers, 200 seamen and 100 "useless people"— married men, women, children and officials. |
| *Number of additional settlers* | 1,500 soldiers were sent to St. Augustine in July 1566. Settlers were sent to the colony from Spain, but as the ships always stopped in Havana first, many deserted and stayed on the island or made their way to Mexico or Peru to look for gold and silver. |
| *Percentage that survived* | Not known |
| *Initial supplies* | Menéndez had ample supplies aboard his ships but sent the two largest ones, which were carrying much of the food, away to keep the French from seizing them. Therefore, food, tools and equipment were in short supply. |
| *How often supplies arrived* | The settlement depended on supplies from Mexico to sustain it, and those supplies were very slow in coming. The first resupply occurred in December 1565, but it was long overdue and the settlers felt the amount was insufficient for their needs. Lack of food was a big problem at the settlement. The soil was sandy and the people were able to grow only a little corn and pumpkins to feed themselves. |
| *Stability of the mother country* | Spain was stable at this time. |
| *Fate of settlement* | St. Augustine was the first permanent European settlement in North America and is still in existence today. |

# FIVE

# English Colonization Efforts

## Prelude to Settlement — Early English Explorations

John Cabot, a Genoese mariner, became intrigued with the idea of finding a northern route to the Orient after Columbus reached what was thought to be the southern coast of China in 1492. Spices, silks, and other luxuries were highly desirable in Europe and very expensive, as the voyage to acquire them was long and dangerous. Cabot hoped to improve on the length of this voyage by finding a shorter northern route. He approached the monarchs of several European countries for sponsorship without success and then decided to try his luck in England. He thought England was a good choice, since the English were at the end of the line for receiving goods from the Orient and therefore paid the highest prices. In 1495 he moved with his wife and three sons to Bristol, England, and petitioned the king to sponsor his voyage. In 1496 he was successful. King Henry VII granted Cabot letters of patent, which gave him "full and free authoritie, leave, and power, to sayle to all partes, countreys, and seas, of the East, of the West and of the North, under our banners and ensigns."[1]

Cabot agreed to pay for the voyage out of his own pocket; but he was to be allowed to bring back items for sale duty-free and required to pay the crown only a fifth of the proceeds. He was also granted the licensing rights to the areas he discovered, which meant that only people who had obtained a license from Cabot or one of his associates would be allowed to trade in the region.[2] After receiving the letters of patent from the king, Cabot began making preparations for his journey. In May 1497, he and his crew of 18 sailed west and, in June, landed in Newfoundland, which he thought was an island off the coast of China. He claimed this land for England. After exploring the coastline and discovering the cod banks off the southern coast, he returned home in July, anxious to tell the King of his discovery. Then he immediately began making preparations for a second voyage. In May 1498 he set sail with five ships to explore the area east and south of Newfoundland. One of the ships was forced to return to port for repairs shortly after departing and the other four, including the one commanded by Cabot, sailed off, never to be heard from again.

In 1501 an Anglo-Azorean association, composed of three merchants from the Azores who were living in Bristol and two English merchants, successfully petitioned the king for letters of patent with provisions similar to those granted to Cabot. From 1501 until 1507 this group apparently sailed to Newfoundland several times and brought back numerous gifts for the king, including birds, wildcats and even three natives who were "clothid in beastys skinnys and ete Rawe Flesh."[3] Although they made numerous voyages, the partners discovered nothing new and could not even interest English fishermen, who were looking for new fishing grounds, to venture out to the cod banks of Newfoundland.

When Henry VIII ascended the throne in 1509, interest in the New World waned. It was not until 1527 that the English undertook another exploratory voyage. In that year Robert Thorne persuaded Henry VIII to sponsor an expedition to discover the Northwest Passage and in May 1527 John Rut headed up the voyage in two ships. Losing one ship in "a marvailous great storme,"[4] Rut arrived in Newfoundland in July. He tried to sail to the north but was forced to retreat south down the coast of Newfoundland owing to the presence of sea ice and eventually made his way to the cod banks at St. John's. He continued heading south, finally ending up in the West Indies. While there, he traded with the Spanish and arrived back in England in the spring of 1528. Rut's voyage discovered no Northwest Passage and found nothing new, and he apparently left little behind in the way of descriptions of the New World.

It was not until Elizabeth I had been on the throne for almost twenty years that English mariners began to explore the seas in earnest. In 1576 a book was published called *A Discoursse of a Discoverie for a new Passage to Cataia* [China], *Written by Sir Humfrey Gilbert, Knight. Quid non?* (Why not?: the motto of the Gilbert family). In his book, written ten years earlier, Gilbert stressed the need for England to find the Northwest Passage and to establish colonies in the New World for the sake of trade and as a place where the unemployed could be put to work. Like Cabot, Gilbert was confident that a short northern route to China existed somewhere in the area around Greenland and Canada. He painted such a vivid picture of the advantages to finding this passage that Martin Frobisher was inspired to explore the ice-choked seas just below the Arctic Circle in order to discover it.

From 1576 to 1578 Frobisher made three voyages looking for the elusive passage. On his first voyage he thought he had found the strait and excitedly named the water passage after himself: Frobisher Strait.[5] After a long and hazardous voyage during which he explored the shores of his "strait," he returned to England with some samples of rocks he had picked up on land. These contained metallic flecks, and when two of the several assayers assigned to test the ore swore that it was gold, enthusiasm for the venture grew and Frobisher was hailed as a hero. The next two voyages were mainly spent in collecting more of the rocks and trying unsuccessfully to colonize the area rather than determining whether the water passage actually led to the Pacific Ocean. A young artist named John White sailed on one of Frobisher's expeditions and made drawings of the Inuit people whom they found living on the shore. It was not until five years later that the expedition's sponsors finally admitted that the rocks contained iron pyrites and not gold.

Meanwhile, Sir Humfrey Gilbert was quietly making his own plans to sail to the New World, both to search for the Northwest Passage and to establish a colony in Norumbega, a vague area somewhere on the coast of present-day Maine. In June 1578 Queen Elizabeth I granted Gilbert letters of patent, which were so broad that they have been called the first English colonial charter. These stated that Gilbert was "to discover, searche, finde out and viewe such remote heathen and barbarous lands countries and territories not actually possessed of any Christian prince or people."[6] He could claim land anywhere from Labrador to Florida and plant settlements with any willing English subjects; he could also remove intruders and dispose of lands. Those English subjects who agreed to settle these regions were to "have and enjoy all the privileges of free denizens and persons native of England and within our allegiance, in such like ample manner and form as if they were born and personally resident within our said Realm of England."[7]

Gilbert left on his first voyage from Dartmouth on September 26, 1578, which was late in the season to begin a northern voyage. He got as far as Ireland and then was forced by bad weather to return to England. He was not deterred, however, and soon went to work to put together a new fleet. For his second voyage he gathered a complement of five ships and around two hundred sixty men, including carpenters, masons, refiners, and mineral men. Edward Hayes, captain of one of the ships, wrote that

> Besides, for the solace of our people, and the allurement of the Savages, we were provided of Musike in good variety not omitting the least toyes, as Morris dancers, Hobby horsse, and Manylike conceits to delight the Savage people, whom we intended to winne by all faire meanes possible. And, to that end, we were ... furnished of all petty haberdasherie wares to barter with these simple people.[8]

The ships sailed on June 11, 1583, and headed west toward Newfoundland. They arrived at their destination on July 30 and sailed down to St. Johns, where they came across a number of fishing vessels from a variety of nations. Gilbert claimed the land for England, which Cabot had already done in 1497, with no opposition from the others of foreign nations who were anchored there.

Gilbert left St. John's on August 20 and headed for Sable Island off the coast of Nova Scotia with only three ships, the others having returned to England with those who had fallen ill during the voyage. When the fleet reached Sable Island, a rainstorm accompanied by thick fog hampered their efforts to land, and a number of men were drowned in attempting to row ashore. It was late in the season, supplies were low and Gilbert had lost many of his men. He therefore decided to sail back to England. Unfortunately, on the return voyage, the fleet ran into a terrible storm and Gilbert's ship was swamped. No one on board survived.

The failure of Frobisher and Gilbert to find the strait to the Pacific Ocean did not discourage others from taking up the search in the same area. Adrian Gilbert (Humfrey's younger brother) formed an association with the English philosopher John Dee, Secretary of State Walsingham, and others to pursue the search for a northern route to the East. In February 1585 Queen Elizabeth granted them a charter empowering them to sail to the north, northwest or northeast, taking as many ships as they chose, giving them a monopoly of trade in any land they discovered and the right to colonize the land under the same terms as had been granted to Adrian's brother Sir Humfrey. Under this charter John Davis made three voyages in 1585, 1586 and 1587 to search for a northern route to the East. While his voyages added to the fund of knowledge about the Arctic, they did not achieve the goal of finding the strait or establishing colonies or trade in the region.

# Roanoke Island Settlement, 1585

Gilbert's charter, which was due to expire in 1584, was renewed by Walter Raleigh, his half-brother, who was anxious to pick up where Gilbert had left off. In April Raleigh dispatched an expedition under Captains Philip Amadas and Arthur Barlowe to explore the North American coast south of Norumbega, the site of Gilbert's proposed colony, and locate an area for settlement.

The expedition took the southern route to the New World, just as Verrazzano had done on his voyage in 1524, arrived along the Outer Banks of present-day North Carolina in July. The Outer Banks, a number of narrow islands beginning at Cape Fear and extending north to Currituck, lie like a barrier between the Atlantic Ocean and Pamlico Sound — that body of water Verrazzano had thought was the Pacific Ocean. Verrazzano had looked in vain for a way to enter through the chain of islands to reach the body of water on the other side, and for several days Amadas and Barlowe could not find an entrance either. Finally, on July 13, Simon Fernandez, the pilot, found an inlet, and the two ships were able to enter but "not without some difficultie."[9] In honor of his achievement in finding it, the inlet was given the name Port Ferdinando.

Having anchored their ships, the men manned the longboats and, traveling south from the inlet, landed on an island called Hatarask by the Indians, of which they promptly took possession for Queen Elizabeth I. The men were delighted with the island, even though it was low and sandy, and began exploring and collecting samples. Friendly relations were established with the Roanoke Indians, who had a village on the northwestern end of Roanoke Island. It was located slightly to the north of Port Ferdinando. Trading took place for several days, and good rapport was established with the Roanoke King Wingina and his brother Grangamineo. So much so that when Amadas and Barlowe left in September, they were able to take two willing Indians, Manteo and Wanchese, with them. The Indians attracted a great deal of attention when they arrived in England and, coupled with the glowing reports of the countryside given by Amadas and Barlowe, a great deal of public interest was aroused. Queen Elizabeth knighted Raleigh and authorized him to name the new land after herself—"Virginia," for the Virgin Queen.

Raleigh had hoped that the queen would undertake the financial backing of the settlement, but although she gave him some assistance in the form of gunpowder, the use of a ship and permission to commandeer other ships and crews, she could not be persuaded to take on the whole financial burden. Raleigh was left as the principal financial backer for the colony, and he needed to augment his personal fortune in some manner in order to fund his settlement. He therefore turned to the time-honored tradition of gaining wealth through privateering, and the timing could not have been better for his enterprises. Relations between England and Spain had been slowly deteriorating, and now the two countries were on the brink of war. The queen began to issue letters of marque for plundering Spanish ships, and Raleigh, like Roberval in 1541, used money made from raids on foreign shipping to finance his settlement.

Raleigh quickly assembled men, provisions and ships, and by April 1585 his expedition was ready to sail to Virginia for the purpose of establishing a permanent settlement, exploring for natural resources, engaging in trade and establishing a base from which to attack Spanish shipping. The fleet of seven ships carried approximately six hundred men: 300 seamen, 200 soldiers and gunners and 108 colonists, all under the command of Sir Richard Grenville, general of the expedition, admiral of the fleet and captain of *Tiger*, the flagship, which was apparently a gift to Raleigh from the queen. Master of the flagship and master pilot of the fleet was Simon Fernandez. Captain Amadas, "admiral of Virginia" designate,[10] was also aboard *Tiger*, and Barlowe may have commanded one of the other ships in the fleet.

Supplies on board the seven ships are not specifically mentioned in the documents relating to the voyage. However, we know that Grenville had on board all the equipment needed to build a pinnace: iron, a forge, sails, cordage and a wheeled truck. Evidently the fleet was not fully supplied with all the food needed for the colony, for Grenville spent a considerable amount of time in the West Indies capturing "prizes" in the form of ships, ransoming passengers and trading the cargoes for "hogs, sows, young cattle, mares, and horses—to stock the colony, and foodstuffs and probably plants of sugar-canes, bananas, and other fruits which it was intended to grow there."[11]

Once established in Virginia, the colony was to be governed by Ralph Lane, a young gentleman of means who had been recalled from the fighting in Ireland to lead the colony. The colonists also included the artist John White, who was there to record the natural history of Virginia with his drawings, Thomas Harriot, a mathematician and scientist who taught at Oxford; Thomas Harvey of the London Company of Grocers, who was the "cape-merchant" or businessman of the expedition; some German miners; a Jewish mineral expert from Prague; several men listed as gentlemen and several soldiers who had served with Lane in Ireland. There were no women in the group.

The seven ships sailed from Plymouth, taking the southern route down the coast of Europe to the Canaries before heading west. While en route, the ships were scattered in a storm and one of them, a pinnace belonging to the flagship, sank. The *Tiger* continued on alone and landed at the "Baye of Muskito" in Puerto Rico in May. Grenville waited there for the other ships to arrive, and since Amadas and Barlowe had stopped there on the previous expedition, it is reasonable to assume that this had been agreed upon as a rendezvous point. Ralph Lane was sent ashore in order to supervise the construction of an earthwork. Also, construction began on a pinnace[12] to replace the one that sank during the storm. On May 19 the *Elizabeth* sailed into Mosquito Bay and joined up with the *Tiger*. Considering the state of war between Spain and England, it was lucky for Grenville that he arrived in Puerto Rico at a time when the nearby Spanish garrison at San German was reduced in strength. A small Spanish patrol of eight horsemen from the garrison appeared but left when challenged by ten English soldiers with arquebusiers. When another larger group of Spanish soldiers arrived, Grenville sent out men to parley, assuring the Spanish that they had stopped in Puerto Rico only temporarily and were anxious to trade and to purchase food. A rendezvous in two days was established to exchange goods in trade, but the Spanish did not keep the appointment. Before departing, Grenville burned the huts Lane's men had built inside the fort and destroyed the embankments, and left an inscription on a post to inform any of the missing ships calling there of the date of the departure of *Tiger* and *Elizabeth*. The three ships, including the newly built pinnace, then resumed their journey. They had been in the area only 11 days.

Since the other four ships had not arrived yet, Grenville needed supplies, especially salt. Shortly after resuming their journey, the English were able to capture two Spanish ships, and since they were close to the southwestern tip of Puerto Rico, which was known for its salt, Grenville dispatched Lane in one of the captured ships to procure it. In three days, Lane and his men constructed an earthwork around two large salt mounds; they were busy loading the salt into the captured ship when a Spanish force appeared in the distance. Lane was surprised, as Grenville had assured him that there were no Spaniards in the area. It was only the garrison from San German, and they did not challenge Lane's encampment. Thus he was able to bring his men and the salt off safely. However, Lane was furious at Grenville for placing him in jeopardy by sending him into Spanish territory to procure salt with only a small number of men.

Upon his return to the *Tiger*, Lane complained bitterly to Grenville — the first of a series of conflicts between Lane and Grenville that plagued the expedition. In a letter to Secretary of State Walsingham written almost three months later from Roanoke Island and sent home with the returning fleet, Lane complained excessively about Grenville's behavior to him and said that once Grenville actually threatened to put him on trial for his life when he offered a conflicting opinion. Simon Fernandez, the pilot, Thomas Cavendish, the expedition's high marshal, Francis Brooke, the treasurer, and Captain John Clarke of the *Roebuck* all apparently sided with Lane in his dislike of Grenville.

In spite of the dislike many of the senior members of the expedition felt for its commander, the voyage continued. In June Grenville sailed to the Island of Hispaniola and anchored in the port of La Isabela, a place known to be amenable to illegal trading with foreign ships, where he was able to arrange a meeting with the governor. After hosting the Spanish to a lavish banquet, Grenville traded the captured ships, passengers, and cargo for much-needed supplies. After a week they departed and headed for the coast of present-day North Carolina.

Grenville had spent over a month in the Caribbean, and alarm bells began to go off in the minds of the Spanish officials in the area. What were the English up to? Rumor had it that the English were going to establish a settlement on the east coast of North America, so why were they spending so much time in the West Indies? Were they also planning an attack on Spanish possessions in the area? Warnings to be on the alert for an English attack were issued to all governors. Pedro Menéndez Marqués, the governor of the Spanish settlement at St. Augustine, began to gather men and supplies for an expedition to discover any settlement the English might have established on the east coast and destroy it.

Grenville and his fleet of ships reached the headland, probably Cape Fear, off the southern coast of present-day North Carolina on June 23 and began to probe the coast for an entrance through the Outer Banks. On June 26 they found an inlet called Wococon, where all the ships with the exception of the *Tiger,* which was lying offshore, went aground on the shallow bar. They were easily floated off. However, when Fernandez attempted to take the *Tiger* through the tricky inlet, he ran her aground and she began to sink. The entry for June 29 in the *Tiger'*s journal states that "wee weighed anker to bring the Tyger into harbour, where through the unskifulnesse of the Master whose name was Fernando, the Admirall[13] strooke on ground, and sunke."[14]

Most of the *Tiger'*s cargo of corn, salt, meat, rice, biscuit and other provisions was lost before the *Tiger* could be beached. While the ship was being repaired, 30 Englishmen were found on Croatoan Island near Cape Hatteras. They had been left there three weeks earlier by the captain of the *Lion,* which was one of the missing ships.

By July 11 Grenville was somewhat settled and ready to explore the area. Taking the pinnace and three boats with 60 men, he crossed Pamlico Sound

The artist John White, a member of the 1585 English expedition to Roanoke Island, made several drawings of the area. This is an engraving done by De Bry from one of his drawings — the Indian town of Pomeiooc. The town consists of several buildings and is enclosed by a palisade of wooden posts. The inhabitants are shown dancing around a large fire in the center (in "Wunderbarliche, doch warhafftige Erklärung, von der Gelegenheit und Sitten der Wilden in Virginia..." [America, pt. 1, German], Frankfort: Theodore De Bry, 1590, p. 81. North Carolina Collection, Wilson Library, University of North Carolina at Chapel Hill).

and landed on the mainland, where the party split into two groups: John Arundell accompanied by Manteo as guide went in one direction and Grenville and his group went in another. During a week of exploring, Grenville's party visited three Indian villages, where they were cordially entertained and John White was able to make several drawings. The harmony that had been established between the Indians and the English was marred, however, by an incident at the Indian village of Aquascogoc. When the English party was leaving the village, Grenville noticed that a silver cup was missing, and he was very displeased over the apparent theft. The werowance, or chief of the village, promised Grenville that he would recover the cup from whomever had taken it and return it to the English. When Grenville's party had finished their explorations and were ready to return to the main fleet, the journal entry states: "One of our boates with the Admirall was sent to Aquascococke to demaund a silver cup which one of the Savages had stolen from vs, and not receiving it according to his promise, we burnt, and spoyled their corne, and Towne, all the people being fledde."[15]

Meanwhile, Arundell and Manteo had explored the mainland and, having previously sent word of their arrival to Wingina on Roanoke Island, headed to the island to survey the area. After extensively examining the region, Arundell made some notes in his journal and the party then returned to the inlet of Wococon and rejoined the rest of the expedition.

Now that his exploring was complete, Grenville in the repaired flagship along with the rest of the group set sail up the coast to Port Ferdinando, where they probably met up with the rest of the missing ships, thus finally uniting the entire expedition. On July 29, Grangamineo, brother to Wingina, came on board the *Tiger* along with Manteo; it is thought that at this time a site for the English fort was chosen. Unfortunately we have no details on when it was decided to build the fort on the northern end of Roanoke Island or under what terms the Indians agreed to the establishment of an English fort near the village of Wingina and his people. However, the beginning of August saw the English on the northern end of Roanoke Island constructing Fort Raleigh. It was an earthen fort, and archeologists excavating the site in the 20th century found no evidence of a palisade of any kind. Evidently there was one large stout building inside the fort while the two-storey houses of the colonists stood between the fort and the Indian village.

On August 2 Captain Amadas was sent with a party to explore Albemarle Sound, and on August 5 Grenville sent a ship back to England to inform Raleigh of their arrival in Virginia and to hasten the sailing of a relief ship with supplies to replace those lost in the *Tiger*. On August 25 Grenville himself set sail for England, promising to return by the following Easter with additional colonists and supplies. He left only 108 men behind, even though he had about three hundred at his disposal. It is possible that the shortage of food and supplies precluded leaving a larger group at the site, but one wonders whether Grenville would have left more men and ships if he felt that Roanoke offered a suitable harbor to serve as a refuge for privateers.

Lane was left in charge in Grenville's absence and was confident that the limited amount of supplies in the colony would prove no hardship, as he and the others could live off the land. In early September Amadas returned from his expedition across Albemarle Sound and gave a good report of the area — the soil was fertile, they found a variety of maize that produced sugar from its stalks, there was medicinal earth and plants to produce medicines, and there were flax and grapes. They also reported the existence of a sizable population on the northern bank of the sound.

By the middle of the month the rest of the fleet was ready to return to England carrying at least three letters from Lane, one of which was dated September 3 from "the new fort in Virginia."[16] These letters dwelt at length on his disagreements with Grenville but also carried information about the area. Lane wrote enthusiastically about the countryside and what had been found there; the only thing he seemed not to be pleased with was the lack of a suitable deep-water harbor for ships.

Details on the winter of 1585–1586 are sparse. We know that Lane sent a group of men to explore the region to the north. Lane was not satisfied with the harbors in the area of Roanoke Island, and since establishing a base for preying on Spanish shipping was a priority for the settlement, he wanted to find a better location for the colony. The group wintered somewhere in the vicinity of the Chesapeake Bay, probably Kecoughtan, and received visits from a number of Virginia Indians. Either John White or Thomas Harriot or both must have been part of the mission, for a detailed map of the area was drawn during the expedition — a feat no one else in Virginia at that time could have accomplished.

Apparently relations between the English settlers and Wingina had become strained over the winter. It is possible that Wingina began to resent the settlers' constant demands for food, which he could ill afford to spare, for although Lane had confidently asserted that the English would live off the land, it was the Indians who provided most of the food for the settlers during the winter. Perhaps also, the proximity of the fort to the Indian village helped to exacerbate the relationship between the two groups. Whatever the reason, Wingina sent messengers out to the various tribes asking them to join in an alliance with him to drive the English out of the area.

Although Lane gives us very few details of the winter months, he began writing a detailed narrative of his explorations and activities in March 1586. He started his explorations on the Chowan River and arrived at the Indian village of Chawanoac only to find representatives from several tribes assembled there to discuss the alliance proposed by Wingina. Lane marched into the village and took Menatonon, the Chawanoac werowance, prisoner and dispersed the rest of the assembly. Lane kept Menatonon handcuffed for two days, during which he questioned him and tried to get as much information from him about the area as he could. Lane was especially interested in possible harbors, inland water channels and sources of minerals and pearls.

Lane wrote:

> The King of the sayd province is called Menatonon, a man impotent in his lims, but otherwise for a Savage, a very grave and wise man, and of very singular good discourse in matters concerning the state, not onely of his owne Countrey, and the disposition of his owne men, but also of his neighbours round about him as wel farre as neere, and of the commodities that eche Country yeeldeth.[17]

Menatonon was extremely helpful and showed Lane some pearls that he had acquired from a large nation to the northeast near a deep-water bay. He told Lane that the territory of this large nation was three days' journey up the Chowan River by canoe and four days overland to the north. Lane's plan was to search for this bay, but since it was already March and Grenville would be returning soon with supplies and reinforcements, which he could use for his expedition, Lane decided to postpone his search. To make sure that Menatonon would supply guides to help him when he was ready to look for the bay, he took his son Skiko prisoner and sent him back to Roanoke Island.

Before being released, Menatonon told Lane about a place called Chaunis Temoatan, located up the Roanoke River in the mountains, where large amounts of gold and copper could be found. This place, said Menatonon, was also near a salt sea. Gold and a passage to the Far East — it was a double lure and Lane could not resist. He set out immediately in two boats with 40 of his own men and several Indians, including Manteo, to row up the Roanoke River against the current with only a few days' worth of supplies. Lane thought that he would be able to get food from the Indians along the way, but the woods around the river were strangely quiet and deserted. Forewarned by Wingina, the Indians in the area had simply left; therefore the villages Lane's party came across were empty and void of food.

Running low on supplies, the party continued on until they heard some Indians in the distance. Hoping at last to be able to trade for some food, Manteo called out to them, but they were not friendly. A volley of arrows struck the boats, but no one was hurt, and when the English returned fire with their muskets, the Indians fled. The next morning the party headed back down the river, after killing two dogs they had with them to make a stew. Very weary and nearly famished, they finally returned to Roanoke Island the day after Easter, but there was no sign of Grenville and his supply ships.

By the time Lane returned from his expedition, relations with Wingina and his Roanoke tribe had improved slightly and Wingina was willing once again to help the English settlers with food. Wingina called all of his werowances together, and they decided that they would help feed the English by setting out weirs for them to catch fish and by planting a field of crops just for them, besides setting aside more ground that the settlers could work themselves. But this was

April and the crops would not be ripe for a at least two months. Until the harvest, therefore, the English faced a dismal situation and were dependent on Wingina and his people, who supplied them with fish and dried roots.

Lane was expecting supplies to arrive from England at Easter time. When they had not come by June, he began to worry, especially as Wingina, unhappy with the English once again, moved his village from Roanoke Island to a place on the mainland called Dasamonqueponke, and he stopped supplying the fort with food. In desperation, Lane sent some of his men to Cape Hatteras and others to Port Ferdinando to fend for themselves and to keep a lookout for the supply ships. This left Fort Raleigh with a limited number of men to defend it.

Once again Wingina tried to rally the neighboring tribes in the area against the English, calling for a gathering of warriors to assemble on June 10 to drive the English away. Warned of the plan by Skiko and other friendly Indians, Lane devised a plan of his own. On the night of June 1, Lane crossed the sound with 25 men and landed on the mainland close to Dasamonqueponke, Wingina's village. The party was met by some of Wingina's warriors; Lane told them that he wanted to send word to Wingina that the English were moving to Croatoan Island, but first he had a complaint to make. One of Wingina's men had released the prisoner Skiko. The ruse worked, and Lane and his armed men were allowed to enter the village. Once inside, Lane yelled out the prearranged signal for attack, which was "Christ our victory." In the ensuing battle, Wingina was wounded and fled into the woods, followed by one of Lane's men, who subsequently killed and beheaded him. In his narrative, Lane does not mention what happened after Wingina's death. We have to assume that the remaining Indians pledged allegiance to the English or fled inland.

Lane was hoping that the settlers would be able to hold on until July, when the crops would be ready to harvest. After the harvest, he estimated that the colony would have food to last for at least a year. When Grenville arrived with more supplies and settlers, Lane planned to send two expeditions to the deepwater bay. One group would follow the land route set down by Menatonon, establishing a number of small fortified posts behind them as they went. He would send another expedition in pinnaces to approach the area by water, and when the two expeditions met, they would establish a base to which the remaining settlers from Fort Raleigh could be moved. He would then have a settlement on a deep-water harbor to act as a base from which to attack Spanish ships and he would also have an open line of communication with the Chowan River by his series of outposts. From the Chowan River he would be able to access the gold mines and look for the saltwater sea located up the Roanoke River. All he needed were the men and supplies to arrive at the colony.

Meanwhile, in England, Grenville and Raleigh were having trouble getting the supply fleet ready to sail. Raleigh had to find additional funds, which was proving to be a time-consuming task. However, one ship with provisions was sent ahead of the main fleet to tide the colonists over until the larger supply arrived. In early June a large flotilla of ships was spotted off the coast of Hatteras Island, but it was not the expected supply fleet from England; rather, it was a squadron of 27 ships under the command of Sir Francis Drake.

Drake, who had just finished a successful campaign against the Spanish in the West Indies, which included the destruction of St. Augustine, had decided to stop by Roanoke Island to see how things were progressing in Raleigh's new colony. When he learned of the situation there, he offered Lane two choices. He would leave Lane a ship and a couple of smaller boats with a crew and a month's worth of supplies, or he would take them all back to England. After meeting with his top people, Lane decided that they would stay another month. Then the time-consuming task of transferring supplies began.

On June 13, however, all these plans changed. A "great storme" arose, which lasted three days. Several of Drake's larger ships put out to sea for fear of being blown on shore. Once the hurricane passed, it was discovered that the ship that was to be left for Lane had disappeared and several of the smaller ships had been wrecked. Also, some of the supplies Drake had with him were lost as well. Drake gave Lane the choice of one ship and limited supplies or giving all of them passage back to England. Drake's principal ship and its supplies had been lost in the storm, and the colonists were in a weakened state and uncertain of when or if Grenville would arrive. Lane then decided that they would all return to England.

To make room for Lane and his men, Drake supposedly abandoned on shore some Indian and African slaves that he had captured from the Spanish. Three of Lane's men could not be located before the ships sailed, so they were left behind. The remnants of Drake's fleet left Roanoke on June 18. Shortly after their departure, the single ship that Raleigh sent ahead of Grenville's main fleet arrived at Roanoke and finding no one there, returned to England.

Grenville's fleet of three ships and 400 men left England about two weeks after the first ship. The journey was not made quickly, since Grenville stopped to capture several prizes on the way. When he arrived at Roanoke Island, he found the place abandoned. He searched the area and captured three Indians, two of whom escaped. From the third he learned that Drake had come and taken all the Englishmen away. Even though he had 400 men with him and a quantity of supplies, he left only 15 behind, along with enough supplies for two years, and returned to England.

## *Breakdown of the First Colony at Roanoke*

| | |
|---|---|
| *Nationality of settlement* | English |
| *Sponsored by* | Charter granted by Queen Elizabeth I to Walter Raleigh |
| *Physical location* | On the north end of Roanoke Island, which lies between North Carolina's Outer Banks and the mainland, close to a break in the barrier islands |

| | |
|---|---|
| | which was named Port Ferdinando in honor of the ship's pilot. The fort was located near the shore on the east side of Roanoke Island between the "North Point" of the north end of the Island and a "creek." |
| *Why that location* | Being sheltered from the sight of passing Spanish ships, near a break in the barrier islands, this location made a good defensive place to settle, where they could launch raids against the Spanish. |
| *Purpose of settlement* | To establish a colony with the idea of exploiting natural resources and local trade — also to establish a base from which to conduct raids against the Spanish. |
| *When settled* | June 26, 1585 |
| *Climatic conditions* | Hurricanes |
| *Relationship with Indians* | Good at first, despite Grenville's burning of the village of Aquascogok. But it quickly deteriorated into open conflict. |
| *Internal quarreling* | Ralph Lane, second in command, Simon Fernandez, the pilot, Thomas Cavendish, the expedition's high marshal, Francis Brooke, the treasurer, and Caption John Clarke of the *Roebuck* all apparently had problems with Sir Richard Grenville. |
| *Number of initial settlers* | 108 |
| *Makeup of initial settlers* | All men, including John White, an artist, Thomas Harriot, a mathematician and scientist, Doughan Gannes, mineral expert, and miners. |
| *Number of additional settlers* | 0 |
| *Percentage that survived* | 94 percent |
| *Initial supplies* | Considerable supplies were lost when the Tiger ran aground and started to sink. |
| *How often supplies arrived* | A supply ship arrived a year later, but the colonists had left shortly before its arrival. |
| *Stability of the mother country* | Stable |
| *Fate of settlement* | Abandoned June 1586 |

## Roanoke Island Settlement, 1587

After the return of Lane and the settlers from Roanoke Island in the fall of 1586, Raleigh took time to rethink his position in Virginia. He had established a garrison on Roanoke Island to provide a base for privateering, and although the first group of settlers had abandoned the area, Grenville had sailed in June with more men and supplies and surely must have left an adequate number of men on the island to hold Fort Raleigh. Lane's report was interesting, and John White, one of the returning settlers, spoke optimistically of the area. Why not set up another colony in Virginia in addition to the one at Roanoke Island? This one would be a civilian, not a military, organization and he would locate it on the Chesapeake Bay in a place recommended by Lane. Families would be encouraged to participate in the venture and an English community would be established in Virginia, with perhaps a privateering base close by. Thus the city of Raleigh in Virginia was created, though it was never established.

In 1587 Raleigh's personal fortune was running low; however, he was able to enlist the financial support of 19 merchants and 13 gentlemen. Some of the colonists themselves, the people who "volunteered" to go to Virginia, were also investors. Five hundred acres of land were offered to each volunteer, regardless of the amount of his investment in the corporation. John White was chosen as governor, and he and 12 named assistants were given a charter and were incorporated by Raleigh as the governor and assistants of the city of Raleigh. White was instructed to stop by Roanoke Island and confer with the men left there and deposit Manteo, who was returning to his people, before proceeding to Chesapeake Bay to settle in the place recommended by Lane.

On May 8, 1587, three ships departed from Plymouth, England, to sail to Virginia and establish a permanent settlement, explore the area for natural resources, engage in trade and establish a safe haven for privateers. On board the three ships were the 85 men, 17 women and 11 children who would make up the new colony. Some of the men were undoubtedly soldiers, as White later writes that he assembled "thirtie shott, ten pikes and ten targets, to man the pinnesse, and to goe a land for salt."[18] The occupations and social class of the remaining passengers are not known. It is estimated that there were about 14 families, including White's daughter and her husband, in the group. The vessels apparently carried supplies, but as on the previous voyage, they were preparing to pick up more supplies in the West Indies.

John White sailed as captain of the flagship *Lion* with Simon Fernandez, who was one of the assistants of the city of Raleigh, as master. Edward Spicer was master of the flyboat,[19] while Captain Edward Stafford commanded the pinnace. The voyage was not a pleasant one, as it was fraught with quarrels between White and Fernandez. White, as commander of the expedition, was superior to Fernandez, but Fernandez went his own way with no apparent concern for White's wishes. As early as May 16, White was recording his displeasure with Fernandez: "Simon Ferdinando Master of our Admirall, lewdly forsooke our Flie boate, leaving her distressed in the Baye of Portingall."[20] The flyboat was left behind to find her own way to Virginia, which she did with no apparent difficulty.

White states that Fernandez

> purposely left them in the Baye of Portingall, and stole away from them in the night, hoping that the Master therof, whose name was Edward Spicer, for that he never had beene in Virginia, would hardly finde the place, or els being left in so dangerous a place as that was, by meanes of so many men of warre, as at that time

were aboord, they should surely be taken, or slaine: but God disappointed his wicked pretenses.[21]

The *Lion* and the pinnace had stopped at St. Croix in the Virgin Islands to take on supplies when White became annoyed with Fernandez once again. White complained that Fernandez had put them all in danger by assuring them that the island was uninhabited, when in fact they found evidence that there were Caribs, who were supposedly cannibals, in the area. Then, in search of fresh meat, Fernandez promised them that they could find some sheep on the nearby Island of Vieques. No sheep were found, so they headed to Puerto Rico to Rojo Bay, where two years earlier Lane had landed to procure some salt. The colonists had made a number of sacks for collecting the salt and White had assembled some armed men to guard those gathering it when Fernandez had a change of mind. His concern was that the ship could be wrecked if a storm arose, especially in that part of the bay. White later claimed that this was not true and that Fernandez, having taken the ship into shallow water, began to swear, and crying great danger proceeded to take the ship out to sea. Thus no salt was obtained.

The next day White wanted to go ashore to gather some plants that he was planning to transplant in Virginia, but Fernandez would not stop. He told White that they would be able to obtain everything they needed on the island of Hispaniola, where on the previous voyage Grenville had entertained the officials in the port of La Isabela and bought supplies from them. According to White, Fernandez said he would obtain the necessary supplies from his friend, a Frenchman named Alençon. But as they drew nearer to La Isabela, Fernandez found excuses for not calling there. The two ships then headed toward the Caicos Islands, where Fernandez said there were two salt ponds. No salt was found and White wrote that Fernandez's assurance of the presence of salt "prooved as true as the finding of sheepe at Beake [Vieques]."[22]

There was no apparent reason for the friction between White and Fernandez. It could have been just a clash of temperaments or have had something to do with privateering, or perhaps it was a combination of both. Fernandez was used to sailing with men who placed great emphasis on capturing "prizes" in the form of ships with passengers to ransom and cargoes to sell at a profit. White, however, was not of that breed. His main interest was getting safely to Virginia with the civilians, including women and children, who were on board the ships and to pick up plants, salt, and other supplies on the way. It may have been that Fernandez, balked of his desire to capture Spanish ships, decided to get his revenge by not accommodating White's wishes. This was unfortunate, as the extra supplies would have been extremely useful.

On July 7, 1587, the two ships at last headed toward Virginia, but White wrote that Fernandez mistakenly thought that they had reached Cape Hatteras when in fact they were much farther to the south. White claimed that they came very close to the coast and would have been wrecked were it not for Captain Stafford. "Such was the carelesnes, and ignorance of our Master [Fernandez]."[23]

On July 22, the two ships arrived at Port Ferdinando and White and 40 of his men immediately went ashore, intending to confer with the men left the previous year by Grenville and then to return to the ships and sail up the coast to the Chesapeake Bay. No sooner had the men entered the pinnace than one of the sailors told them that Fernandez had said the colonists in the boat were to remain on land and not to return to the ships with the exception of White and a few others approved by him. According to White, the sailors said that Fernandez felt the summer was too far advanced for them to travel farther and therefore the settlers were to be left on Roanoke Island. White maintained that all the sailors were in agreement with Fernandez, so that "it booted not the Gouernour to contend with them."[24] With no more protest than that, White and his party landed on Roanoke Island. White wrote that they

> Went aland on the Island, in the place where our fifteene men were left, but we found none of them, nor any signe, that they had bene there, saving onely we found the bones of one of these fifteen, which the Savages had slaine long before.
>
> The 23 of Iuly, the Govvernour, with divers of his companie, walked to the north ende of the Island, where Master Ralfe Lane had his forte, with sundry necessarie and decent dwelling houses, made by his men about it the yeere before, where wee hoped to finde some signes, or certaine knowledge of our fifteene men. When we came thither, wee found the forte rased downe, but all the houses standing unhurt, saving that the neather roomes of them, and also of the forte, were overgrown with Melons of divers sortes, and Deere within them, feeding on those Mellons: so we returned to our companie, without hope of ever seeing any of the fifteene men living.
>
> The same day order was given, that every man should be imploied for the repairing of those houses, which we found standing, and also to make other newe Cottages, for such as shoulde neede.[25]

What was Fernandez's motive for not wanting to take the settlers on to the Chesapeake Bay? It might have been that he and his crew were anxious to reach the Azores, as the Spanish treasure fleet was due to arrive there in August or September.[26] With no apparent demur, the settlers prepared to go ashore and the long process of unloading the supplies began. On July 25 they were pleasantly surprised by the arrival of the flyboat, the one that White maintained had been callously abandoned by Fernandez in the Bay of Portugal. All the colonists had now arrived. They numbered 111.

On July 28 George Howe, one of the governor's assistants, searching for crabs some distance from the settlement, was ambushed and killed by Indians. The settlers were dismayed, as they had expected to live in friendship with the Indians in the area. In an attempt to establish some rapport with the Indians, Captain Stafford and some of the colonists went with Manteo to visit his people on Croatoan Island. Once the Croatoans were assured by Manteo that the members of the party were friendly, they embraced them and entertained them in a friendly manner.

The Croatoans told the colonists that the remnants of the Roanoke Indians living at Dasamonqueponke were responsible for the recent death of George Howe and had also killed some of the men Grenville left the previous year. Indians from the various tribes in the area were gathering at Dasamonqueponke to join the Roanokes against the English. White was anxious to make peace with all the Indians in the region, and the Croatoans offered to intercede on the colonists' behalf and let the principal tribes in the area know of their friendly intents. All the leading members of these tribes would be invited to come to Roanoke Island within seven days for a meeting. The Croatoans would either bring the people to the meeting or would send a messenger to the English with the tribes' responses to their overtures of friendship.

After the seven days had passed and no message had been received, the settlers feared the worst. John White, with Captain Stafford and 24 men, decided to attack the town of Dasamonqueponke to revenge the deaths of Grenville's men and the death of George Howe. Unfortunately the Roanoke Indians had already deserted the village and in their place were the friendly Croatoan Indians, who had heard of the flight of the Roanokes and had come over to "gather the corne, and fruite of that place."[27] Manteo, who was with the attacking English, quickly realized the mistake and was able to halt the fighting, but not before one of the Croatoans was shot. Although he was greatly grieved by the attack on his people, Manteo realized that the Croatoans were partly to blame, as they had neglected to send the expected message, and he was able to defuse the situation.

It should be noted that the Croatoans had made a point of telling the colonists "not to gather or spill any of their corne, for that they had but little."[28] This, coupled with the fact that they were scavenging for food in another tribe's deserted village, demonstrates the Indians' lack of resources. Tree-ring data from centuries old bald cypress trees has now shed some light on the climatic conditions during this time. The data indicate that the colonists settled Roanoke Island during the most extreme drought in 800 years (1587–1589).[29] This would explain the Croatoans' concern for lack of corn and why they had to scavenge in order to supplement their diet.

The colonists had arrived too late in the season to plant crops and the Indians had little food to spare. The settlers pleaded with Governor White to sail back to England in order to hasten the arrival of a resupply fleet. With great reluctance he agreed to do as they asked. Reading between the lines there is a slight hint here that the settlers might have been anxious for White to leave, for while they had confidence in his integrity, they had little confidence in his leadership abilities. It must have been a sad leavetaking for White. He was not only leaving his daughter in Virginia but on August 18, just before he sailed, his granddaughter Virginia Dare was born. She was the first English child known to be born in the New World.

The settlers formed a plan to leave information about their whereabouts in case White should return to find that they had left the area. If the colonists decided to move to a more suitable location, which was, of course, the original plan, the name of the new place would be carved into a tree. If a cross were carved above the name, it would mean that they left under distress. White left the colony on August 27, sailing in the flyboat, while Fernandez took command of the *Lion*. Just after White boarded the flyboat, an accident occurred involving the capstan; this injured half the crew and made it impossible for them to raise the anchor. They were forced to cut the anchor loose so that they could get under way. Thus with no anchor and a limited crew the ship set sail for the Azores, struggling valiantly to keep up with the *Lion*. Upon reaching the Azores, the two ships parted company — the one to cruise the area in search of "prizes" and the other to limp home with little water or food and a ship full of disabled and ailing sailors. On November 8, 1587, White finally arrived at Southampton.

When White arrived in England he found the country in turmoil and preparations under way to defend the country from the Spanish Armanda. The queen commanded that no ship that could be used to fight the Spanish was to leave port. White met with Raleigh on November 20, and Raleigh began to make arrangements for a pinnace to be sent out right away with supplies for the colonists. A larger supply fleet headed by Grenville would follow later. The pinnace was never sent because of the queen's order, but in March 1588 Grenville's ships were ready to sail. However, he was ordered at the last minute to keep his ships in home waters so that they could assist the navy.

Apparently at White's urging, Grenville was able to release two small ships, the *Brave* and the *Roe,* which were not needed for the defense of England. They were loaded with supplies and a small number of additional colonists, including some women, and sailed on April 22. The captains of both ships were apparently more interested in piracy than the fate of the colony. After chasing and boarding some foreign ships, the *Roe* and the *Brave* separated and, as luck would have it the *Brave,* which carried John White, was captured by a French ship, whose crew took all the supplies intended for the Roanoke colony. During the battle, White "was wounded twise in the head, once with a sword, and another time with a pike, and hurt also in the side of the buttoke with a shot."[30] With no supplies aboard, the ship had no choice but to return to England. When the *Brave* arrived, it was found that the *Roe* had also returned.

The Spanish armada attacked England in July 1588 and was defeated, but it was not until March 1590 that relief ships were sent out to Virginia. White secured passage with the privateer John Watts and his fleet of three ships. According to White, Watts refused to take on additional colonists and stores and only reluctantly accepted White as a passenger. After privateering in the Caribbean, the fleet sailed up the coast to the Outer Banks and at last anchored offshore from Port Ferdinando.

White must have eagerly scanned the horizon for any signs of habitation as they approached the inlet, and he may have been cheered when, off to the northwest where the settlement would have been located, he saw a thin column of smoke rising in the air. The next morning, White and crews from two of the ships piled into two small boats and began making their way toward Roanoke Island. Unfortunately a wave hit one of the boats and it capsized. Four of the men were rescued but seven, including Edward Spicer, one of the captains, were swept away. Despite this tragedy, they pressed onward but overshot their landing place on Roanoke Island, as it was now dark They saw light from a fire and sounded their trumpets and sang English songs to attract the attention of any settlers on the island — but there was no response.

At dawn the next day they landed and walked toward the fire, only to discover that it was merely grass and old rotting trees that were burning. They walked through the woods to the place where the colonists had been left in 1587 and, on top of a timbered dune, White saw a tree on which had been carved the letters CRO without a cross above it. They continued on and White later wrote:

> We passed toward the place where they were left in sundry houses, but we found the houses taken downe, and the place very strongly enclosed with a high palisade of greate trees with cortynes and flankers very Fort-like and one of the chiefe trees or postes at the right side of the entrance had the barke taken off, and 5. foote from the ground in fayre Capitall letters was graven CROATOAN without any crosse or signe of distresse.[31]

Inside, the stockade was empty except for some iron bars, pigs of lead, iron saker-shot and four cannon. Down by the creek White looked in vain for some sign of the colonists' boats. He was returning to the empty stockade when he was met by one of the sailors, who had found five chests that had been buried in a nearby ditch, probably the trench that had been dug around the first fort in 1585. The chests had been dug up presumably by the Indians and their contents taken or scattered about. White recognized the remains — they were his framed pictures and maps, his books, his armor — all damaged by pillaging hands and the elements. He was not dismayed, though, for he was certain that he would find the settlers on Croatoan Island 50 miles across the sound.

Unfortunately, before White could go out to Croatoan to search for the colonists, a violent storm arose damaging the ships and forcing the fleet to leave the area. Supplies aboard the ships were running low. There were plans to revictual in the West Indies and return to Virginia to look for the settlers, but bad weather intervened and the ships headed back to England. White had no opportunity to look for his people and was never able to return to the area to make a prolonged search for them. Other attempts were made to find the colonists, but to no avail. No trace of the settlers was ever found, and the Roanoke settlement has gone down in history as the "Lost Colony."

In a letter dated February 4, 1593, White wrote "Thus committing to reliefe of my discomfortable company the planters in Virginia, to the merciful help of the Almighty, whom I most humbly beseech to helpe & comfort them, according to his most holy will & their good desire."[32]

## Breakdown of the Second Colony at Roanoke

| | |
|---|---|
| *Nationality of settlement* | English |
| *Sponsored by* | Charter granted by Queen Elizabeth I to Walter Raleigh. With his personal fortune running out, Raleigh was able to enlist the financial support 19 merchants and 13 gentlemen. |
| *Physical location* | On the north end of Roanoke Island, which lies between North Carolina's outer banks and the mainland, close to a break in the barrier islands, which was named Port Ferdinando in honor of the ship's pilot. The fort was located near the shore on the east side of Roanoke Island between the "North Point" of the north end of the Island and a "creek." |
| *Why that location* | Originally the colonists were only to stop by Roanoke Island to confer with the men left behind by Grenville and then proceed to the Chesapeake Bay region. The pilot Fernandez refused to take them any further, and thus they settled on the island. |
| *Purpose of settlement* | To establish a colony with the idea of exploiting natural resources and local trade—also to establish a base in which to conduct raids against the Spanish. |
| *When settled* | July 22, 1587 |
| *Climatic conditions* | Tree-ring data indicate that the colonists settled Roanoke Island during the most extreme drought in 800 years (1587–1589). |
| *Relationship with Indians* | The Indians were still hostile, killing George Howe, one of the governor's assistants. Through the intercession of the Indian Manteo, who had relatives on the barrier island of Croatoan, friendly relations with the Croatoan Indians were re-established, but the others remained aloof. The colonists mistakenly attacked the Croatoan Indians, thinking that they were the Roanokes. |
| *Internal quarreling* | John White and Simon Fernandez did not get along. |
| *Number of initial settlers* | 111 |
| *Makeup of initial settlers* | Men, women, and children—approximately fourteen families |
| *Number of additional settlers* | 0 |
| *Percentage that survived* | 0 percent |
| *Initial supplies* | Arrived too late in season to plant crops and Indians had little food. |
| *How often supplies arrived* | Relief ships arrived three years later, but the colonists were not there. |

| | |
|---|---|
| *Stability of the mother country* | Unstable; England was at war with Spain. |
| *Fate of settlement* | It disappeared and so has gone down in history as the "Lost Colony." |

# Popham Colony

The English failure to establish a settlement on Roanoke Island did not diminish England's desire for colonization but it did lessen the enthusiasm of potential backers for such an enterprise. It was estimated that Sir Walter Raleigh had lost £40,000[33] in his colonizing effort, and no one, especially the crown, was willing to fund such an expensive and unpredictable project again. This was a problem that had to be solved if England was to take her place as one of the major powers in Europe. The Spanish were established in Florida and the French were actively engaged in Canada. That left Virginia for the English, and it was felt that a permanent settlement was needed to strengthen England's claim to the region.

In March 1602, Bartholomew Gosnold and Bartholomew Gilbert, son of Sir Humphrey Gilbert, set sail with a group of 32 men for the coast of present-day Maine. Having arrived there, they gathered some sassafras, animal skins and cedar then sailed southward. They visited an area they named Cape Cod and an island they called Martha's Vineyard. They spent some time in these areas and, on their return to England, reported that although they liked the region, they were uneasy about the Indians. Martin Pring, commanding two small ships outfitted by Richard Hakluyt and some Bristol merchants, visited the northeastern coast in the spring of 1603. He was able to explore and trade and returned to England confirming the earlier reports on the quality of the land.

Unfortunately, the English colonizing movement was about to lose one of its most assiduous advocates—Sir Walter Raleigh. Queen Elizabeth I died on March 24, 1603, and was succeeded by King James I, who lost no time in securing a peace treaty with Spain. When Raleigh jeopardized this treaty by continuing his privateering activities against Spanish interests in the Caribbean, James I had him arrested for high treason. In November 1603 Raleigh was convicted and imprisoned in the Tower of London, thus ending his association with colonizing the New World.

Other backers came forth to take his place, however. Most likely by the end of 1604, Thomas Arundell was involved in a plan to send English Catholics to America, notably to the area north and south of Cape Cod. Since James I had established peace with Spain, it was thought that there would be no opposition to this plan from either country. To the contrary: the Spanish made it known that they would not tolerate any kind of English settlement in North America, and English Catholic leaders felt that an exodus of Catholics from England would weaken the Catholic cause in that country.

In spite of the resistance, Arundell went ahead with his plans. In early 1605 he made an agreement with Captain George Waymouth, who was also involved with a group of Plymouth merchants, to explore the coast of present-day Maine. Waymouth sailed on March 5 and was back in England in July, having explored a group of Islands off the coast that would offer good fishing for his merchant backers as well as a suitable place for settlement.

Waymouth and his party "found the land a place answerable to the intent of our discovery, viz. fit for any nation to inhabit." As such, they "used the people [Indians] with as great kindness as we could devise, or found them capable of."[34] They described the Indians as "very civill and merrie: shewing tokens of much thankefulnesse, for those things we gave them. We found then (as after) a people of exceeding good invention, quicke understanding and readie capacitie."[35]

While exploring, they traded "knives, glasses, combes and other trifles"[36] with the Indians for animal skins including beaver, otter, and sable. They appear to have traded fairly with the Indians, for Waymouth would not accept a gift of tobacco without giving them something in return.[37]

Shortly before they were ready to leave the region, Waymouth decided they should take Indian captives back with them to England. When two canoes with three Indians in each came to the ship to trade, the English decided to take advantage of the situation by enticing all six on board ship. The three Indians in the first canoe acquiesced, but the Indians in the second refused and paddled back to shore. Seven or so of the English crew followed them and, under the guise of trade, managed to capture two, while the third fled into the woods. The five Indians with their canoes and bows and arrows were then transported back to England.

When Waymouth arrived in England, he found that Arundell was no longer interested in establishing a settlement for Catholics. However, Waymouth's favorable report of the area, along with the good accounts given by Gosnold and Pring, were incentive enough to cause other backers to consider establishing a settlement in the region. All that was needed was a solution to the problem of financing the colony. If no one man could bear the expense of sponsoring a settlement, could a group of men invest their money in a company that would bear the financial responsibility for colonization?

For decades commercial companies involved in international trade had flourished in England. These companies were granted trade monopolies in a particular area by the crown in return for a certain percentage of the profits. In 1600 this idea was expanded into a new kind of corporation called a joint-stock company, also chartered by the crown but open to a wider range of investors than the previous companies. Investors could "adventure" their money for a single voyage or for a longer period of time, and the profits were in proportion to the money invested. The most successful and best known of these companies was the East India Company.

The idea of using a joint-stock company to undertake the financing of a permanent English settlement in North America began to take hold. The king would issue a charter giving exclusive rights to the company to explore and settle a certain area, and the investors would provide the money for the enterprise. In this manner, investors could "adventure" as much as they could afford, the risk to each investor would be small and all would have a share in the profits. Enough money could be raised in this manner to finance a settlement and support it until the profits began to accrue. The idea was very appealing, and on April 10, 1606, James I granted a charter to a group of men to form a joint-stock company called the Virginia Company in order to explore the land for natural resources, search for the Northwest Passage, plant permanent settlements and bring Christianity to the Indians.

The first charter established one company with two branches—the Virginia Company of London and the Virginia Company of Plymouth—with the right to settle and develop the land in North America known as Virginia, which included all the land between Spanish Florida and French Canada—that is, from Cape Fear in present-day North Carolina to modern Halifax, Nova Scotia. The London Company was given the right to settle all the land between 34 and 41 degrees latitude (the land between Cape Fear, North Carolina, and Long Island, New York) and the Plymouth Company had the right to settle all the land between 45 and 38 degrees latitude (the land between Nova Scotia and the present-day borders of Maryland and Virginia). Since there was a portion of the territory each company could settle that overlapped, a buffer zone of 100 miles was to be left between the settlements.

The two branches operated under the same terms—they were given permission to send as many people to Virginia as were willing to undertake the voyage, and they were responsible for providing adequate supplies for their settlements. The king granted them the right to trade and to collect and keep all duties for the first 21 years. When they had chosen the sites for their settlements, they were allowed to expand and to have the benefits of all the resources found within 50 miles to the north and south, 100 miles inland and 100 miles out to sea. The king reserved for himself one fifth of the gold and one fifteenth of the copper found in Virginia. James I, as his predecessor Elizabeth I had done, promised the colonists that they and their children would have the same rights in Virginia as his subjects had who were living in England.

There were three ways for people to invest in the Virginia Company. They could "adventure" their money by buying a share or shares of stock and remain in England, they could "adventure their person" by actually going to Virginia to settle and paying for their own passage and provisions, or they could go as contract workers for a certain period of time, after which they would have a share of the profits. Initially there was no public offering of the stock, and the first investors were wealthy merchants or influential members of government. Most of these investors remained in England, but a few decided to adventure their person and were members of the first expeditions to settle Virginia.

Sir John Popham, a chief justice of the Queen's Bench, who happened to have presided at the trial of Raleigh in 1603, was in charge of the Plymouth Company. He and his brother Sir Ferdinando Gorges were the major backers of the colony. Having heard about the colonization efforts, the Spanish ambassador Zúñiga warned Popham that encroaching on Spanish territory was a violation of the peace treaty. Popham brushed this objection aside, telling the ambassador that the main purpose of the plan was to rid England of "thieves and traitors" and have them "drowned in the sea."[38]

With the charters in place, both branches of the Virginia Company began making arrangements to establish a colony. The Plymouth Company was the first to get the project under way. In August 1606 their ship *Richard* prepared to set sail for the land Waymouth's Indian captives called Mawooshen and the English called Northern Virginia — the coast of present-day Maine. The ship was captained by Henry Challons and carried 31 men including two of the Indians taken on Waymouth's voyage. In November they were in the Florida Straits, sailing north up the American coast amid a thick blanket of fog and rain, when Challons discovered that he had accidentally wandered into the middle of a Spanish flotilla. The Spanish fired on the ship, and immediately Challons asked to speak to the admiral of the fleet in order to present his credentials: a pass from the king giving him permission to sail to Virginia. However, as she approached the flagship, the *Richard* was attacked, her main sail was shot to pieces, and she was boarded by the Spanish, who ruined or took all her cargo and also "most cruelly beate us all and wounded two of our Company in the heads with their Swords, not sparing our Captayne nor any."[39]

The *Richard's* men were scattered as prisoners among the Spanish ships and thus ended up in different locations. One of the Spanish ships, damaged in a storm, landed in France, where four of the Englishmen were released by the French and sent home. The other men were imprisoned in Spain. Over the next 18 months some of the men were given bail and some were kept imprisoned and treated severely, one being stabbed in the stomach and dying 14 days later. Constant requests by the English ambassador to free the remaining men only met with a decree from the Spanish that all voyages to Virginia should cease. The English claimed the right of free passage on the seas along with the right to settle anywhere they chose in Virginia. This situation put the crown in an uneasy position, as James I was trying to form closer ties with Spain.

In order to put more pressure on the English to give up their colonizing expeditions, Spain sent a number of the English prisoners to the galleys. However, this only served to increase England's resentment, since Spain was seeking English support in her dealings with the Spanish Netherlands. In an effort to win English favor, the prisoners were finally released in 1608. The results were not exactly what the Spanish had anticipated, as the whole affair made the royal government all the more determined to stand behind the Virginia Company in its endeavor to establish a permanent settlement in Virginia.

Two months after Challons sailed, a ship carrying supplemental supplies for the colony was sent out under the command of Thomas Hanham, with Martin Pring as the master. Not finding any settlers in the area, they left and went back to England. Nevertheless, they brought back more detailed information and such favorable reports of the region that Popham and the other members of the Plymouth Company decided that another attempt was in order.

On May 31, 1607, two vessels, a fly-boat called the *Gift of God*, under the command of Captain George Popham, John Popham's nephew, and a ship called *Mary and John*, captained by Raleigh Gilbert, set sail with a little over one hundred settlers. Some of the settlers were listed as gentlemen and included a physician, draftsman, shipmaster, and chaplain. Roughly one hundred other unidentified colonists made the voyage; these included a number of soldiers, carpenters, craftsmen and possibly farmers.[40] The supplies on board the two ships are not specified, but we know they were limited. The Plymouth Company's finances had been severely strained by the loss of the *Richard* and her cargo, and although Sir John Popham, whose health was failing, expended his last bit of energy in an attempt to enlarge the number of subscribers to the company, he was unsuccessful. Therefore the company had been able to acquire only a limited quantity of low-priced supplies for the voyage. Artifacts found by archeologist Jeffrey Brain at the site of the settlement confirm the fact that the colony was supplied with inexpensive wares. The only expensive items found were in the area identified as Raleigh Gilbert's house — a gentleman adventurer who would have brought his own supplies with him.[41]

Just after the departure of the *Gift of God* and the *Mary and John*, Sir John Popham died in England. Popham's death was a major blow to the colonization effort, since he seems to have made the settlement his own personal project. Francis, his son and heir, was to take his place, but it would be his uncle Sir Ferdinando Gorges who would be the main supporter of the settlement in the future.

The two ships had an uneventful voyage and met at the mouth of the Sagadahoc (Kennebec) River on August 17, 1607. Popham and Gilbert with 48 men in two of the ships' boats sailed

up the Ryver of Sagadehock for to view the Ryver and also to See whear they might fynd the most Convenyent place for thear plantation. We fynd this river to be very pleasant with many goodly Illands in ytt and to be both Large and deepe Watter havinge many branches in ytt, that which we tooke bendeth ytt Selffe towards the northeast.

Tuesdaye beinge the 18th after our return we all went to the shore and thear mad Choies of a place for our plantation which ys at the very mouth or entry of the Ryver of Sagadehocke on the West Syd of the Ryver beinge almoste an Illand of a good bygness.

Thursdaye being the 20th of Auguste all our Companyes Landed and thear began

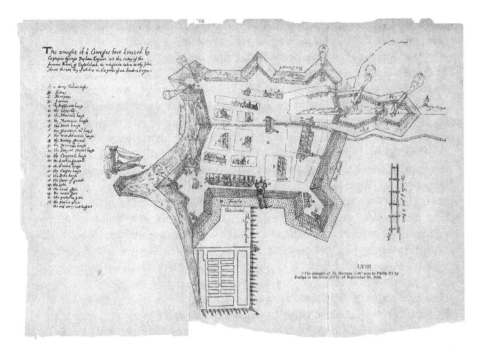

John Hunt, one of the Popham colonists, was a cartographer and drew this map of Fort St. George. Modern archeologists working at the site have confirmed that much of the map is correct, but it is not certain if all the buildings depicted here were actually built. Notice the walled garden outside the ramparts of the fort (Harvard College Library, Widener Library, US 18382.40 vol. 1).

to fortefye. Our presedent Captain Popham Sett the fryst spytt of ground unto ytt and after hem all the rest followed and Labored hard in the trenches about ytt.

Frydaye the 21st of Auguste all hands Labored hard about the fort. Som in the trentch Som for fagetts and our ship Carpenters about the buildinge of a small [pinnace] or shallop.[42]

Captain George Popham was to be the president of the council that was to govern the colony, and he was to be assisted by Captain Raleigh Gilbert, admiral; Captain Edward Harlow, master of the ordnance; Captain Robert Davis, sergeant-major; Captain Elis Blest, marshall; Master Seaman, secretary, Captain James Davis, captain of the fort and Master Gome Carew, chief searcher.[43]

On October 6 the *Mary and John* was sent back to England under the command of Captain Robert Davies to give a report on all that had been accomplished in the colony and to urge the dispatch of a resupply ship early in the next year. It is probable that the ship also carried a number of settlers, as later reports claim that only 45 men wintered in the colony that first year. The second ship, *Gift of God*, had not been completely unloaded when the *Mary and John* sailed for England, so she remained at the settlement with the intention of following in a few weeks.

After the departure of the *Mary and John*, the remaining men worked on the fort, which they decided to call Fort St. George in honor of the patron saint of England. Fort St. George was surrounded by a trench and fortified with 12 pieces of ordnance. Inside the fort there was a church, a storehouse and some houses. The carpenters framed a 30-ton pinnace which was christened *Virginia*, and Gilbert was able to accomplish some expeditions in the area before the weather became too cold for exploring.

There were problems, of course. Relations with the Abenaki, the local Indian tribe, were tenuous at best, and though some trading took place between the two groups, the English sometimes found the Indians elusive and unwilling to offer their best animal pelts for trade. The English suspected that the Abenaki were "in hand" with the French, who had established an extensive trade network in the area, and indeed, the colonists reported that the Indians' language was interspersed with French words. The settlers were afraid that the French were pressing the Abenaki not to trade with them and even to drive them out of the country in return for French aid against their enemies. The coast was full of harbors and coves where French ships could hide and mount an attack on the fort. Therefore, when shortly before the *Gift of God* was due to sail for England, friendly Indians warned of a possible attempt by the French to lay siege to Fort St. George, the president and council immediately ordered the ship to remain in port to keep a lookout for French ships.

Not only were the settlers having trouble getting along with the Indians, they were having trouble getting along with each other as well. Ferdinando Gorges later wrote that he was displeased with the colonists' inability, through "pride and arrogansay, faction, and privat resolution,"[44] to follow the directions they had been given. Raleigh Gilbert was not on good terms with George Popham, the president of the council. Popham was later described by Gorges as "an honest man, but ould, and of an unwieldy body, and timorously fearful to offende, or contest with others that will or do oppose him, but otherways a discreete, careful man."[45]

Raleigh Gilbert thought the colony should be under his control, as his father, Sir Humphrey Gilbert, had been given a patent to it late in the previous century. He began to assert his rights for control, gathering a group of men around him to oppose the president. Gilbert was described by Gorges as "desirous of supremacy, and rule, a loose life prompte to sensuality, little zeale in Religion, humerouse, head stronge, and of small judgment and experience, other wayes valiant inough."[46]

Thus Gorges later reported to Lord Salisbury (Robert Cecil, secretary of state and chief backer of the Virginia Company) that the settlement was getting into trouble because of "childish factions, ignorant, timerous and ambitious persons."[47]

The next difficulty to face the settlers was the weather. By late November winter had set in on the Sagadahoc River with a vengeance. It was cold and windy, with snow falling in abundance and great floes of ice appeared on the river, endangering the *Gift of God* as she rode at anchor in the harbor. One night, when the force of the ice pushed in a plank on the side of the ship, it was decided to send her home before she was damaged beyond repair. The difficulty was that there were not enough provisions to victual the ship for the return voyage. Taking what supplies they could, the crew laded the ship with a cargo of masts, and on December 16, 1607, set sail for the Azores, where they sold the masts and pawned the ship's cannon to buy food and so were able to return to England.

The colonists inside Fort St. George survived the winter with apparently little sickness, "although theyr Cloathes were but thinne and theyr Dyets poore."[48] There was a fire at the fort and the storehouse burned, with the loss of some of their provisions, but these English settlers fared much better than the French had during the winter of 1604–1605 just a little to the north, on an island in the St. Croix River. There were some deaths, though, the most notable being that of George Popham on February 5, 1608. Raleigh Gilbert was now in control of the colony.

The *Mary and John* returned to England, arriving at Plymouth on December 1 with about half of the settlers and mixed reports. Gorges wrote to Lord Salisbury that the ship had returned with news of "a fertill Contry, gallant Rivers, stately Harbors, and a people tractable, (so discreete Courses bee taken with them), but no returne, to satisfy the expectation of the Adventurers."[49]

Gorges tried to be optimistic when he wrote that it was not reasonable to expect very much to be accomplished because the settlers had been there only about two months; there were so few of them and they had many things to do. However, when the *Gift of God* arrived in Plymouth on February 6, 1608, with nothing but the report that the "extremity of the weather hath been great" and the colonists were divided into factions, "each disgracing the other, even to the Savages."[50] Gorges remarked:

> These often returnes without any commodity, hath much discouraged our adventurers ... although in common reason, it bee not to bee looked for, that from a savage wilderness, any great matters of moment can presently be gotten, for it is arte, and industry, that produceth those thinges ... and therfor I am afrayde, wee shall have much a doo, to go forwardes as we ought.[51]

Still trying to put the best face on the situation, Gorges tried to persuade Lord Salisbury to prevail upon the king to take over the Plymouth Company. He listed all the advantages: the fertile soil, the excellent fishing, the abundance of naval stores for the building of ships, the ability to settle hundreds of England's poor in a place where they could be self-sufficient and satisfied. Last, but not least, he stressed the importance of preventing the French from encroaching on the region. His pleas were not successful and in the end Gorges was obliged to raise the money himself to outfit three resupply ships for the colony.

The first two ships were small and left at the end of March, carrying "victualles & other necessaryes"[52] to the settlers. The third ship of 200 tons, under the command of Captain Davies—laden with food, arms, instruments and tools—sailed in May and did not reach the colony until the end of the summer. At Fort St. George, Captain Davies "found all things in good forwardness, and many kinds of furrs obteyned from the Indians by way of trade; good store of sarsaparilla gathered, and the new pynnace all finished."[53]

Captain Davies brought letters with him for the settlers; one in particular was for Raleigh Gilbert, president of the council. It informed him that his elder brother, Sir John Gilbert, had died in England and that he, Raleigh Gilbert, was heir to the family property. He decided to return to England to take up his inheritance. No one among the remaining settlers was willing to assume the post of president, and with the prospect of facing another harsh winter at Fort St. George ahead of them, they all elected to abandon the settlement and return to England. On September 30, 1608, they loaded up the relief ship and the new pinnace *Virginia* and set sail for home, arriving in Plymouth in late 1608.

After the colonists returned, the London Company tried to get the backers of the Plymouth Company to support an expansion to the southern colony at Jamestown, which apparently some did. The Plymouth Company then became involved in a series of lawsuits, pointing out the fact that too little money had been invested for colony to have had much chance of success. The lack of money also contributed to the fact that too little time had been allowed to determine if the settlement could have been successful as at least a trading post.[54]

The loss of the *Richard* and her cargo had been a devastating blow for the colony, not only financially but emotionally as well. If the *Richard*'s voyage had been successful, the Plymouth Company would have had the honor of establishing a colony in Virginia in the fall of 1606—before the Jamestown settlers had even left England. The Popham colony would have been the first, and all the publicity and momentum would have been theirs.

The series of lawsuits slowed the Plymouth Company's activities down for a while, although some seasonal fishing and trading still took place along the New England coast. However, after John Smith visited it and determined that it was not suitable for human occupation, no settlement was proposed for this area. Thus it would be another 12 years before another settlement was attempted, this time at Plymouth, Massachusetts.

## Breakdown of the Popham Colony

| | |
|---|---|
| *Nationality of settlement* | English |
| *Sponsored by* | The Plymouth Company, a division of the Virginia Company, which was granted a charter from the king |

| | |
|---|---|
| *Physical location* | At the mouth of the Kennebec River |
| *Why that location* | Positive reports of the area from Gosnold, Pring, and Waymouth. Also, Waymouth said it was a suitable place for a settlement. |
| *Purpose of settlement* | To establish a colony with the idea of exploiting natural resources and local trade, especially animal skins. Also to keep the French out of the area. |
| *When settled* | August 18, 1607 |
| *Climatic conditions* | According to the Waymouth, who was there in the summer, the weather was similar to that of England but somewhat hotter. The colonist, however, reported that the winter was very harsh. |
| *Relationship with Indians* | Tenuous, although some trading did take place. |
| *Internal quarreling* | George Popham and Raleigh Gilbert were not on good terms. Gilbert began to assert his rights for control under his father's earlier patents. |
| *Number of initial settlers* | Approximately 107 landed in the colony but only 45 remained for the winter. |
| *Makeup of initial settlers* | Six gentlemen, including a physician, a draftsman, a shipmaster and a chaplain. Roughly 100 other unknown colonists, possibly including soldiers, craftsmen, and farmers. |
| *Number of additional settlers* | None. About half the colonist went back to England at the end of 1607. |
| *Percentage that survived* | It appears that a majority of the colonists survived, although exact numbers are not known. |
| *Initial supplies* | Initial supplies proved inadequate. |
| *How often supplies arrived* | Three supply ships were sent out in the summer of 1608. |
| *Stability of the mother country* | Stable; England was at peace with Spain. |
| *Fate of settlement* | Abandoned in the fall of 1608. |

# SIX

# *Jamestown*

The charter giving the Virginia Company the right to settle the land claimed by England in North America was issued by the king in April 1606, and the two branches of the company immediately began to recruit investors for their proposed voyages. While the Plymouth company was busy preparing for an expedition to plant a settlement in northern Virginia in the summer of 1606, the London company was equally busy planning to send its expedition to settle southern Virginia in December of that year.

Under the first charter, the king established the system of government that would be used in the colonies. There was to be a royal council in England, whose members were to be chosen by the king, and it was their responsibility to oversee and direct all matters concerning both colonies. There was also to be a council in each colony, whose members were to be selected by the royal council in England. Their responsibility was to govern the colony subject to the laws and instructions of the king. The council in Virginia was to select, by majority vote, one man among them to act as president for a term of one year, and the council had the power to remove and/or replace its members. Under this system the president had two votes and the other council members had one; all decisions were to be made by majority vote.

On December 20, 1606, the London Company's fleet of three ships carrying 105 men sailed from London for the New World for the purpose of exploring the land for natural resources, to search for the Northwest Passage, to plant a permanent settlement and to bring Christianity to the Indians. The settlers were all men and included gentlemen "adventurers," some of whom had military experience, two surgeons, carpenters, laborers, soldiers, bricklayers, a minister, a mason, a barber, a tailor, a fisherman, a blacksmith, and four boys.[1] On board the ships were all the provisions and supplies that would be needed in Virginia, including seeds for planting and domestic animals such as chickens and dogs. The fleet of three ships was under the command of Captain Christopher Newport, the admiral.

The Virginia Company of London had issued very precise instructions intended to help the settlers avoid the pitfalls that had plagued other settlements.

The settlers were instructed upon arrival on the coast of Virginia to seek a "safe port in the entrance of some navigable river,"[2] and if there was more than one suitable river, they were to choose the one "which bendeth most towards the northwest, for that way shall you find the other sea."[3] They were advised to settle on a site that was as far up the river as possible so they would not "be surprised as the French were in Florida by Melindus [Menéndez], and the Spaniard in the same place by the French."[4] To keep potential mutineers from stealing the ship that was to be left in Virginia, they were told to take the sails and anchors ashore.[5]

Once they had decided on a site, the leaders were to divide the men into three groups. One group was to fortify and build, taking care to build a store-house first for their provisions, while the second group was to prepare the ground to sow corn[6] and roots. When that had been done, ten men from the second group were to go to the mouth of the river and act as sentinels. The last group was to go exploring and, it was hoped, would find the passage to the "other sea" or deposits of gold and silver.[7]

The London Company gave advice on how to deal with the Indians:

> In all your passages you must have great care not to offend the naturals, if you can eschew it; and employ some few of your company to trade with them for corn and all other lasting victuals.... For not being sure how your own seed corn will prosper the first year, to avoid the danger of famine, use and endeavor to store yourselves of the country corn.[8]

There was advice on how to choose a place to settle also, for they were warned not to select an area that was heavily wooded, for it would be difficult to clear the land and the woods "may serve as a covet for your enemies round about you."[9] The instructions continued with, "Neither must you plant in a low and moist place, because it will prove unhealthful."[10] Ending with a request that the leaders send a report with Captain Newport of all they had done, they were reminded that they should all work together for the good of their country and wished the best of luck.

The voyage did not have a promising start, as the three ships had no sooner entered the English Channel than they encountered contrary winds. They were forced to spend six weeks in the Channel until a favorable wind came up, allowing them to continue their journey. The settlers, bobbing up and down on their ships in the English Channel, confined in close quarters with little or nothing to do for six weeks, must have been extremely bored and no doubt became short-tempered and irritable. By the time the fleet reached the Canary Islands in late February, disagreements had broken out aboard ship to the extent that three of the men were accused of trying to start a mutiny and clapped in irons for the remainder of the trip. Ironically, one of these men was Captain John Smith, who was destined to play a prominent role in the settlement of the colony and would also write extensively about it. The situation aboard the ships did not improve, and by the time the fleet arrived in the West Indies, it had deteriorated to the point that Christopher Newport, the admiral, came very close to hanging Smith.

However, after a few weeks on the islands in the West Indies, tempers improved; they were able to proceed with the voyage, and on April 26, 1607, reached the coast of Virginia. Captain Newport and 30 of the men went ashore, where they took great delight in the "fair meadows and goodly tall trees"[11] they found there. They named that point of land Cape Henry in honor of Prince Henry, the oldest son of James I, and it was there they had their first encounter with the Indians—a skirmish in which two men were wounded. The Indians ran into the woods when they had "spent their arrows,"[12] and although the English marched inland the next day, they did not find any Indian people, only a deserted campsite.

The colonists spent four days on Cape Henry where, following the instructions of the London Company, they opened a black box containing the names of the members of the council in Virginia. The council in England had chosen seven men to be on the council and placed their names in a black box that was to remain locked until the fleet reached Virginia. All seven of the men had military experience and, to the delight of some and the chagrin of others, Captain John Smith's name was on the list. The men voted on a president and selected Edward Maria Wingfield, the oldest among them.

Four days later the ships moved into the Chesapeake Bay and began their search for a navigable river. The James River, flowing down from the northwest proved suitable, which, as the settlers wrote, was to their "good comfort,"[13] so they named the point of land at the mouth of the river Point Comfort. The men spent two weeks exploring the river, going as far as the Appomattox River near present-day Richmond before deciding on the best site for their fort.

The place they chose was a small peninsula connected to the mainland by an isthmus that, at high tide, was flooded, making the peninsula an island. The semi-island was low, but at the western end there was some higher ground and a channel in the river ran close to the shore there, so that the settlers were able to moor their ships "to the trees" on shore "in six fathom water."[14] It was a good defensive site,[15] as the river channel ran away from the island at the eastern end, preventing enemy ships from landing soldiers to attack the fort by land, and at the western end it ran close enough to the shore for enemy ships to come under fire from the cannons in the fort but not so close that the ships could fire effectively at the fort. The colonists decided to build their fort on this western end.

In a letter to the council in England, the settlers wrote enthusiastically of the site: "We are set down 80 miles within a river for breadth, sweetness of water, length navigable up into the country, deep and bold channel so stored with sturgeon and other sweet fish as no man's fortune hath ever possessed the like."[16] John Smith called it "a very fit place for the erecting of a great city."[17] There were no springs of fresh water on the island, but with a river full of "sweet water," that was not seen as a problem.

The colonists arrived at the island on the evening of May 13, 1607. They landed the next day and set about fulfilling their instructions by erecting a fort. John Smith recorded: "Now falleth every man to work; The council contrive the fort, the rest cut down trees to make place to pitch their tents, some provide clapboard to relade the ships, some make gardens, some nets, etc."[18]

The fort was apparently not a very substantial structure, for according to Smith it was "but the boughs of trees cast together in the form of a half-moon."[19] It had been erected by the effort of Captain Kendall, a member of the council. Smith wrote that Wingfield, the president, showed little interest in the building of a proper fort and did not hold any military exercises during those first weeks; however, he did put men to work clearing fields for planting.

On May 21 Newport was ready to explore the countryside as the London Company had instructed him. Taking 5 gentlemen and 18 men in the pinnace, he sailed up the James River all the way to the falls, beyond which the boat could not go, and erected a cross with the inscription "Jacobus Rex 1607." On the trip the Englishmen had friendly encounters with various Indians, learning from them that all the tribes in the region were under the control of a powerful chief named Wahunsonacock but called Powhatan. Approximately thirty to thirty-two tribes paid an annual tribute to Powhatan — produce from their fields or copper they had received in trade — in return for protection from their enemies.

When Newport and his men reached the falls of the river, the Indians in that area refused to provide guides to take the English to the land beyond the falls. Newport wisely refrained from pressing the matter and had to be satisfied with a barrelful of earth that he believed contained gold and the image of the great necklaces of pearls worn by the Indians. When he returned to England, Newport joyfully reported his impressions of the area, and soon Virginia was being called the Promised Land, but instead of milk and honey it was said to be full of gold and pearls.[20]

The men then journeyed back to the fort, where they were met with the disturbing news that the day before the Paspaheghs, in whose territory the fort was located, had attacked the fort, surprising the men who were busy planting in the fields. Most of the muskets had not been unpacked as yet, and if it had not been for the artillery on board the ships, which frightened the Indians and made them run away, the fort would have been overrun. In the attack several members of the council were wounded and a boy in the pinnace was killed.

It was then that Wingfield ordered a proper fort to be built. George Percy wrote: "[it] was triangle-wise, having three bulwarks at every corner like a half moon, and four or five pieces of artillery mounted in them."[21] The men worked hard, and even though they were interrupted frequently by Indian attacks, they finished their fort by June 15. They called it Jamestown in honor of James I, and they called the river on which it was built the James River, also in honor of the king.

On June 22 Christopher Newport and his men sailed for England in two of the ships, leaving the smallest ship behind for the settlers to use. He took with him a letter to the royal council in London. In it the settlers wrote:

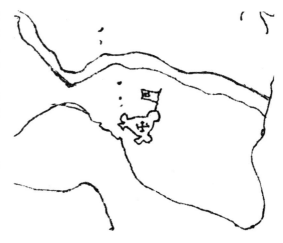

> Within less than seven weeks, we are fortified well against the Indians; we have sown good store of wheat; we have sent you a taste of clapboards; we have built some houses; we have spared some hands to a discovery; and still as God shall enable us with strength we will better and better our proceedings.[22]

But there was a cloud on the horizon, as they continued:

> Our easiest and richest commodity being sassafras, roots were gathered up by the sailors with loss and spoil of many of our tools, and with drawing of our men from our labor to their uses against our knowledge to our prejudice. We earnestly entreat you — and do trust — that you take such order as we be not in this thus defrauded, since they be all our waged men.[23]

This is the only known drawing of the English fort at Jamestown. It was sent in September 1608 from Zúñiga, the Spanish ambassador in London, to the Spanish king. It is not known how the ambassador acquired it, but the map was discovered in the Spanish archives in the late 19th century. For years the object at the top of the central image was interpreted as a large flag. Now, however, it is thought to be a walled garden similar to the one shown on Hunt's map of Fort St. George (Harvard College Library, Widener Library, US 18382.40 vol. 1).

Before he left, Newport had noticed a feeling of discontent among the settlers and, hoping to avoid a future confrontation between the president and some of the council members, he called them together for a serious talk. He tried to persuade the men to work together for the good of all, and when he sailed he was confident that his efforts had been successful. He left the 104 settlers well protected in their fort, vowing to put aside their grievances and work together, but he also left them very short of provisions.

The voyage had taken twice as long as had been expected, and they had used more of their food supply than was planned. And by their late arrival in Virginia, as John Smith wrote,

> we ... lost the opportunity of the time and season to plant.... What toil we had with so small a power to guard our workmen adays, watch all night, resist our enemies, and effect our business to relade the ships, cut down trees, and prepare the ground to plant our corn, etc. I refer to the reader's consideration.[24]

Moreover, the settlers were obliged to provide food out of their supply to the ships for their voyage home. When Newport left on June 22, 1607, Smith said they had provisions for 13 or 14 weeks.[25] Newport promised to return within 20 weeks with new settlers and fresh provisions.

The first summer in Virginia proved to be devastating to the English settlers, for not only did the Paspaheghs keep up their sporadic attacks on the fort but the hot, humid weather and the lack of fresh water to drink caused many men to sicken and die. George Percy, one of the gentlemen adventurers, wrote "Our men were destroyed with cruel diseases, as swellings, flixes, burning fevers, and by wars, and departed suddenly, but for the most part they died of mere famine. There were never Englishmen left in a foreign country in such misery as we were in this new-discovered Virginia."[26]

The sweet water in the river had changed, as Percy wrote "Our food was but a small can of barley sod in water to five men a day; our drink cold water taken out of the river, which was at flood very salt, at a low tide full of slime and filth, which was the destruction of many of our men."[27]

In the spring the snows in the mountains to the west melt and flow into the James River and then down to Chesapeake Bay. At this time of the year the water in the river is mostly fresh, but in the summer, fall and winter the tide sweeps up river past Jamestown Island all the way to present-day Richmond. The salty tidal water mixes with the fresh, making the water in the river brackish. Since the English arrived at Jamestown Island in the middle of May, the water in the river was fresh and they were satisfied that there would be no problem with the water supply, only to discover their mistake during the summer. Percy wrote of "slime and filth" in the river at low tide, which was more than likely the result of sewage being dumped down river from the fort and then being swept up past the fort by the tide. Fish from the river, possibly contaminated by the raw sewage, constituted a large part of the diet of the settlers that first summer. It is thought that dysentery, saltwater poisoning and typhoid fever were responsible for the many deaths in the fort.

During that first summer the men were often so weak that at times there were barely enough among them with adequate strength to act as sentries. To make matters worse, there was dissension among the members of the council. According to Wingfield, "Master Kendall was put off from being of the council, and committed to prison, for that it did manifestly appear he did practice to sow discord between the president and the council."[28]

In their weakened state, the men in the fort were fully expecting the Indians to attack and kill them all. But surprisingly that did not happen; instead, the Indians began to bring food to the settlers. By fall the 38 survivors began to revive, thanks to the food brought to the fort by the Indians and the advent of cooler weather. Migrant birds soon made an appearance in Jamestown, giving the men a welcome change in their diet.

The colonists had suffered greatly during their first summer in Virginia and were not happy with the situation in the fort. John Smith, in his *True Relation*, wrote: "As yet we had no houses to cover us, our tents were rotten, and our cabins worse than nought."[29] Discontent was prevalent and, as might be expected, the blame for conditions in the colony fell on Edward Maria Wingfield, the president. He was consequently deposed from office and Captain Ratcliffe elected in his place.

In the fall, seeing that the food supply was getting low, the council asked John Smith to trade for corn among the Indians. Smith made several trips to nearby Indian villages and came back with enough food to last for some weeks. The added food along with the change in leadership and the cooler weather had brought some improvement in conditions in the fort, but there was still dissension among the leaders and the men continually grumbled and complained. Some even became rebellious—one of the men, the blacksmith, was on the point of being hanged for insubordination when he "declared a dangerous conspiracy, for which Captain Kendall as principal was by a jury condemned and shot to death."[30] Details as to the nature of this conspiracy are disappointingly few. Wingfield called it a "mutiny"[31] but gave no details, and there are no records of Kendall's trial. The only details we have are from a deposition by Francis Maguel, an Irishman, a sailor from a town just outside of London, who was more than likely a spy.[32] His deposition was translated into Spanish and sent to the king of Spain by the Spanish ambassador in London.[33] In it, Maguel, who said that he had been in Virginia for eight months, stated:

> they have tried in that fort of theirs at Jamestown an English Captain, a Catholic, called Captain Tindol [George Kendall], because they knew that he had tried to get to Spain, in order to reveal to His Majesty all about this country and many plans of the English, which he knew, but which the narrator does not.[34]

By November conditions in the fort had settled to the point that John Smith, who was anxious to explore the countryside, felt that he could be spared to set out on an expedition. It was during this trip that Smith was captured by the Indians and taken to Powhatan's favorite village on the Pamunkey River (now the York River) to meet Powhatan himself. According to Smith, Powhatan greeted him "proudly lying upon a bedstead a foot high, upon ten or twelve mats, richly hung with many chains of great pearls about his neck ... with such a grave and majestical countenance as drave me into admiration to see such state in a naked savage."[35]

Powhatan asked Smith why the English had come to his land, and Smith told him they had been in a fight with their enemies, the Spanish, and had come to his land to refit their ships and rest a while. Then Powhatan wanted to know why they had traveled up the river (the James River) to the falls. Smith replied that they had some grievance with the Monacans (Powhatan's enemies) and were anxious to go beyond the falls to make war on them. It was understood that Powhatan would be glad to accept the help of the English against his enemies, and when Smith left to return to the fort, he took with him Powhatan's promise to aid the settlers with food or anything they needed.

Soon after Smith returned to the fort in January 1608, Christopher Newport arrived with the first supply of settlers and provisions. Two ships had been sent from England, but they had become separated during the voyage. After several weeks, when the second ship, *Phoenix*, did not arrive at Jamestown, it was presumed that she was lost at sea. The settlers' joy at Newport's arrival turned to dismay as fire swept through the fort, destroying it and most of the settlers' possessions, including all the books of the Reverend Hunt, the minister.

The arrival of Newport and his mariners proved to be a mixed blessing. Although Newport's men helped the settlers to rebuild the fort and the houses, the mariners began to trade with the Indians in such a generous way that Smith complained, "But in a short time it followed that could not be had for a pound of copper which before was sold us for an ounce."[36] And that was not his only complaint about the mariners. He continued:

> This hap'ned in the winter in that extreme frost, 1608. Now though we had victual sufficient — I mean only of oatmeal, meal, and corn — yet the ship staying 14 weeks when she might as well have been gone in 14 days spent a great part of that, the beef, pork, oil, aqua vitae, fish, butter and cheese, beer and near all the rest that was sent to be landed. When they departed, what their discretion could spare us to make a little poor meal or two we called feasts to relish our mouths. Of each somewhat they left us, yet I must confess those that had either money, spare clothes, credit to give bills of payment, gold rings, furs or any such commodities, were ever welcome to this removing tavern.[37]

Powhatan kept his promise and frequently sent messengers to the fort with gifts of grain, beans and meat. Often his ten-year-old daughter Pocahontas[38] accompanied the messengers. Francis Perkins, one of the new arrivals, wrote home that Powhatan also sent some of his people to teach the settlers how to "sow the grain of this country [and] to make certain tools with which they are going to fish ... [but] it is more in clearing out the wood than in the multiplying of the grain that the difficulty arises."[39]

On April 20, while the settlers were busy cutting down trees and planting their corn, they were surprised by the arrival of *Phoenix*, which they had all thought lost at sea. Master Nelson, the captain, had been forced by storms to winter in the West Indies, where he was able to live off the land, thus preserving the provisions he had aboard. He brought both new supplies and a group of healthy settlers to the fort. His arrival was very welcome to say the least.

In the summer of 1608, Smith took a small group of men to explore the Chesapeake Bay, making two trips there. The expedition traveled all the way to the head of the bay and Smith drew maps of the area, which were remarkably accurate considering the technology, or rather lack of it, at the time. One of the reasons for the trip was to try to discover the existence of silver mines. The

Powhatan Indians had some silver-colored metallic dust that they had gotten from the Patawomeck Indians. Newport was convinced that it was silver and wanted the settlers to search for the mine. They found it, but the "glistering metal"[40] proved to be of no value.

The second reason for the expedition was to search for the Northwest Passage, and Smith and his men had high hopes that they had found it. According to what the Indians at the head of the bay told them, the bay "stretched into the south sea or somewhere near it."[41] Smith returned to the fort from his first expedition on July 21 to find that the settlers from *Phoenix* were all sick and the rest of the men so disgusted with Ratcliffe, the president, that they were on the point of "tormenting him with revenge."[42]

According to Smith, the men in the fort asked him to take over as president, which he did; but since he wanted to continue his explorations, he appointed Matthew Scrivener in his place and more honest officers to assist him. Evidently Ratcliffe had misappropriated some of the food supplies, which Smith promptly distributed equally among the men. "And in regard of the weakness of the company and heat of the year — they being unable to work — he left them to live at ease to recover their healths, but embarked himself to finish his discovery."[43]

Smith returned to Jamestown on September 7 to find that although some of the new settlers were recovered, many in the fort had died and others were still sick. Thanks to Matthew Scrivener, the harvest had been gathered, but some of the provisions in the storehouse had been spoiled by the rain that had come in through the leaky roof. On September 10, 1608, Smith was elected president of the colony. He had the church repaired, the storehouse recovered, buildings prepared for the next supply, "the fort reduced to a five-square form"[44] and squadrons trained.

Soon after Smith took over as president, the "second supply" of settlers and provisions arrived in Jamestown, including the first two women — Mistress Forrest, who had accompanied her husband to Virginia, and her maidservant, a young girl named Ann Burras. Mistress Forrest appears to have either died or returned to England, as nothing more is heard of her, but in December Ann, who had just turned 14, married a laborer named John Laydon. The next fall their child, a little girl, was born at the fort and appropriately named Virginia. She was the third English child born in the New World — Virginia Dare and an unnamed child having been born in the Roanoke Colony in 1587.

After Newport arrived at the fort with the "second supply" in the fall of 1608, he traveled up the James River above the falls into the land of the Monacans in search of the passage to the South Sea and also to look for gold and silver mines. The London Company also wanted Newport to follow up on the information that the settlers had gotten from the Indians about English people living among Indian tribes outside of Powhatan's territory. There were rumors that a group of English people, presumably the Roanoke colonists, had traveled to the land of the Chesapeake Indians from the south and lived among them for many years. According to the information given by an Indian named Mechumps, Powhatan had attacked the Chesapeakes, killing almost everyone, including the English, shortly after the arrival of the Jamestown settlers in 1607. However, Mechumps said, seven of the English—four men, two boys and a young girl—had escaped and were living in the village of Chawwonoke.[45] Twice men were sent to visit the area and, as John Smith reported, "but nothing could they learn but they were all dead."[46] Newport had no luck finding either the passage to the South Sea or mines of gold and silver.

While Newport was obeying his instructions from the London Company, Smith left to try to trade with the Indians for food, as their harvest was "newly gathered ... our own not being sufficient for so great a number."[47] The relationship with the Indians so far had been tenuous at best, with the Paspaheghs being the most troublesome and tribes farther from the English settlement being more friendly and willing to trade. The constant demand for food by the English, however, strained the relationship to the breaking point.

Smith tried cajolery to obtain food but most often was forced to resort to threats to get what he needed from the Indians—telling them that if they did not load his boat with corn, he would load it with their dead bodies, or threatening to burn their houses if they did not bring him food. He maintained that he always paid for the food with trade goods or pieces of copper, which the Indians valued highly, and never took it from them by force. However, the Powhatans had only so much food available to them and needed to make their supply last until summer, when their first crops matured.

In January 1609 Smith was at Werwocomoco trying to procure food from Powhatan, and the wily chief wanted swords and guns in return for the food, items that he must have known Smith would not trade. Smith wrote that Powhatan asked to see the commodities for trade, "But none he liked without guns and swords, valuing a basket of corn more precious than a basket of copper, saying that he could eat his corn but not the copper."[48] Powhatan had only a limited amount of food and obviously preferred to keep it rather than trade it for copper. Whether he would have traded it for guns and swords is another matter.

In the early spring of 1609 the relationship with the Paspaheghs, never good, worsened and finally culminated in an attack by the English on the Paspahegh village, in which several of the Indians were killed and others made prisoners. The English burned their houses and took their boats with all their fishing weirs—a serious loss, as the Indians' diet consisted mostly of fish at this time of year.

The Paspahegh chief came to Smith and said:

> We perceive and well know you intend to destroy us that are here to entreat and desire your friendship, and to enjoy our houses and plant our fields, of whose fruit you shall participate. Otherwise, you will have the worse by our absence, for we

can plant anywhere, though with more labor; and we know you cannot live if you want our harvest and that relief we bring you. If you promise us peace, we will believe you; if you proceed in revenge, we will abandon the country.[49]

The English response was positive and "upon these terms the president promised them peace till they did us injury, upon condition they should bring in provision. Thus all departed good friends and so continued until Smith left the country."[50]

Having gathered a sufficient amount of food from the Indians, Smith turned his attention to other matters. He had made a rule that "He that will not work shall not eat, except by sickness he be disabled."[51] He divided the men into squadrons of ten or fifteen and they worked six hours a day and spent the rest "in pastime and merry exercise."[52] He wrote:

Now we so quietly followed our business that in three months we made three or four last of tar, pitch and soap-ashes, produced a trial of glass, made a well in the fort of excellent sweet water ... built some twenty houses, recovered our church, provided nets and weirs for fishing ... built a blockhouse in the neck of our isle [on the isthmus at the land approach to the island], kept by a garrison to entertain the savages' trade, and none to pass or repass—savage nor Christian—without the president's order.

Thirty or forty acres of ground we digged and planted. Of three sows in eighteen months increased 60 and odd pigs, and near 500 chickings.... But the hogs were transported to Hog Isle, where also we built a blockhouse with a garrison to give us notice of any shipping....

We built also a fort for a retreat near a convenient river upon a high commanding hill, very hard to be assaulted, and easy to be defended.[53]

Smith was not without his critics during his term as president, for according to the charter granted by the king, decisions were to be made by majority vote of the council. Smith dispensed with this practice and made the decisions himself— much to the annoyance of some of the settlers. However, under his guidance progress was undoubtedly being made and the future looked promising. Then disaster struck. Upon inspecting the stored corn, the settlers found "it half rotten"[54] and much of the rest of it consumed by rats that had arrived in the colony aboard the English ships. This was a very serious situation, as it was spring and the fields of corn, beans and squash had not yet ripened. The settlers were forced to live off the land as best they could. The Indians brought deer, turkeys and squirrels to the fort and Smith quartered some men among the Indian villages, paying them for their hospitality with pieces of copper. Some men he sent down to Point Comfort to live off the oysters and others to the falls near modern Richmond, but all they found there were berries and acorns.

In the summer of 1609 Captain Argall and Master Sedan arrived in Jamestown to "truck with the colony and to fish for sturgeon."[55] They brought news of a large fleet preparing to sail to the colony with many provisions and settlers. They also brought letters to the president criticizing him for his harsh treatment of the Indians and for not sending the ships back loaded with profitable materials. When the two ships returned to England, they took back the colonists' reply, in which they said none of these things could be remedied unless "they would send us men and means that could produce what they so much desired."[56]

The news that the Royal Council in England had been receiving from Virginia was not encouraging. The samples of gold that had been sent back proved to be worthless and the products that were forthcoming—sassafras root, clapboard, a few chisels made from bog iron and some glass—were not creating much revenue for them or their investors. The inability of the leaders in Virginia to cooperate with each other was disturbing, as was the high death rate among the settlers.

The council in England decided that the problems in Virginia stemmed from "the form of government and the length and danger of the passage by the southerly course of the Indies."[57] The council felt that settlers arrived in the colony in a debilitated state because of the length of the voyage and the exposure to the extreme heat in the Indies and that this, in turn, caused the high death rate. They took steps to correct this by commissioning Captain Argall to find a shorter, more northerly route to Virginia, which he did, making the crossing in 9 weeks in spite of being becalmed 14 days.

The council felt that the form of government, which fostered dissensions and factions, was responsible for the lack of food in the colony and everything else that was wrong. They therefore decided to change it and so petitioned the king for a new charter. The second charter granted more power to the London Company and gave them the sole right to decide on the type of government that would be established in the colony. It also opened investment in the London Company to the public at large and stipulated that the company was obliged to pay a dividend to its investors in seven years.

The greatest change that the council made was to put the government of the colony in the hands of a newly created governor and captain general. The person holding this position would have full authority to govern the colony and have a council of men in Virginia to advise him. In the absence of the governor, there was to be a lieutenant governor to serve in his place.

With the opening of investment to the public, a large amount of money was made available. Gondomar, the Spanish ambassador wrote: "Fourteen Counts and Barons have given 40,000 ducats, the merchants give much more and there is no poor little man or woman who is not willing to subscribe something."[58]

With this influx of capital, the company outfitted the largest supply fleet ever to sail to Virginia. It was known as the "third supply" and included nine ships with 500 people on board. For the first time families were encouraged to participate, so there were women and children among the passengers. Thomas West, Lord de la Ware, was named governor and captain general of Virginia, and as he was not ready to sail with the fleet, he sent Sir Thomas Gates as the lieutenant general of the colony. Gates, carrying the new charter with him, sailed on *Sea Venture,* which was the fleet's flagship. Since it was the largest of the ships, it also carried most of the provisions for the new settlers for the next year.

The ships left England in early June and had a very uneventful voyage for seven weeks. Then, eight days before they reached Cape Henry, they were hit with a powerful hurricane that scattered the ships and drove them off course. By mid–August, six of the nine ships reached James Fort, but *Sea Venture* was not one of them. About six weeks later, the seventh ship, *Virginia,* appeared, but still there was no sign of the flagship.

The settlers watched anxiously for the ship and the provisions she carried, for the situation at the fort was very serious. There was hardly enough food to feed the former inhabitants and certainly not enough to feed the almost three hundred new arrivals. To make matters worse, arguments broke out between Smith and a few of Smith's critics who had returned to the colony with the third supply after a short absence. They insisted that the form of government had been changed and that he was no longer in charge. Smith replied that he would not step down until he had seen the official charter, which was with Gates on *Sea Venture.*

Meanwhile, Smith continued as president and, knowing that the fort could not house and feed so many people, sent his men to live in camps away from the fort. He sent some to live on the Nansamond River and a large group to live near the site of present-day Richmond in a village he had acquired from the Indians. The latter group proved very troublesome; they were having difficulties with the Indians and Smith traveled there to sort things out. On his way back to the fort, he was injured by an ignition of gunpowder on his thigh. Because his wound was serious, he decided to return to England with the fleet when it sailed in early October 1609.

George Percy was asked to take over as president of the colony and immediately faced a very difficult situation. Many of the new settlers had arrived in a much-weakened condition because of the hurricane, and there was wholesale sickness on one of the ships (the settlers said it was the plague). Because of the lack of food and the crowded conditions in the fort, many of the new arrivals began to die.

Percy then sent Captain Ratcliffe with some men to Point Comfort to build a fort there, knowing that the men would be able to live on what they could find on land and in the bay and thus relieve the fort of the necessity of feeding them. However, just as he had managed to reduce the number of people in the fort, half the men who had been stationed at the falls returned with the report that the Indians had killed the rest of their company.

Percy, seeing "our number at James Town increasing and our store decreasing,"[59] appointed Captain Tucker to calculate how much food was left and how it should best be rationed. According to Percy, there was enough food to last three months, but Captain Tucker, "by his industry and care," figured he could make it last four months.[60] Knowing that he could not expect relief from England in so short a time, Percy sent 50 men under the command of Captain Ratcliffe to trade with Powhatan for food, but to no avail. Of the 50 men, 33, including Ratcliffe, were killed; the 17 survivors returned to the fort empty-handed.

The fate of the men sent to live on the Nansamond River was not any better, as they were found dead, their mouths stuffed with bread. They had wanted to set up their camp on an island in the river near an Indian village and offered to buy the village from the inhabitants. When the messengers sent to negotiate the transaction did not return, the men attacked the village, "burned their houses, ransacked their temples, took down the corpses of their dead kings from off their tombs, and carried away their pearls, copper and bracelets."[61]

Seeing that he could expect no help from the Indians in the Powhatan chiefdom, Percy sent Francis West and 36 men to the Potomac River to trade for maize and beans with the Indians there. West was successful, even though, according to Percy, he "used some harsh and cruel dealing by cutting off two of the savages' heads and other extremities."[62] With his ship loaded with food, West and his men were on their way back to Jamestown when, coming by Point Comfort, the men stationed there yelled out to them to make haste as the people in the fort were in dire need of food. Percy wrote "upon which report Captaine West, by the persuasion, or rather by the enforcement, of his company, hoised up sails and shaped their course directly for England, and left us in that extreme misery and want."[63]

The settlers in the fort were indeed in great want, and it was to get worse, as the Indians, seeing they had a chance to get rid of the English with no danger to themselves, kept the settlers penned up inside the fort. In 1610 Lord de la Ware, the new governor, wrote: "the Indian as fast killing without as the famine and pestilence within."[64] What followed was the terrible "winter of the starving time," in which the settlers trapped inside the fort ate all the hogs, dogs, and horses that were available and then started on the rats, snakes, and mice. They ate the leather from their shoes and the starch from their shirts, and there were instances of cannibalism. By spring, according to Percy, there were only 60 people left alive at Jamestown.

In May the settlers in the fort were surprised to see two English pinnaces in the James River and even more surprised when they discovered that the boats carried the survivors of *Sea Venture*. The ship had been wrecked on the coast of Bermuda and the passengers had escaped to spend ten months marooned on the island. They managed to build two boats and the whole party had boarded and made their way to Jamestown. Lieutenant Governor Gates was dismayed to find the fort falling apart and its inhabitants emaciated and on the brink of starvation.

Food was the greatest need, for although the Bermuda survivors had some food supplies left, they were not enough to feed everyone for very long, and there was no food at all at the fort. The governor sent men over to Hog Island, where he had been told the colonists had placed their hogs to forage, but the Indians had killed them all. The men were set to fishing in the river, but one of the survivors of the shipwreck wrote that they were unable to catch enough fish to give the people "one pound apiece at mealtime.... But let the blame of this lie where it is, both upon our nets and the unskillfulness of our men to lay them."[65]

Gates then made the decision to leave the fort and take all the people down to Point Comfort, where the 30 men who spent the winter there had survived very nicely on what they found on land and in the river. There he would wait for a time to see if a relief fleet from England arrived. If it did not come within ten days, he would take the people to Newfoundland, where they would be able to augment their meager food supplies and then make their way back home.

Fortunately, the three ships from the fort had not gone ten miles when they saw a longboat coming toward them bringing the news that the relief fleet had arrived with the governor and Captain General Lord de la Ware, more settlers and the much-needed food supply. The ships returned to the fort. Lord de la Ware took charge of the colony and Sir Thomas Gates returned to England.

In early September, Gates reached England and although the Royal Council was pleased to hear of the safe arrival in Jamestown of the survivors of *Sea Venture*, they were troubled by the situation in the colony.

> The Councell of Virginia (finding the smalnesse of that returne, which they hoped should have defraied the charge of a new supply) entred into a deepe consultation, and propounded amongst themselves, whether it were fit to enter into a new contribution, or in time to send for home the Lord La-ware and to abandon the action.[66]

They decided to send for Gates to get his opinion. Gates told the council that Virginia was "one of the goodliest countries under the Sunne"[67] and that he could not wait to go back. At the same time a letter arrived from Lord de la Ware in which he pledged his support for the colony, adding that if the Virginia Company were to abandon the colony, he would "lay all his fortune"[68] upon continuing it himself. The company decided to continue the colony and petitioned James I to give them a new charter, granting them the Bermuda Islands also.

In September of 1610 the Spanish ambassador in London wrote to his king that the English were preparing to send more ships with settlers, including women and Protestant ministers to Virginia. He earnestly urged Philip III to send a force to Virginia to eliminate the settlement. In 1611 a Spanish ship appeared off Point Comfort and landed three men on the shore. The men were quickly apprehended and taken to Jamestown as prisoners, where they remained for several years. The leader was a man named Don Diego de Molina, and he spent his time at the fort observing the situation in the colony. He was finally allowed to leave in 1616 and promptly wrote to Philip III for permission to take soldiers to attack the settlement in Virginia. He thought that the fort was poorly defended and would be easy to conquer, and he told the king that the people in the colony were so unhappy that they would welcome the Spanish. He was given six ships for that purpose, but unfortunately for him, when he had been at sea for a month, the crew mutinied and stabbed him to death. The proposed attack on Virginia came to nothing.

Lord de la Ware left Virginia in the spring of 1611 because of an illness he had contracted in the colony. His arrival in England caused the London Company again to doubt the feasibility of the Virginia colony and to discuss its abandonment; however, Lord de la Ware was able to persuade them to continue the colony. For the next seven years Lord de la Ware, who had been named governor and captain general of Virginia for life, would oversee the affairs of the colony from England, while Gates and Dale ran the colony in Virginia.

The reign of Sir Thomas Gates as governor and lieutenant general and Sir Thomas Dale as marshall heralded a new era in Virginia. Lord de la Ware had established martial law in the colony and Gates and Dale expanded on what de la Ware had started with the "Laws Divine, Moral and Martial" under which the colony was to be governed for the next several years. The laws were very harsh and the punishments very severe; in fact, they were more severe than was usual in England. During the martial law period, all written correspondence was strictly censored, so that discouraging or bad news did not reach people in England. This was not entirely successful, for news of events in the colony did spread to England. Therefore not many settlers were willing to come to Virginia and investment in the London Company dropped.

Dale felt that the site of Jamestown was not healthy and wanted to establish a new settlement farther up river. He took 200 men and traveled to the falls and, on a high bluff overlooking the river, founded Henricus near present-day Richmond. Gates, however, stayed at Jamestown, and since he was the governor, Jamestown remained the seat of government.

In 1613 conditions began to improve as Dale put into effect a new system. One third of the men were given three acres of cleared land each on which to grow food, which they were allowed to keep for themselves after yielding 2½ barrels of corn yearly for the common storehouse. These "farmers" were to be excused from much company service and, except for clothing, were not to draw supplies from the common storehouse. One third of the men were set to building and repairing and the other third were to serve as soldiers to fight the Indians, for the settlers were engaged in all-out war with the Powhatans. The builders and soldiers were to receive food from the common storehouse.

Dale started his system of setting men to farming three acres of land in 1613 — the year the drought that had been plaguing the colony ended. Tree-ring data gathered in 1998 and reported in the *Science Magazine* of April 24 has indicated that the period from 1606 to 1612 was the driest seven-year period in southeastern Virginia in 770 years.[69] Certainly the ending of the drought helped to make Dale's system successful, but there was another reason for its success, and that was the incentive offered to the farmers. Until this time men worked in the fields to grow food for the common storehouse and there was no incentive for one man to work any harder than the next.

John Rolfe had been one of the passengers on *Sea Venture*; when he arrived in the colony in 1610, he began to experiment with growing tobacco. The Spanish had introduced tobacco to Europeans in the sixteenth century, and a great demand was created for it, as Europeans took quickly to its use. The Indians in North America grew tobacco and used it for religious and ceremonial purposes, but it was harsh and Europeans did not like it, preferring the Spanish tobacco instead. Rolfe worked with the tobacco seeds he had brought with him, which according to rumor had been obtained illegally in Trinidad, and by 1612 had developed a strain of tobacco that he thought would appeal to European taste. As a consequence he soon afterwards sent his first trial of tobacco to England, where it was well received. Excitement over its possibilities began to grow in England.

Also in 1613 the English, in an attempt to force Powhatan to make peace with them, kidnapped one of his favorite daughters, Pocahontas, and held her for ransom. Powhatan, however, would not acquiesce to all of their demands, so Pocahontas remained with the English, eventually converting to Christianity. She and John Rolfe met, fell in love and married in the church at the fort in Jamestown in April 1614. The marriage signaled an era of peace between the two peoples.

With the improving food supply, peace with the Indians, and the relaxation of strict laws, life was better in Virginia. Then 1616, the magic year when dividends were supposed to be paid to investors, arrived and the London Company had nothing to give its investors except land on which to grow tobacco. Up to this point all the land in the colony belonged to the London Company, and settlers came to Virginia either as adventurers (investors) or employees of the company. There was no private ownership of land.

The London Company made the decision in 1616 to offer investors land in the colony in proportion to their investment, but it was not until 1618–1619 that the company was in a financial position to implement the system in the colony. Adventurers who had come to the colony at their own expense before 1616 were given 100 acres of land; in addition, employees of the London Company, when their term of employment was over, were also offered 100 acres. And from 1619 on, those persons who came to Virginia at their own expense would receive a "headright" of 50 acres of land. And if they transported others to the colony, they would receive an additional 50 acres for each person whose passage they had paid.

The headright system would enable countless numbers of English men and women to become landowners—an ambition that would have been impossible for most of them to realize in England. On that land they would grow tobacco and become prosperous. Some of those coming to Virginia hoped to make their fortune and return to England to live "the good life" there, but many who came to the colony decided to stay. They settled on their land, built their homes, married and raised families and in general lived better lives in Virginia, in spite of the hardships, than they could have hoped to have lived in England.

Those who could not afford to pay for their passage had the opportunity to come to Virginia as indentured servants. Servants were in great demand in the colony to work in the tobacco fields, for tobacco was a very labor-intensive crop, and the more labor a planter had, the more tobacco he could plant, which in turn led to greater prosperity. When the servants' terms of indenture, usually four to seven years, were over, they were given "freedom dues"—sometimes land but generally food or tools to help give them a start in their new lives. Life was difficult for the indentured servants, as they were not always given enough to eat, appropriate clothing or adequate shelter and, indeed, in some cases suffered great physical abuse. However, this system gave some of the impoverished people in England a chance for a better life and many were willing to take advantage of the opportunity.

Landownership in England gave the landowner the right to be represented in the House of Commons, and Sir Edwin Sandys, treasurer of the Virginia Company, felt that the landowners in the colony should have the same right. He is generally believed to have written the Great Charter of 1618 establishing representative government in Virginia. The General Assembly met for the first time in the church in Jamestown in August of 1619.

The first General Assembly consisted of the governor and the Council of Government, who were elected by the stockholders of the Virginia Company, and the House of Burgesses, whose members were elected by the inhabitants of the colony. These two bodies met together as the legislative branch of government; in addition both bodies also had judicial responsibilities, with the governor and council acting as justices in the General Court and the House of Burgesses hearing appeals. As the governor and council met separately to consider the state of the colony and to recommend legislation, they also represented the executive branch of government. Therefore the three branches of government that exist in the United States today were present in the General Assembly in 1619. King James I was not happy with the establishment of the General Assembly, but under the terms of the second charter, it was the Virginia Company that had the right to determine the form of government used in the colony, not the king.

In 1622 there was an Indian uprising that resulted in the deaths of almost a quarter of the population and completely eliminated the settlement at Henricus. Despite this setback, the colony was strong enough to survive, but unfortunately the Virginia Company was not, as it was both bankrupt and out of favor with the king. The Indian uprising gave James I the excuse he needed to dissolve the company, and in 1624 the king revoked the charter of the Virginia Company and made Virginia a royal colony. By this time the English had established a settlement in Bermuda, in Newfoundland and in Massachusetts—they were firmly entrenched in North America.

In 1624 there were 1,200 people living in the colony of Virginia. Their plantations lay up and down the James River from the point where it empties into Chesapeake Bay up to the falls near modern Richmond. In the next ten years settlement would spread to the York River and the population would reach 5,000. There would be not only English people living in the colony but people from other countries as well. In 1619 the first Africans arrived, and soon there would be Portuguese, Spanish, Turks and Dutch settlers in the colony.[70]

Jamestown itself never developed into a large town, despite the efforts of several governors to encourage growth there. People were drawn to Virginia by the lure of land ownership, and most people lived on widely scattered plantations raising tobacco, which they then traded for the household goods, clothing and tools brought to the colony by merchant ships. The few craftsmen and artisans who came to Jamestown to practice their trade did so only long enough to earn the money to buy land, so Jamestown remained small. However, Jamestown was the seat of government in the colony of Virginia for 92 years.

## Breakdown of the Virginia Colony at Jamestown

| | |
|---|---|
| *Nationality of settlement* | English |
| *Sponsored by* | The Virginia Company of London |
| *Physical location* | A semi-island in the James River about sixty miles from the mouth of the river. At high tide the isthmus connecting it to the mainland was flooded, making it an island. |
| *Why that location* | It was a good defensive position and the river channel ran close to the shore on the western end, enabling the settlers to moor their ships to trees on the shore. There were no springs of water on the island, but in the spring the water in the river was fresh. The rest of the year it was brackish. The land was also low and swampy. |
| *Purpose of settlement* | To explore the land for natural resources, search for the Northwest Passage, plant a permanent settlement and to bring Christianity to the Indians. |
| *When settled* | May 14, 1607 |
| *Climatic conditions* | The period from 1606 to 1612 was the driest seven-year period in southeastern Virginia in 770 years. |
| *Relationship with Indians* | The tribes living closest to the fort were hostile, but other tribes were friendly. The first summer the Indians brought food to the settlers and saved their lives. Later, the Indians kept the settlers penned up in the fort in an effort to starve them to death. |

| | |
|---|---|
| *Internal quarreling* | The first president of the council was removed from office, one of the council members was executed for "heinous crimes" and there was much discontent and argument among the settlers in the early years. |
| *Number of initial settlers* | 105, though one died on the voyage to Virginia. |
| *Makeup of initial settlers* | Gentlemen "adventurers," who paid their own way and some of whom had military experience, two surgeons, carpenters, laborers, soldiers, bricklayers, a minister, a mason, a barber, a tailor, a fisherman, a blacksmith and four boys. |
| *Number of additional settlers* | The first supply arrived in January 1608 and brought 120 men. The second supply arrived in October 1608 and brought 68 men and 2 women. Six ships of the third supply arrived mid–August of 1609 and brought 500 settlers. |
| *Percentage that survived* | In September 1607 only 38 of the 104 settlers who had arrived in the colony were left alive, or 37 percent. Saltwater poisoning, dysentery and typhoid are believed to have been responsible for the deaths. |
| *Initial supplies* | Food, muskets, ammunition, tools, seeds for planting and some domestic animals such as chickens and dogs. |
| *How often supplies arrived* | January 1608, October 1608, August 1609, June 1610 and from then on supplies came on a fairly regular basis, but the colony continued to suffer from a shortage of food for several years. |
| *Stability of the mother country* | England was at peace with both Spain and France at the time of settlement. |
| *Fate of settlement* | Jamestown became the first permanent English settlement in North America and was the seat of government for the colony until 1699. |

# SEVEN

# Acadia —
# The French Return to Canada

French interest in establishing a colony in North America suffered a severe setback in 1565 with the destruction of Fort Caroline and the killing of most of its defenders by the Spanish. It was to receive another devastating blow in 1572. The religious civil wars that had caused the abandonment of Charlesfort in 1562 were still simmering in France. One of the main leaders of the French Protestants, the Huguenots, was Admiral Gaspard de Coligny, the man who had been so instrumental in the efforts to establish Charlesfort and Fort Caroline. Joined with him in furthering the Huguenot cause was Henri of Navarre, a member of the French royal family, a Protestant and ruler of the kingdom of Navarre, a small independent country north of the Pyrenees Mountains which form a border between France and Spain. In an attempt to make peace between the Huguenots and the Catholics, a marriage was proposed between Henri of Navarre and Marguerite of Valois, sister of Charles IX, the French king.

On August 18, 1572, Henri and Marguerite were married in Paris. Thousands of Huguenots, expecting that the marriage would bring peace to France, had flocked to the city to celebrate the wedding. But during the festivities a plot was formed to assassinate Admiral Coligny. On August 24, the feast day of St. Bartholomew, a group of men seized the admiral at his home, stabbed him to death, cut off his head and put his body on public display. This act was followed by an attack on all Huguenots in Paris; it lasted for several days and resulted in the deaths of over a thousand men, women and children. The attack, known as the St. Bartholomew's Day Massacre, caused wholesale bloodshed throughout the country as Huguenots by the thousands were hunted down and killed.

The intense fighting that ensued put all thoughts of colonization on hold for a time. However, the idea of establishing a permanent settlement in the New World was not completely forgotten. In 1576, tired of fighting, the two sides signed a peace treaty signaling a period of respite, and suddenly men began to contemplate voyages to North America once again. As thoughts of settling the New World took shape, it was to the north that Frenchmen directed their attention. The voyages of Jacques Cartier gave the French a strong, legitimate claim to Canada, and it was far away from the Spanish settlement at St. Augustine. French fisherman had been visiting the Grand Banks off Newfoundland for almost a century and had even penetrated into the St. Lawrence, hunting walruses and whales. Since the area was well known to the French, it made sense to establish a permanent settlement there.

In 1577 Troilus de Mesgouëz, the marquis de la Roche, a Breton nobleman, was granted permission by the king to settle Newfoundland and other lands in that vicinity for France. However, La Roche was not able to do anything in the way of colonization for the next seven years, owing primarily to the religious civil wars that were still raging in France. In the meantime, while Frenchmen were busy fighting at home, French fishing vessels continued to visit the Cod Banks off Newfoundland and the waters of the St. Lawrence. Soon these ships were bringing another commodity back with them along with their cargoes of fish — a commodity that had great commercial potential.

Many of the fishing vessels visiting the Grand Banks remained at sea during their stay in the area, salting their catch aboard ship before returning home with their cargoes and having little or no contact with the Indians. Other captains, however, preferred to establish seasonal camps where their crews could come ashore periodically to lay out their catches to dry. These crewmembers were sometimes obliged to travel inland to hunt and to gather wood for their fires, thus making contact with the Indians. Quite often the two groups traded for food and other objects of interest. Frenchmen, since the days of Cartier and Roberval, had noted that the Indians gathered large quantities of animal pelts every winter, which they then bartered among themselves. Soon the fishermen began to trade with the Indians for some of the pelts to bring home as souvenirs.

The fur pelts created a great deal of interest in Europe. Furs, of course, were prized for their warmth and beauty and were a sign of wealth and position, but they were also the source of a material called felt, and felt was the fabric used to make hats. The fur most preferred by European hat makers was beaver, as it was easily made into a strong, thick, waterproof felt with a glossy sheen. European hatters had been using beaver felt to make hats since the 14th century, and by the 1580s the breeding grounds of the beaver in Europe were beginning to decline. Therefore, although all the furs brought back to France from Canada attracted interest, it was the beaver pelts that attracted the most notice. Before long fishing vessels were bringing back furs along with their cargoes of fish. In 1581, the merchants of St. Malo, Rouen and Dieppe began to send ships to the New World purposely to trade for furs. The five ships outfitted by merchants of St. Malo for trade in the St. Lawrence in 1584 were so successful that the merchants planned to send ten ships the next year. Cod fishing would always be important, but during the last quarter of the 16th century furs, especially beaver pelts, were to take center stage.

Also in 1584, during a temporary lull in the religious wars, La Roche was able to obtain financial backing from the archbishop of Rouen and Admiral de Joyeuse with which to organize an expedition to settle the lands granted him by the king. His fleet with 300 colonists on board, along with all the necessary provisions, set sail for Canada but was forced to turn back when the largest ship was damaged near Brouage. La Roche did not follow this expedition with another, as religious fighting broke out once again in France.

In 1589 France's King Henri III died, leaving the throne to his Protestant cousin Henri of Navarre. Turmoil followed, as many in France, especially the citizens of Paris, were not ready to accept a Protestant monarch, and the new King Henri IV had to fight for his kingdom. The issue was finally resolved in July 1593 when Henri converted to the Catholic faith. He was crowned king on March 22, 1594, and began to bring order and stability to the country.

In 1597 the king renewed La Roche's grant, making him the king's lieutenant in New France. La Roche began to prepare for an expedition to settle the lands he had been granted in the spring of 1597. He sent a re-

In Europe, fashionable hats similar to these were made of beaver felt. By the late 16th century, the beaver had been hunted almost to extinction in Europe and merchants gratefully turned to the New World for the needed furs. It was the lucrative beaver trade that financed the French settlement at Québec (drawing by Caroline S. Taylor).

connaissance voyage to Sable Island — a 25-mile-long island 90 miles off Cape Canso on the northeastern coast of present-day Nova Scotia. The ship's captain brought back a report describing Sable Island as a treeless land covered with shrubs but with a good supply of fresh water. Moreover, livestock, which had been left on the island 60 years before by the Portuguese, had multiplied and would provide a reliable food source for anyone living there. There were walruses and seals in plentiful numbers to supply pelts, ivory and oil.

Pleased with the report, La Roche obtained the king's permission to take prisoners and "strong tramps and beggars, both men and women"[1] from France to form a settlement there. Although the grant allowed him to take 200 men and 50 women convicts and vagabonds along with 100 soldiers, it is thought that he took only 50 people along with a few soldiers when he set sail in March 1598.[2] La Roche settled his reluctant colonists on Sable Island and set them to work gathering seal and walrus pelts. The settlers evidently worked hard, and when La Roche left Sable Island in the fall to return to France, he took a valuable cargo with him.

La Roche himself did not return to Sable Island, but in 1599 he sent a ship with wine, clothing and tools to the colony. The ship's captain brought back a cargo of skins and oil and reported that the settlers were getting along well, had started gardens and appeared to be able to produce enough food to be self-sufficient. La Roche sent a ship to the island in 1600 and again in 1601 to bring supplies to the workers and transport the furs they had gathered back to France. Then in 1602, for some unknown reason, no vessel arrived at the island. The settlers, rebelling against the harsh conditions and lack of fresh supplies, attacked and killed the guards and then turned on each other. A ship finally arrived in 1603, and finding only 11 survivors, took them back to France.[3]

While La Roche was busy with his colony on Sable Island, another man entered the picture — Pierre Chauvin, a Protestant merchant from Dieppe who had served Henri IV as a military commander during the wars of religion. Chauvin persuaded the king to grant him the title of the king's lieutenant in Canada (all the land north of the St. Lawrence) and Acadia (the area from present-day Montréal to modern Philadelphia). This was changed, however, as La Roche complained that he was being defrauded of his rights under his grant. Chauvin was made, instead, a lieutenant under La Roche and given a monopoly on the fur trade along 100 leagues of the St. Lawrence so as to help finance the stronghold he was expected to build there.

Chauvin chose as his assistant a man named François Gravé du Pont, a Catholic born in St. Malo, who was also a military man turned merchant and a sea captain. Gravé had already made several voyages to the St. Lawrence to trade with the Indians, sailing all the way past Québec to Trois Rivières. Also on board, as an observer, was Pierre Du Gua de Monts, who was a Protestant and, like Chauvin, had fought in the religious wars for the Huguenots.

Chauvin sailed for Canada in the spring of 1600 with four ships, heading directly for Tadoussac, where he intended to establish his settlement. Tadoussac, located on the northern bank of the St. Lawrence at the mouth of the Saguenay River, was well known to the French, as Cartier had visited it in 1535 on his first journey up the St. Lawrence and Roberval had stopped there in 1542. Over the years European fishing vessels hunting for walruses and whales in the St. Lawrence had occasionally anchored at the entrance to the river to barter with the Indians. Thus Tadoussac had gradually become the center of the European fur trade in Canada. Indians came there in the spring with their birch bark canoes loaded with furs they had gathered during the winter months, either by trapping or in trade with Indian people living in the remote northern regions. Here they were met by European ships loaded with goods for barter and crews anxious to do business with them.

As a trading site, Tadoussac had much to recommend it, but as a site for settlement it left something to be desired. The area was mountainous with, as Champlain later described it, "little soil, if not all rocks and sand ... the most disagreeable and unfruitful place there is in this country."[4] He went on to say that the cold at Tadoussac was much more intense than it was upriver at Québec. Gravé and de Monts would both have preferred to plant the settlement somewhere else, but Chauvin was more interested in trading than in exploring for a better location.

After spending the summer at Tadoussac fishing and bartering for furs, Chauvin was ready to return to France. He left 16 men at Tadoussac to spend the winter. He had built a shelter for them there — a wooden structure that measured 24 feet by 18 feet. This building, 8 feet high and covered with wooden planking, was surrounded by a light fence around which a small ditch had been dug. When it was finished, Chauvin left the men food for the winter, told them that he would send a ship with more supplies in the spring and then sailed off to France.

The wooden building proved to be grossly inadequate to protect the men from the harshness of the winter. They quickly ate up all the food and fell to bickering among themselves. Some of the men died and the rest sought refuge with the Montagnais Indians until relief arrived in the spring. The ship sent by Chauvin spent the summer in the area fishing and trading for furs, but it returned to France in the fall with the settlers, as they were not interested in spending another winter there. Chauvin sent another ship to trade at Tadoussac in 1602, but there was no attempt to re-establish the settlement. Tadoussac was a seasonal trading post and would remain so for decades to come.

It became increasingly apparent to the king and officials in France that they needed to establish a permanent settlement in Canada if they were to protect the resources of the St. Lawrence and ensure the continuance of French power and authority in the region. By 1598 Henri IV had managed to stabilize the country by putting down Spanish threats to his kingdom, subduing the powerful French nobles who had been fighting for control of the country and settling the religious situation by issuing the Edict of Nantes, giving Protestants the right to worship publicly in many areas of France. All the energy and resources that had been devoted to fighting could now be used to accomplish the goal of establishing a colony in Canada.

However, how was such a venture to be financed? Chauvin had been granted a monopoly on the fur trade with the expectation that the profits would provide the necessary money for colonization, but the results had not been satisfactory. Something on a larger scale was needed if a permanent settlement was to be established. In the fall of 1602 the king decided that, since Chauvin could not by himself accomplish "the discovery and inhabitation of the province of Canada,"[5] a company should be formed. Therefore he invited the merchants of St. Malo and Rouen to join Chauvin as partners in a company that would be granted a monopoly of trade in Canada in return for financing the establishment of a permanent settlement.

At the end of January 1603 the king sent Vice-Admiral Aymar de Chaste to Rouen to meet with the merchants of both Rouen and St. Malo. The merchants were faced with a difficult problem. On the one hand, none of them wanted a monopoly on trade in the area of the St. Lawrence to be granted to an exclusive group of merchants—they were all in favor of free trade. If a monopoly were to be granted, they could choose to become partners in the monopoly; but then they would be forced to pay the expenses of colonization, which they feared would cut heavily into their profits. It was a dilemma that would plague the French efforts to colonize Canada for years to come. The merchants of St. Malo decided that it was not in their best interest to enter into a partnership with Chauvin and the merchants of Rouen, and they withdrew from the meeting.

In February 1603 Chauvin died and Aymar de Chaste was chosen to replace him. He quickly formed an association of merchants from Rouen and organized a reconnaissance voyage to Canada under the command of François Gravé, who was to be his representative there. The fleet sailed in March 1603 with a passenger aboard who was to be of the greatest importance in the establishment of a French colony in Canada. His name was Samuel de Champlain, a soldier who had fought with Henri IV's army, a navigator, geographer and writer. He had spent three years traveling in the Caribbean and returned to France in 1601, where he was granted a pension by the king and made the acquaintance of Admiral de Chaste. He was invited by the admiral to join the expedition to "see this country and what its promoters were doing there."[6] Whether he was requested to do so or not, he later brought back a written report on the area.

The expedition reached Tadoussac on May 26, 1603, and spent several weeks there bartering with the Algonquin and Montagnais Indians for furs. Champlain was given an opportunity to study the Indians and learn from them about the great water routes followed by the nations of the north, who came down to barter with the Montagnais for goods they had obtained in trade with the French. He established a friendly relationship with these people and promised that in the future he would help them in their fight against their enemies.

On the 18th of June Gravé, Champlain and five others continued their travels up the St. Lawrence all the way to the Lachine Rapids, which Gravé on his many trips to the area had never seen. Champlain was impressed with the area and noted sites suitable for cultivation and habitation. He gathered more information from the Indians about a great lake whose waters were undrinkable "so big is it, that they will not risk putting out into its midst."[7] Today we call it Lake Huron, but Champlain thought it might be the Asian Sea — the Pacific Ocean.

By July 11 the expedition had returned to Tadoussac and Gravé and Champlain immediately headed for Gaspé for a few days of fishing, which gave Champlain a chance to study that area. From the Indians and French mariners who had traveled in the region of present-day Cape Breton and Nova Scotia, Champlain heard of iron and copper mines, even the possibility of silver mines, but also of a beautiful countryside with magnificent trees. Champlain began to think about the easiest way to find the lake the Indians had told him about. He wrote:

> It would be a great benefit to find in the coast of Florida [the Atlantic coast] some passage which would lead close to this great salt-water lake, both for the navigation of vessels, which would not be subject to so many perils as they are in Canada, & for the shortening of the route by more than three hundred leagues.[8]

On August 16, 1603, the expedition returned to France, reaching Le Havre on September 20. Upon arrival, Champlain immediately set about to publish his notes on the voyage in a book entitled *Des Sauvages,* which contained geographic details of the area and information about the Indians. Gravé and Champlain also learned that Aymar de Chaste had died in June and the association of merchants that had sponsored their expedition to Canada was without a leader.

By the fall of 1603 news of the failure of the colony at Sable Island had reached France. Henri IV no longer had confidence in La Roche's ability to found a successful colony and was not inclined to appoint him to replace de Chaste as head of the merchant association. On November 6, 1603, Pierre du Gua, Sieur de Monts, who had accompanied Gravé and Chauvin to Tadoussac in 1600, petitioned the king for permission to settle lands in Acadia.

De Monts chose Acadia as the site for his settlement over the St. Lawrence. He had visited Tadoussac in 1600 with Chauvin and knew that the settlement there owed its failure in great part to the extremely cold winter. He was determined to avoid that possibility by locating his own settlement farther south, in Acadia, where there were favorable reports of the fertility of the countryside and the possibility of copper, iron and silver mines, not to mention the opportunity of searching more easily for the Northwest Passage.

On November 8, 1603, King Henri IV created Pierre du Gua, Sieur de Monts,

> Our Lieutenant Generall, for to represent our person, in the Countries, Territories, Coasts and Confines of La Cadia. To begin from the 40th degree unto the 46 [from Montréal to Philadelphia]. And in the same distance, or part of it, as farre as may bee done, to establish, extend and make to be knowne our Name, Might and Authoritie.[9]

De Monts was given the power to make war and alliances, grant pardons and privileges, distribute lands and assign titles and seigneuries.[10] The king stipulated that de Monts was to settle and maintain 60 people each year in his colony, "equal number at the least, notably artisans, architects and other expert men for the building and fortification."[11] However, the king also allowed him to include prisoners and vagabonds among the settlers. De Monts was to establish a permanent settlement in Acadia, develop profitable trade with the Indians, convert them to Christianity and search for the Northwest Passage.[12]

He and his merchant associates were to pay two thirds of the cost while the other third was to be paid by Monsieur de Danville, the admiral of France and Brittany. In return, de Monts and his associates were to receive a ten-year monopoly on trade with the Indians on the Atlantic coast as well as the St. Lawrence. No one was allowed to trade in this area without permission from de Monts, under penalty of a fine of 30,000 livres. Although investment in the association was open to all, most investors felt that the colonization effort would take up most of the profits, and they were unwilling to take the risk. In the end it was merchants from Rouen, St. Malo, La Rochelle and St. Jean de Luz who agreed to finance the first two voyages.

Champlain has left us an account of the expedition in his book *Les Voyages.* In it he wrote:

> The Sieur de Monts, having by virtue of his commission made known throughout all the ports and harbors of this Kingdom the injunction against fur-trading granted to him by his Majesty, collected about 120 workmen whom he embarked in two vessels: one ... wherein commanded the Sieur de Pont-Gravé [François Gravé] and the other ... wherein he himself took passage along with several noblemen.[13]

There were two Catholic priests—one of whom was traveling as an observer—one Huguenot minister, noblemen, a miner, a surgeon, carpenters, sailors, a pilot and personal servants mentioned as being part of the expedition. No women were included in the group of settlers and it is not known if the party contained any of the convicts and vagabonds that de Monts was authorized to take with him. The ship carried provisions, artillery, ammunition, seeds for planting, tools and other necessary equipment.[14]

Sailing with de Monts on board his ship were Champlain and all the noblemen who accompanied the expedition either as volunteers or observers. One of these noblemen was Jean de Biencourt de Poutrincourt, a former soldier who had fought against Henri IV in the siege of Paris but who had become one of his supporters after Henri converted to Catholicism. Henri IV evidently valued the Sieur de Poutrincourt, as he appointed him gentleman of the chamber and also governor of Méry-sur-Seine. He came on the expedition, according to Champlain, with the king's permission "for pleasure and to explore the country and the places suitable for a settlement which he desired to found."[15]

On April 7, 1604, de Monts sailed from Havre de Grâce, followed three days later by Gravé. The first landfall was made on May 13 at Port Mouton on the southeastern coast of present-day Nova Scotia. The men disembarked and set up a temporary camp on the shore, as de Monts intended to remain there only long enough to find a suitable port where an interim base could be established. From this base he would then search for the best possible site for his settlement.

While the men were busy setting up the camp, de Monts sent Champlain, his secretary, Sieur Ralleau, and ten men in a pinnace to explore the coast for a good harbor. The group sailed south around Cape Sable, investigating all the islands in the area, and then headed up the southwest coast of present-day Nova Scotia, inspecting all the coves for evidence of the mines reported by previous explorers. They were in luck, for Master Simon, the miner who was part of Champlain's expedition, found evidence of both a silver and an iron mine. After noting that St. Mary's Bay provided good anchorage for ships, the expedition headed back to Port Mouton.

The next day de Monts ordered his ships to St. Mary's Bay while he, Champlain, Poutrincourt and the other noblemen took off in the shallop to inspect the islands Champlain had found and to view the "infinite number of birds there."[16] When the party arrived at St. Mary's Bay, they began an inspection of the area looking for a suitable place for their temporary camp. While acknowledging that the bay was an adequate harbor, de Monts was not satisfied that the region was suitable for his interim settlement. Champlain wrote: "Having found in St. Mary's Bay no place where we might fortify ourselves, except after a long delay, we determined to ascertain whether there might be some more suitable place in the other bay [the Bay of Fundy]."[17]

The party then headed north and almost immediately came upon a large inlet. Champlain wrote: "We entered one of the finest harbors I had seen on all these coasts, where a couple of thousand vessels could lie in safety ... which I named Port Royal."[18]

They explored the area and, in spite of the fact that "this place was the most suitable and pleasant for a settlement that we had seen,"[19] de Monts decided to continue the search by traveling up the coast and then down the opposite shore, the coast of modern New Brunswick. On the voyage they noted the presence of copper and iron mines.

Their travels finally took them to a large bay (Passamaquoddy) into which a large river emptied. Four miles up the river they came upon an island situated in the middle of the river. Champlain wrote:

> The island is covered with firs, birches, maples and oaks. It is naturally very well situated, with but one place where it is low, for about forty paces, and that easy to fortify. The shores of the mainland are distant on both sides some nine hundred to a thousand paces, so that vessels could only pass along the river at the mercy of the cannon on the island. This place we considered the best we had seen, both on account of its situation, the fine country, and for the intercourse we were expecting with the Indians of these coasts and of the interior, since we should be in their midst.... This place was named by the Sieur de Monts the island of Ste Croix.[20]

The island also boasted a small land-locked harbor.

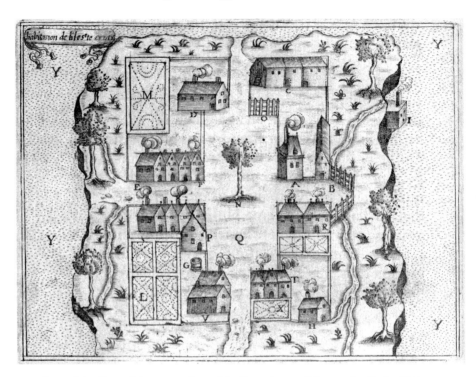

Samuel de Champlain, a member of the French expedition to Acadia in 1604, was a cartographer and drew this map of the settlement at Ste. Croix. After spending a miserably cold winter there, the French moved to a different location in June. They dismantled the buildings at Ste. Croix and used the wood to construct a new settlement at Port Royal. Key (translated from the original French): A. the lodging of Sieur de Monts; B. the public house (for passing time when it rains); C. the storehouse; D. lodgings for the Swiss; E. the forge; F. lodgings for the carpenters; G. the well; H. the oven (where bread was made); O. palisade; P. the lodgings of the Sieurs d'Orville, Champlain and Chandore; Q. the lodgings of the Sieur Bonlay and other artisans; R. the lodgings of the Sieurs de Genestou, Sourin and other artisans; T. the lodgings of Sieurs de Beaumont, La Motte Bourioli and Fougeray; V. lodgings of our priest; X. other gardens; Y. the river which surrounds the island (courtesy of Houghton Library, Harvard University. Can 205.4).

The men went to work immediately to erect a barricade on a small islet near the island to mount their cannon. Champlain reported: "Each worked so efficiently that in a very short space of time it was put in a state of defense, though the mosquitoes (which *are* little flies) gave us great annoyance while at work."[21] De Monts then sent his longboat to St. Mary's Bay to bring the rest of the expedition to Ste. Croix to join them.

When everyone had landed, the work of erecting the necessary buildings was begun. De Monts chose the site for the storehouse; then the workers were divided into groups of five or six and assigned living spaces. Champlain wrote:

"After that all set to work to clear the island, to fetch wood, to cut timber, to carry earth, and other things necessary for the construction of the buildings."[22]

The carpenters in the group were set to work building the storehouse, which when finished was "fifty-four feet long, eighteen broad and twelve feet high."[23] They then began work on de Monts' house, while the other men worked on their own dwellings. Champlain reported:

> An oven was also built, and a hand-mill for grinding our wheat, which gave much trouble and labour to most of us, since it was a painful task. Afterwards, some gardens were made, both on the mainland and on the island itself, wherein many kinds of grain were sown which came up very well, except on the island where the soil was nothing but sand."[24]

With everything going well at Ste. Croix, de Monts decided to send his ships back to France. Gravé, as the captain of one of the ships, was to return, and he took with him de Monts' secretary, Ralleau, who had to attend to some business, and Poutrincourt, who had only come on the voyage for pleasure and to find a suitable site for his own planned settlement. He had been successful in this endeavor, as he had been very impressed with Port Royal and asked de Monts to give it to him in seigneury. His request was granted on August 31, 1604, and on that day the ships left Ste. Croix for France, leaving de Monts and some 79 others on the island.

The island was defended by a battery of cannon on the south and on the north by a fort, which was composed of three buildings inside a palisade. The settlers lived outside the fort in houses that were arranged, along with the fort, around an open space. On the west bank of the river, the men had built a mill and made their gardens. On the mainland farther upstream, near some rapids (now called St. Stephen), ground was cleared and wheat sown.[25]

It was a promising beginning, but Ste. Croix was not intended to be a permanent settlement — only a temporary one. On September 2, Champlain set out to search for a permanent site. His voyage lasted a month and he got as far as Moscongus Bay, between the Penobscot and Kennebec rivers. He traveled some distance up the Penobscot and formed an alliance with the Etchemins — a nomadic people who lived along the coast. Champlain was not much impressed with the land that he saw on his travels and he returned to Ste. Croix.

Soon after Champlain's return in early October, winter began. Champlain wrote:

> Snow first fell on the sixth of October. On the third of December we saw ice passing, which came from some frozen river. The cold was severe and more extreme than in France and lasted much longer; and it hardly rained at all that winter. I believe this is caused by the north and northwest winds, which pass over high mountains continually covered with snow. This we had to a depth of three or four feet up to the end of the month of April.[26]

The winter that year was unusually severe and the French, not being accustomed to such extreme weather, were not prepared for it. They had not thought to dig a cellar underneath their storehouse in which to keep their provisions; therefore, with the exception of the Spanish wine, all their beverages froze. There were no springs or even a brook on the island to provide water, so the men were reduced to melting snow for drinking water. The cold wind swept into their dwellings through the cracks in the walls, making it colder inside than out. Firewood was in short supply. The men had expected to visit the mainland to obtain both water and firewood, but they were prevented from doing so by the "great cakes of ice carried by the ebb and flow of the tide, which rises three fathoms between low and high."[27] Their diet consisted of salt meat and vegetables.

This diet led to another problem. Champlain described it in his writings:

> During the winter a certain malady attacked many of our people. It is called land-sickness, otherwise scurvy, according to what I have since heard stated by learned men.... In brief, they were in such a state that the majority of the sick could neither get up nor move, nor could they even be held upright without fainting away; so that of the seventy-nine of us, thirty-five died, and more than twenty were very near it. We could find no remedy with which to cure these maladies. We opened several of them to determine the cause of their illness.[28]

The French had experienced scurvy in the days of Cartier and Roberval and had received a cure for it from the Indians at Stadacona, but unfortunately the Indians around Ste. Croix knew of no remedy for the sickness.

The French had grossly underestimated the severity of the winter, owing to their lack of experience in the area. Champlain wrote bitterly:

> It was difficult to know this country without having wintered there; for on arriving in the summer everything is very pleasant on account of the woods, the beautiful landscapes, and the fine fishing for the many kinds of fish we found there. There are six months of winter in that country.[29]

At the end of April the survivors were expecting a supply vessel to arrive. During the first two weeks of May they watched anxiously, but no ship came and they began to have "forebodings fearing lest some accident had befallen them."[30] By the middle of the month de Monts ordered two pinnaces fitted out so that they could sail to Gaspé to find some French vessels to take them home. Then, on June 15, 1605, at 11 o'clock at night, Gravé arrived in a shallop and told the joyous colonists that his ship was anchored six leagues from the settlement.

On June 17 de Monts, accompanied by Champlain, some of the gentlemen, 20 sailors and an Indian guide and his wife, left Ste. Croix "to go in search of a suitable site for a settlement, and one where the climate was milder than where we were."[31] They arrived at Pemaquid on July 1, barely missing George Weymouth, who had departed from the area a short time before after exploring the entrance to the Kennebec River. De Monts and his party explored the river, establishing a friendly relationship with the Almouchiquois, but the countryside did not appeal to them and the river was dangerous for ships.

They continued down the coast, investigating every cove and making friends with the Indians they met until they eventually reached present-day Cape Cod (so named by the Englishman Gosnold in 1602). De Monts had not found a spot for settlement that met all his requirements: friendly Indians, fertile soil, mild climate and good anchorage for ships. By this time the expedition was some four hundred miles from Ste. Croix and running low on provisions. They decided to head back to the settlement, reaching Ste. Croix the first part of August.

Champlain wrote:

> Sieur de Monts decided to remove elsewhere, and to build another settlement to escape the cold and the dreadful winter we had experienced at Ste. Croix island. Having up to that time found no port that appeared to us suitable, and the time being short in which to build houses and to get settled, we fitted out two pinnaces which we loaded with the woodwork of the houses at Ste. Croix, to transport it to Port Royal twenty-five leagues distant, where we judged the climate to be much more agreeable and temperate.[32]

Gravé and Champlain were given the task of finding a site for the settlement. They chose an elevated spot on the north shore that was surrounded by marshes and good springs. Champlain wrote:

> Having seen that the site for our settlement was a good one, we began to clear the ground, which was full of trees, and to erect the houses as quickly as possible. Everybody was busy at this work. After everything had been set in order and the greater part of the dwellings built, the Sieur de Monts decided to return to France to obtain from His Majesty what was necessary for his enterprise. And as commander of the said place in his absence ... the matter was mentioned to Pont-Gravé [François Gravé] who was offered the position, which he accepted.... And I myself, at the same time, determined to remain there as well, in the hope of making new discoveries towards Florida; and of this the Sieur de Monts highly approved.[33]

De Monts left forty to forty-five men at Port Royal (present-day Annapolis Royal, Nova Scotia) to spend the winter. The plan of the settlement was changed somewhat from the one they had adopted at Ste. Croix. All the buildings at Port Royal were placed in a quadrangle. Champlain described it:

> The plan of the settlement was ten fathoms in length and eight in breadth, which makes thirty-six in circumference. On the eastern side is a storehouse of the full width, with a very fine cellar some five to six feet high. On the north side is the Sieur de Monts' dwelling, constructed of fairly good wood-work. Around the courtyard are the quarters of the workmen. At one corner on the western side is a platform whereon were placed four pieces of cannon; and at the other corner, towards the east, is a palisade fashioned like a platform.[34]

Gardens were made in the area outside the habitation.

The French were fortunate that the area was inhabited by a large group of friendly Souriquois or Micmacs, a nomadic people living at times at St. Mary's Bay or Port Royal. Their chief, Membertou, was "of prodigious size, and taller and stronger-limbed than most, bearded like a Frenchman" even though "not

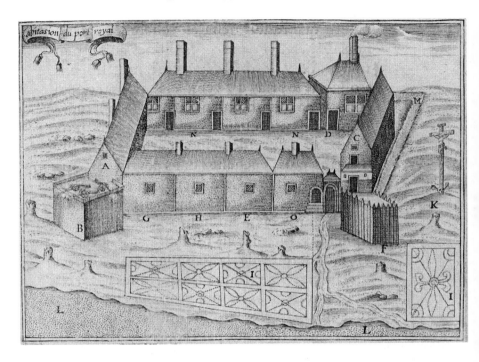

Champlain drew this map of Port Royal, the second French settlement in Acadia. The plan for Port Royal differed from that for Ste. Croix as the buildings were all arranged in a quadrangle. Key (translated from the original French): A. lodgings of the artisans; B. platform for the canons; C. the storehouse; D. the lodgings of the Sieur de Pontgravé and Champlain; E. the forge; F. a palisade of stakes; G. the oven; H. the kitchen; I. small house where we stored the supplies from our barques; having been rebuilt by the Sieur de Poutincourt it is where the Sieur de Boulay lived when the Sieur de Pont returned to France (courtesy of Houghton Library, Harvard University. Can 205.4).

one of the others had hair on his chin."[35] Membertou was said to be over a hundred years old and vowed that he had once met Jacques Cartier. He and his people would prove to be good friends to the French.

Champlain and one of the miners spent the fall consulting with the Micmacs in the area as to the location of mines and going to inspect the places pointed out by them. The winter proved to be much milder than the one at Ste. Croix, as snow did not start to fall until December 12 and was not as deep or last as long as it had the previous winter. Scurvy made its appearance again, "though not so seriously as at Ste. Croix island. Yet, of the forty-five of us twelve died, of whom our miner was one."[36] Two other victims of the scurvy were the Catholic priest and the Huguenot minister, who had spent much of their time in Acadia in heated theological debates. They were placed in the same grave "to see whether they could rest in peace together in death, since they were unable to reach agreement in life."[37] The surgeon again performed autopsies on the bodies and found "the same parts of the body affected as in those opened on Ste. Croix island and could discover no remedy for curing them."[38]

Gravé had been instructed by de Monts to search, in the spring, for a permanent site for the settlement somewhere to the south of Cape Cod. In March 1606 he had the pinnace fitted out for the voyage and on March 15 the expedition set out to explore the coast. The voyage had not progressed very far when a navigational accident caused some damage to the pinnace; then, after it was repaired, bad weather forced a return to Port Royal, where Gravé suffered a slight heart attack. By April 8, he had recovered and the expedition set out once again. They had just passed through the entrance to the harbor when the outgoing tide swept the pinnace out of the passage and drove it onto some rocks near the shore. The men waited until the tide receded, allowing them to wade ashore, and then tried to salvage what they could from the ship. Membertou's people, seeing their plight, came to their rescue, taking them and the goods they had unloaded back to the settlement in their canoes. The pinnace, however, was lost, and although there was another pinnace at Port Royal, it was thought that she could not be fitted out before the arrival of the supply ship from France, which they were expecting sometime in May. Gravé decided to wait.

However, the ship from France had not arrived by June 15, and Gravé decided to make the remaining pinnace ready in case they needed to return to France on their own. De Monts had told Gravé that if the supply ship had not arrived at Port Royal by July 16, he was to return to France with the settlers. On that date, when no ship had arrived, Gravé began preparations to leave Port Royal. He would take his ships and settlers to either Cape Breton or Gaspé, where they could find passage back to France aboard one of the fishing vessels anchored there.

Two men volunteered to stay at Port Royal to look after the settlement, and Membertou assured Gravé that he and his people would take good care of the men until the French returned. Waving goodbye to the two volunteers and the Indians, Gravé and the other settlers left Port Royal, reaching Cape Sable on July 23. The next day they spotted a shallop heading toward them. Aboard was Ralleau, de Monts' secretary, who had come in search of them with the news that de Monts had sent a ship with provisions along with 50 new settlers in charge of Poutrincourt, who had been made lieutenant general of the country. Joyously they all returned to Port Royal.

Port Royal was still not the site that de Monts wanted for his permanent settlement, and he had instructed Poutrincourt to search for a better site south of Cape Cod. Poutrincourt, however, decided, since it was now August and "the four months which remained before winter were not sufficient to seek a new site and make another settlement,"[39] that they would spend the coming winter at Port Royal. He proposed that "during this time we should merely discover some more commodious situation for our abode."[40] He planned to take an expedition to explore the coast as soon as the crops had been sown.

At the end of August Gravé left to return to France, taking with him most of the men who had wintered with him at Port Royal. Three of these men, including Champlain, elected to stay with Poutrincourt and his colonists. Among the new arrivals were a number of workmen: joiners, carpenters, masons, stone carvers, locksmiths, tailors, sawyers and mariners along with several volunteers: Louis Hébert, a young apothecary from Paris, who was first cousin to Poutrincourt, a man from Poutrincourt's hometown of St. Just, Claude de Turgis de Saint-Etienne et de la Tour and his 14-year-old son Charles and the lawyer and poet Marc Lescarbot, who was to entertain his fellow settlers with his verse during the winter and would later write an extensive history of Acadia. There were no priests in the group, and as the only priest who had wintered at Port Royal the previous year was dead, the colony had no one to conduct religious services for them during the winter of 1606–1607. Again there were no women in the party.

Poutrincourt immediately set men to work cultivating land upriver from the settlement. "There he had wheat, rye, hemp, and several other seeds sown to ascertain how they would thrive."[41] With that accomplished, Poutrincourt prepared to set forth to find a new site for the colony to the south. His party, which included Champlain, the apothecary Hébert and several others, left Port Royal on August 24 and, instead of heading directly for Cape Cod and beginning the search for a suitable site there, the party started their journey by re-exploring the same area that de Monts had already visited and found unsuitable. By the time the group reached the cape it was the first of October and too late in the season for them to accomplish much in the way of exploring. When they were attacked by hostile Indians and ran into strong, contrary winds, they reluctantly decided to abandon their search and return to Port Royal. Cape Cod was as far south as the French were ever to go.

Poutrincourt and his party returned to Port Royal to find that those left behind were very relieved to see them, as they had begun to wonder if the expedition had met with some accident. In order to celebrate their safe arrival and lift the spirits of the members of the expedition, Lescarbot "ventured to express the feeling of the moment in a bit of literary mirthfulness."[42] It was a play written in French verse entitled: *Théâtre de Neptune*.

The play heralded the beginning of probably the most pleasant winter to be spent by Europeans in North America for many years to come. Lescarbot wrote that de Monts had furnished them with ample provisions: "For our allowance, wee had Pease, Beanes, Rice, Prunes, Raisins, drie Codde, and salt Fleshe, besides Oyle and Butter. But whensoever the Savages, dwelling neere us, had taken any quantitie of Sturgeon, Salmons, or small fishes ... they brought unto us halfe of it."[43] He added that there was plenty of bread and enough wine so that "every one had three quarts of pure and good Wine a day."[44] Mussels, lobsters and crabs were also gathered in great quantities in the harbor at low tide.

Champlain added to the festivities with a new innovation. He wrote:

We spent this winter very pleasantly, and had good fare by means of the Order of Good Cheer [L'Ordre de Bon Temps] which I established, and which everybody found beneficial to his health, and more profitable than all sorts of medicine we might have used. This Order consisted of a chain which we used to place with certain little ceremonies about the neck of one of our people, commissioning him for that day to go hunting. The next day it was conferred upon another, and so on in order. All vied with each other to see who could do the best, and bring back the finest game. We did not come off badly, nor did the Indians who were with us.[45]

Lescarbot has left us a colorful description of the festivities at dinner:

... for it was a great banquet, where the ... Governor of the feast ... having made the Cooke to make all things ready, did march with his Napkin on his shoulder, and his staffe of office in his hand, with the colour of the order about his neck ... and all of them of the order following him, bearing every one a dish. The like also was at the bringing in of the Fruit, but not with so great a traine. And at night, after grace was said, he resigned the Collar of the Order, with a cup of wine, to his successor in that charge, and they dranke to one another.[46]

Membertou and his people were often present at these dinners, and when they were absent, Lescarbot wrote, they were greatly missed.

The weather was milder than in the two previous winters and the snow did not remain on the ground for so long a time. There were only a few cases of scurvy for, according to Champlain, just seven died of the disease. In the spring the settlers anxiously awaited the arrival of the supply ship from France. If it did not arrive, they would have to leave, as they could not survive on the provisions they had on hand.

On May 24 they were relieved to see a small pinnace sailing toward them. Expecting that the pinnace brought news of the imminent arrival of a larger vessel, the settlers "at once saluted our visitors with four cannon and a dozen small guns."[47] However, the commander of the boat did not bring news of the arrival of a supply ship, only letters from de Monts to Poutrincourt and the news was not good. Lescarbot wrote:

The privilege to trade for beaver furs, given to Monsieur de Monts for ten years, was now withdrawn, a disaster never dreamt of. For this reason no more men were to be sent out to replace us.... Monsieur de Poutrincourt asked of the company who among them would be willing to remain there one year. Eight good companions presented themselves. They were each promised a cask of wine (of that which remained to us) and wheat in sufficient quantity, but they asked besides this such high wages that no agreement could be reached. Nothing remained but to face the return to France.[48]

On August 11, 1607, the French took a last look at their habitation, their gardens and the water mill that Poutrincourt had just built and departed reluctantly from Port Royal. They bequeathed to Membertou and his people possession of the habitation along with ten barrels of flour.[49] Poutrincourt, who held Port Royal in seigneury, was the most unwilling of the party to depart and vowed that he would return even if he could find no one but his family to accompany him. In 1610 he would fulfill this vow and the French would maintain a presence, albeit a small one, in the region for many years.

While the French were preparing to abandon their colony at Port Royal, Raleigh Gilbert and George Popham, two Englishmen, were on their way to establish a settlement (Popham Colony) at the mouth of the Kennebec River. In May of that year, 104 Englishmen had landed on Jamestown Island in Virginia and established what was to be the first permanent English settlement in North America. Only France of the three great European rivals had yet to establish a permanent settlement in the New World.

The French, however, had not given up the idea of founding a colony in North America. They had gained much valuable experience in Acadia, and this experience would serve them well as they entered into their next venture in colonization. This time they would turn their eyes north to the St. Lawrence.

## *Breakdown of de Monts' Colony*

| | |
|---|---|
| *Nationality of settlement* | France |
| *Sponsored by* | Pierre du Gua, Sieur de Monts and merchants from St. Malo, Rouen, La Rochelle, and St. Jean de Luz paid two thirds of the costs while Monsieur de Danville, admiral of France, paid one third. De Monts was given a ten-year monopoly on the fur trade. |
| *Physical location* | Ste. Croix Island in the middle of the Ste. Croix River — the modern boundary between the U.S. and Canada. The second site was located in Port Royal, Nova Scotia. |
| *Why that location* | Ste. Croix was a good defensive site and had sheltered anchorage for the ships. The Indians in the area were friendly. Port Royal was an elevated site with good springs of water and a more temperate climate, and the Indians were friendly there also. |
| *Purpose of settlement* | To establish a permanent settlement, to develop profitable trade with the Indians, to convert them to the Catholic faith and to search for the Northwest Passage. |
| *When settled* | Ste. Croix Island was settled in summer 1604. The colony was moved to Port Royal in June 1605. |
| *Climatic conditions* | The winter spent at Ste. Croix lasted six months and was very severe. Conditions were better at Port Royal. |
| *Relationship with Indians* | The French established cordial relations with the Indians in both areas— Ste. Croix and Port Royal. |
| *Internal quarreling* | None noted. |

| | |
|---|---|
| *Number of initial settlers* | A total of 79 men spent the winter at Ste. Croix in 1604–1605. About forty men spent the winter of 1605–1606 at Port Royal. |
| *Makeup of initial settlers* | Gentlemen, two Catholic priests, one Huguenot minister, carpenters, artisans, surgeons, servants, soldiers and possibly conscripted vagabonds and prisoners. No women were among the passengers. |
| *Number of additional settlers* | On July 25, 1606, 50 settlers came to Port Royal with the first supply ship. They were all men and included Poutrincourt and Lescarbot. |
| *Percentage that survived* | The first winter at Ste. Croix 35 of the 79 men died — a 56 percent survival rate. |
| *Initial supplies* | Not specifically known — there is mention of weapons including cannon, tools, utensils, trade goods and seeds for planting. |
| *How often supplies arrived* | The first supply ship arrived on July 25, 1606, and was late — the settlers had started their voyage back to France, leaving two men behind in Port Royal when a shallop brought them the news of the arrival of a ship from France. |
| *Stability of the mother country* | France was in a period of peace and stability at this time, as Henri IV had settled the religious disputes and ended the Spanish threat to French territory. |
| *Fate of settlement* | Ste. Croix was abandoned in June 1605 and the colony moved to Port Royal in modern Nova Scotia. That settlement was abandoned in the summer of 1607, but a French presence was maintained off and on in the area after 1610. |

# EIGHT

# Québec

In the spring of 1607 Henri IV, succumbing to protests from the merchants of Normandy and Brittany, revoked the monopoly on the fur trade that he had granted to de Monts in November of 1603. In truth, although the venture had begun well, the monopoly had not been a great success for de Monts and his company of merchants. In the first year, 1604, the ships sent by the company to the St. Lawrence had gathered a large share of the fur trade, but the company's ships simply could not monitor the St. Lawrence, the entire coast of the Gulf of St. Lawrence and the Atlantic coast of Cape Breton and Nova Scotia to enforce the prohibition against unauthorized trade. Basques from French Navarre continued to visit the St. Lawrence, hunting for whales and bartering for furs on the side just as they had always done, while the French merchants who had chosen not to join the monopoly sent ships to trade in whatever unguarded areas they could find. By the time the company's monopoly was revoked, its profits had fallen considerably.

Although de Monts had lost money in this venture, he was still interested in colonization if he could find a way to finance it. When Champlain returned from Acadia, he sought a meeting with de Monts and offered a new plan for establishing a settlement. Since the monopoly previously held by de Monts covered too much territory for the ban to be enforced, Champlain suggested that de Monts petition the king for a short-term monopoly that included only the St. Lawrence. He then proposed that a settlement be established upriver to secure the furs coming from the Indian nations to the north and west before they reached the trading center downriver at Tadoussac. Navigation of the St. Lawrence above Tadoussac was uncertain and captains were not inclined to take ships of any size up the river, preferring instead to send smaller boats that could be rowed if needed. A settlement upriver then would not be hampered with the arrival of large ships belonging to the free traders. Moreover, Champlain had traveled the St. Lawrence above Tadoussac and knew that the lands there were suitable both for habitation and cultivation. Also, he now knew that there was no passage to the Asian Sea from the Atlantic coast around Acadia and he was anxious to look for one in the St. Lawrence.

De Monts was intrigued with the plan and petitioned the king for a one-year monopoly on the fur trade in the St. Lawrence. On January 7, 1608, Henri IV granted de Monts his petition since, he said, "we have resolved to continue the settlement which has already been begun in those parts in order that our subjects may go there and trade freely."[1] The terms of the agreement were similar to those issued to de Monts when he went to settle Acadia: he and partners in Rouen were given authority to plant a settlement on the St. Lawrence and were to bear the cost of colonization. In return they were to receive a monopoly on the fur trade in that region for one year.

De Monts named Champlain as his lieutenant in New France and gave him authority over the entire expedition. It was the first time in his two trips to North America that Champlain had been given a position of authority. His qualifications were excellent, as he had gained much valuable experience in the previous five years, traveling up the St. Lawrence in 1603 and then spending three winters in Acadia. During this time Champlain had formed very definite ideas on how colonies should be established, and he was now ready to put these ideas into practice as the leader of an expedition to establish a permanent French settlement in Canada.

De Monts and his associates outfitted two ships for the expedition, one of which was to be commanded by Champlain and the other by François Gravé. Champlain was to establish a settlement on the St. Lawrence and spend the winter there, overseeing the project. Gravé was to sail to Tadoussac and spend the summer bartering for furs with the Indians, after which he would return to France with his cargo. Twenty-eight settlers sailed with the expedition; their numbers included gentlemen, workmen, carpenters, sailors, locksmiths and a surgeon. No priests or women were included in the party. They carried on board a cargo "of the things necessary and appropriate for a habitation."[2] The purpose of the expedition was to plant a permanent settlement on the St. Lawrence, to search for the Northwest Passage, to barter with the Indians for furs and to convert the Indians to the Catholic faith.

The two ships were ready to leave Honfleur in April 1608. Gravé left port on the first of April and Champlain followed on April 13, with a planned rendezvous at Tadoussac. When Champlain arrive on June 3 at Tadoussac, he discovered that Gravé had been there for some days and had been involved in a fight with some Basque free traders who refused to stop bartering with the Indians. They had attacked Gravé's vessel, wounding him and two of his men and killing a third. Upon Champlain's arrival, the Basques began to regret their hasty attack on Gravé and sought to come to some kind of compromise with the newcomers.

Champlain conferred with Gravé and they decided that it was in the best interest of the settlement to come to a peaceful agreement with the Basques and allow the whole matter to be resolved in France. Therefore it was agreed that the Basques would cease trading for furs and Gravé would allow them to hunt for whales unhindered. With this matter settled, Champlain had the carpenters "fit out a small pinnace in which to transport all that would be necessary for our settlement."[3] While he was waiting for the work to be finished, Champlain took the opportunity to explore the Saguenay River and sailed as far as the waterfall above modern-day Chicoutimi.[4]

By the end of June the pinnace was ready and Champlain and his men set out to find a suitable place for their settlement, leaving the two vessels, their crews and Gravé at Tadoussac. On July 3, they arrived at an area that Champlain considered promising, and he began to look about for an appropriate site to build their fort. He wrote:

> I could not find any more suitable or better situated than the point of Québec, so called by the natives,[5] which was covered with nut-trees. I at once employed a part of our workmen in cutting them down to make a site for our settlement, another part in sawing planks, another in digging the cellar and making ditches, and another in going to Tadoussac with the pinnace to fetch our effects. The first thing we made was the storehouse, to put our supplies under cover, and it was promptly finished by the diligence of everyone and the care I took in the matter.[6]

No sooner had Champlain and the settlers arrived at Québec than a conspiracy broke out in the camp. It was started by a locksmith named Duval, who intended to kill Champlain, take over the settlement and yield it to the Basques, who had been trading at Tadoussac. Apparently he won four others to his side and they were successful in persuading a number of the additional settlers to join them by telling them if they turned the settlement over to the Basques, they would become very rich. While four or five of the men close to Champlain were away in the pinnace gathering supplies at Tadoussac, the mutineers planned to attack. However, the plot was leaked by one of the conspirators to Champlain's pilot, and the budding mutiny was stopped.

Duval was hanged, while the three other leaders, who had been sentenced to hang, were taken back to France and handed over to de Monts for punishment. The remaining men swore their loyalty to Champlain and continued working on the settlement. To discourage any lingering thoughts of mutiny, Duval's head was impaled on a pike and placed nearby.

Gravé sailed from Tadoussac on September 18 with the three prisoners, and Champlain continued with the construction of the settlement, which he said:

> contained three main buildings of two stories. Each one was three fathoms long and two and a half wide. The storehouse was six long and three wide, with a fine cellar six feet high. All the way round our buildings I had a gallery made, outside the second story, which was a very convenient thing. There were also ditches fifteen feet wide and six deep and outside these I made several salients which enclosed a part of the buildings, and there we put our cannon. In front of the building there is an open space four fathoms wide and six or seven long, which abuts upon the river's bank. Round about the buildings are very good gardens, and an open space on the north side of a hundred, or a hundred and twenty, yards long and fifty or sixty wide.[7]

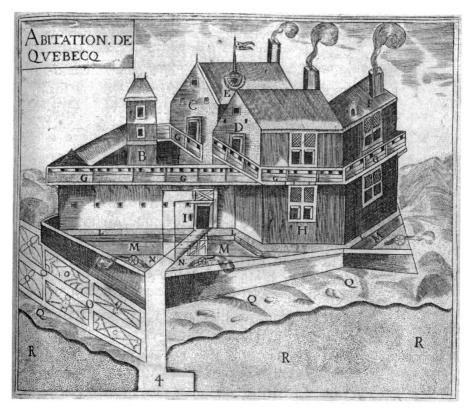

Champlain's drawing of the French habitation at Québec. The habitation resembled a small European fortress. Key (translated from the original French): A. the storehouse; B. the dovecote; C. main building used for storing our arms and for housing workers; D. another main building for housing our workers; E. dial; F. another main building containing the forge and lodging for the artisans; G. galleries going all around the buildings; H. the lodging of the Sieur de Champlain; I. gate to the Habitation where there is a drawbridge; L. walkway around the Habitation 10 feet wide extending to the edge of the ditches; M. the ditches; N. platforms for canon; O. garden of the Sieur de Champlain; P. the kitchen; Q. space in front of the Habitation on the bank of the river; R. the great river of Saint Lawrence (courtesy of Houghton Library, Harvard University. Can 205.4).

When it was finished, it resembled a small-sized European fortress. While the carpenters and other workmen were busy building the Habitation, as it was called, Champlain had the rest of the men clear the land around the settlement. He intended to make gardens to grow grain and vegetables "for the purpose of seeing how the whole thing would succeed, particularly since the soil seemed to be very good."[8]

The men worked hard at their tasks and did all they could to prepare for their first winter in Canada. Champlain reported that they had their first hard frost on October 3 and that the leaves began to fall on October 15. November 18 saw the first snowfall, which lay on the ground for two days, followed by a strong wind. The first deaths were recorded during November — a sailor and a locksmith died of dysentery. According to Champlain:

> snow and ice remain on the ground for three months, that is from the month of January until about the eighth of April by which time it is nearly all melted....
> From Tadoussac to Gaspé, Cape Breton, Newfoundland and the Grand Bay, one still finds ice and snow in most places up to the end of May, at which time the whole mouth of the great river is blocked with ice, whilst at Québec there is none.[9]

In the days of Cartier and Roberval, Québec had been the site of the village of Stadacona, the home of the Iroquois chief Donnaconna and his people. In 1608, however, there were no Indian villages or towns in the area. Stadacona as well as the large, walled town of Hochelaga (Montréal), which Cartier first visited in 1535, had disappeared. The Iroquois, who had inhabited the land 70 years earlier, were also gone, replaced by the Algonquins and Montagnais, nomads who did not till the soil but roamed the country hunting and gathering wild plants for food and trapping for furs to barter.

One fall day the men at the Habitation were surprised to see a band of Montagnais on the river in their canoes. The Montagnais explained that it was their custom to come to this area in the fall to fish for eel, which they would then bring ashore to dry to provide food for the winter. After spending about a month in the area, they suddenly announced that they were off to hunt beaver for a while and asked Champlain if he would store their dried eel and some of their equipment for them until they returned. Champlain kept their provisions at the Habitation until the Montagnais returned in the middle of December. The Indians spent another month near the French settlement, eating their dried eel and, when that had been consumed, took off again to hunt for moose and bear.

In February another band of Indians appeared, this time on the opposite shore and, at great risk to themselves, crossed the ice-choked river to reach the Habitation to beg for food. Winter was a lean time for the nomadic Algonquins and Montagnais, and the people in the band were near starvation. In fact, Champlain reported that he and his men were appalled at their condition and gave them as much food as they could. It was a departure from the usual situation in European colonies, for it was generally the Indians who gave food to the starving settlers, not the other way around.

The winter, however, was not without its problems for the French colonists. Champlain recorded that "The scurvy began very late, that is in February, and lasted until the middle of April. Eighteen were struck down with it and of these ten died: and five others of dysentery."[10] Of the twenty-eight men who had come to Québec there were now only eight left and "half of these were ailing."[11]

Relief was on the way, for on June 5, 1609, a shallop arrived at the settlement with the welcome news that Gravé had returned and was anchored at Tadoussac. Champlain immediately traveled downriver to confer with Gravé, who gave him the good news that de Monts' monopoly had been renewed for another year. The two men then decided that Champlain would take 20 men in the shallop and go in search of their Algonquin allies, who had promised to take him exploring in the interior of the country. When his explorations were finished, de Monts wanted Champlain to return to France to give him a report on his discoveries and the state of the settlement. Gravé was to winter at Tadoussac.

Leaving Gravé at Tadoussac to barter for furs, Champlain headed upriver and had only gone 60 miles before he came upon a party of Algonquins with a group of Indians he had never seen before. The strangers were members of the nation of the Ouendats, who, although culturally and linguistically related to the Iroquois, were allied with the Algonquins. The French called them Hurons, after their manner of wearing their hair, which was thick and wiry and reminded the French of the crest of a boar's head (*hure* in French).[12] The two groups were on their way to attack their common enemy, the Iroquois.

The Algonquins then reminded Champlain of his promise to help them fight their enemies, which he said he was quite willing to do. Before going off to war, however, the Indians wanted to visit the French settlement at Québec. The whole group then headed downriver to the Habitation and, amid much feasting and dancing, a very profitable trade in furs was carried on. Gravé was sent for and came up to Québec with a load of trade goods to participate in the activities. Then Champlain and 11 others set out aboard the shallop along the St. Lawrence to the River of the Iroquois (renamed the Richelieu River in 1642) with their Indian allies on a raid against their enemies.

The shallop had difficulty navigating the river because of the rapids, so Champlain sent it and most of the men back to the settlement while he and two volunteers traveled with the Indians in their canoes. They continued along the Richelieu River until they came to the lake (now called Lake Champlain), where they participated in a victorious battle against the Iroquois.

Champlain parted from the Indians "with great protestations of mutual friendship"[13] and returned to Tadoussac by the end of the summer. Gravé had decided to return to France with Champlain, and after conferring they decided to leave the settlement in charge of Captain Pierre Chavin until de Monts could be consulted. Champlain wrote: "This decision having been taken, we went to Québec to install him and to furnish him with everything required and necessary for a settlement, along with fifteen men."[14] On September 15, 1609, Champlain and Gravé sailed for France, arriving at Honfleur on October 13.

As soon as he returned to France, Champlain had an audience with the king, giving him a report on his explorations and presenting him with a belt of porcupine quills as well as two small scarlet birds and the head of a fish with a long snout and two or three rows of very sharp teeth that he had caught in the great lake of the Iroquois (Lake Champlain). The King was very pleased with what had been accomplished in his name and with the settlement at Québec; however, he refused to extend the fur monopoly to cover the upper region of the St. Lawrence as de Monts had requested. Disappointed but not discouraged, de Monts traveled to Rouen to confer with merchants in the city. They were encouraged by the reports brought back by Champlain and the hopes he had of finding the Northwest Passage and agreed to fund the settlement for another year. However, they were able to send only the barest necessities back with Champlain for the settlers at Québec.

Champlain returned to Canada with "a certain number of artisans,"[15] leaving Honfleur on April 18, 1610. Upon his arrival at Québec he found "Captain Pierre, the commander, and all his comrades, hale and hearty."[16] One of the noblemen who had wintered there told him that "only a very few of them had been slightly ill ... there had been scarcely any winter and that they had generally had fresh meat all winter long. Their greatest trouble had been to amuse themselves."[17]

Champlain again accompanied the Indians on a raiding expedition against the Iroquois but was unable to undertake as much exploration as he would have liked. The Montagnais were supposed to take Champlain up the St. Maurice River to the edge of the body of water known today as Hudson's Bay.[18] They were to return by way of Lac St. Jean and the Saguenay River. The Montagnais decided to postpone the expedition, much to Champlain's disappointment. He was finding some reluctance on the part of his Indian allies to allow him to visit their country. The Indians were afraid that if the French visited the remote regions, they would begin to trade directly with those nations and cut out the Montagnais as middlemen.[19] However, Champlain did persuade one of the Huron chiefs to take a young man back with him for the winter and return with him in the spring. Champlain and Gravé were hoping that the young Frenchman would be able

to learn what was the nature of their country, to see the great lake, observe the rivers, what manner of peoples inhabit them; withal to discover what mines & most rare things may be found among these places & peoples so that on his return we might be informed of the truth thereof.[20]

The chief, while agreeing to take the young man, insisted that Champlain take a Huron named Savignon back with him to France to report to them "all the fine things he has seen."[21] The mutual exchange was made.

Champlain returned to Québec and was engaged in repairing the palisades around the Habitation when bad news arrived from France: on May 14, 1610, King Henri IV had been assassinated, leaving the kingdom to Louis XIII, his nine-year-old son. Henri IV had been a supporter of colonization and Champlain and Gravé both feared that his loss would mean a setback for the colony and a resumption of the political and religious unrest that had plagued the country during the previous century. They were right to be concerned, for France was about to be thrown into another period of instability as opposing factions at court tried to take advantage of the fact that the country was being ruled by a very young monarch with the queen mother as regent.

Champlain and Gravé prepared to return to France in August 1610, leaving 16 men at the Habitation commanded by Du Parc, who had wintered there the previous year and was now replacing Captain Pierre Chavin, who was to return to France to attend to some business affairs. Champlain reported that when they left, the gardens were "well provided with kitchen vegetables of all sorts, as also with very fine Indian corn, with wheat, rye and barley."[22] They sailed on August 13, for France.

The summer of 1610 had not been good for the fur trade, as the Indians had not come in great numbers to barter and competition for the limited number of furs had been intense. As a result, de Monts' association of merchants was not able to supply the colony for the next year. Champlain, however, took an important step in the months following his return to France, which helped to ensure the continuance of the colony. On December 27, 1610, at the age of 40, he became betrothed to Hélène Boullé, a 12-year-old girl, the daughter of Nicolas Boullé, a secretary in the king's service. Her dowry, most of which was paid to Champlain the day before the wedding, would be used to further the settlement at Québec. The marriage took place on December 30 in Paris, but the marriage contract stipulated that the couple would not cohabit for two years owing to the young age of the bride. Champlain then set about helping de Monts plan another voyage to Canada in the spring.

On March 11, 1611, Champlain, leaving his young wife in France, sailed for Canada and, after a difficult voyage and many dangerous encounters with icebergs, reached Tadoussac on May 13. He was pleased to learn that Du Parc and his companions at Québec were well, having suffered no sickness over the winter. However, the fur trade was not progressing well, as the "Indians are now too sharp and crafty"[23] and refused to trade until "several vessels had arrived in order to get our wares more cheaply."[24]

Champlain made his way to Québec and found the Montagnais chief waiting there, but Champlain was unable to persuade him to conduct him to the north country. Champlain then pushed on to the rapids of the St. Lawrence, the site of present-day Montréal, where he had promised the previous year to rendezvous with the Algonquins. Unfortunately news of Champlain's friendship with the Indians had spread among the independent fur traders, who knew that he was heading for a rendezvous. Therefore, as he hastened upriver to keep his appointment, a flock of free traders followed him, 13 pinnaces in all, hoping to take advantage of Champlain's friendship with the Algonquins. However, when he reached the site of the rendezvous, the Indians were not there.

Champlain waited three weeks for his friends to appear. He put his time to good use, though, as he wanted to choose a site for the establishment of another trading station in the area. On Pointe Callières, a point of land at the mouth of the Rivière St. Pierre, he built a clay wall ten yards high, four feet wide and three or four high to ascertain how the "heavy potter's clay"[25] would endure the winter. He had trees cut down, gardens made and laid out a square "flat & ready for building,"[26] which he called Place Royale. A nearby island, which he named Sainte Hélène after his wife, would, he thought, be a good place to build a town.

On June 13 two hundred Hurons, including the young Frenchman who had been living with them and some Algonquins, arrived.[27] They were late in coming to the rendezvous as the independent traders had spread rumors among them that Champlain had made a deal with the Iroquois and was now going to fight with them against his former allies or that he was dead or had decided to remain in France. The Indians were pleased to see Champlain and Savignon, the Huron who had gone to France the previous year and was now safely returned. However, they were not pleased to see the independent fur traders who had followed Champlain to the rendezvous. They complained bitterly about the actions of these traders, whom they described as cruel and dishonest.

The Hurons invited Champlain to accompany them to the head of the Lachine Rapids—a place he had been most anxious to see—for further conferences. During their talks, the Indians indicated that they were quite willing to trade with Champlain and men under his control but they preferred not to do business with the free traders. Champlain tried his best to reassure them about the fur trade and was able to convince them to take another Frenchman back with them. He was also able to add to his knowledge of the interior region, both as a result of his visit and from conversations with the young Frenchman who had spent the past year with the Hurons. Although he parted from the Hurons and Algonquins in great friendship, with promises of a rendezvous in that area for the next summer, he was nonetheless troubled by the actions of the free traders and the effect they had on his Indian allies.

In the fall of 1611, Champlain returned to France. De Monts was no longer in charge of the company of merchants who had funded the colony in the past. His monopoly had expired and the merchants were not interested in continuing the association without the benefit of a monopoly. De Monts was forced to buy back the shares of the merchant associates, and since he could not support the colony alone, he relinquished ownership of it to the merchants of La Rochelle, who held it for one year.

Champlain knew that the fur trade was essential to the survival of the colony. There had to be a way to control or regulate the trade so the Indians would be willing to participate in it. With that thought in mind, Champlain went to Paris to try to find a powerful figure who would be willing to take over the enterprise and see that the king's wishes regarding the monopoly were enforced. He was able to persuade Charles de Bourbon, Comte de Soissons, to take on the task, and consequently Soissons was named lieutenant-general for the king in New France. He, in turn, made Champlain his lieutenant and gave him full control of the fur trade in Québec and the authority to enlist the aid of anyone he thought necessary to settle and explore the country.

When the Comte de Soissons died suddenly, Champlain found a replacement in Henri de Bourbon, Prince de Condé, a royal prince who was second in line to the throne. On November 13, 1612, Marie de Médici, the queen mother, acting as regent for her son Louis XIII, appointed Condé viceroy of New France, giving him a 12-year monopoly on the fur trade at Québec and above. He, in turn, appointed Champlain as his lieutenant in New France, with the same authority as had been granted him by Soissons. De Monts, who had been lieutenant-general of New France since 1603, stepped down, replaced by a royal prince whose power and prestige were expected to achieve better results than had previously been attained.

There was great optimism for the colony in the fall of 1612, and Champlain did his best to promote the settlement that autumn by printing a number of maps of the areas he had visited. In the winter of 1613 he published two books of *Voyages* dealing with the Acadian years (1604–1607) and the settling of Québec from 1608 to 1612. However, his endeavors produced no great interest among merchants to form an association to trade in the St. Lawrence. All the prince de Condé was able to do was issue permits to individual companies to trade in the area. As a result, there was no cooperation between the companies and competition was intense and often violent.

When Champlain returned to Québec in the spring of 1613, he found the Indians unhappy with the French traders and on the point of severing their relationship with them. As the entire structure of the fur trade was in jeopardy, Champlain made the decision "to go into their country, so as to encourage those remaining there with the good treatment they shall receive" and "with my concern for assisting them in their wars."[28] At the end of August he was once again at Québec making plans to return to France.

In Paris that fall Champlain continued to promote the colony by publishing accounts of his explorations, while he also persisted in his attempts to negotiate an agreement with the merchants. At long last these transactions were successful. On November 15, 1613, the merchants of Rouen and St. Malo signed a contract to form an association that included a right of participation for the merchants of La Rochelle. The association was known officially as the Company of Canada and received an exclusive monopoly to trade on both sides of the St. Lawrence for 11 years. The company agreed to pay a yearly fee to the prince de Condé as viceroy of New France, to give Champlain an allowance as the lieutenant to the viceroy, and to pay for the transport of six families to boost the colony at Québec.

As the viceroy's representative in Canada, Champlain had broad powers and was not a subordinate of the Company of Canada, which paid his salary, but in effect "its superior in authority and rank."[29] Nevertheless, Champlain had a difficult job as commander of Québec. In 1616 the colony only had fifty or sixty year-long residents—mostly fur traders, a few priests and two or three families. Almost all the inhabitants except the priests were employed by the company and worked for low pay.

No matter how hard Champlain tried to promote settlement at Québec, very few were willing to live there. The merchants in charge of the company were supposed to encourage settlement, but in reality they did not want a colony with a large population because the settlers might set themselves up as middlemen in the fur trade and so diminish their profits. Few of the employees of the trading company brought their wives with them, and even fewer were interested in growing their own food. There was only one family in the settlement that had a garden, and that belonged to the apothecary—the same Louis Hébert who had wintered at Port Royal in 1606 and who had been so successful in establishing a garden there. He had come to Québec in 1617 with his wife and three children. The colony survived on food supplies from France, which left the inhabitants anxious and on the brink of starvation when these supplies were late arriving.

There were, however, some signs of progress. In 1618, when Champlain returned to Québec, he found the garden planted by Hébert prospering. A marriage took place that summer between Etienne Jonquest and Louis's daughter Anne—the first to be performed in New France. However, in 1619 the plan Champlain had drawn up in France with the Company of Canada to supply eighty new settlers to the colony came to nothing and Champlain himself came very close to being replaced as commander of the Habitation. He was obliged to spend the summer in France and eventually had his command restored to him. In the spring of 1620 Champlain was able to return to Québec with his young wife, Hélène.

On his return he found the Habitation so desolated that it pained him to look at it, and he set men immediately to work repairing it. He had a fort called St. Louis built on Cape Diamond almost 170 feet above the Habitation. Although it was only a wooden structure, by 1621 Champlain was able to man it in case of danger. Courts were established in the colony, and the country's first laws were published in 1621. In February 1623 Louis Hébert was given the land he had occupied during his employment with the Company of Canada, and the next year Quillaume de Caën, whose family had taken over the Company of Canada in 1620, was granted Cap Tourmente, the Isle of Orléans and other islands in seigneury. In 1624 the Habitation, which had been built of wood and was in constant need of repair, was rebuilt—this time of stone. It had two wings and a turret at each corner and the whole building was surrounded by a moat.[30]

In 1627 Cardinal Richelieu, a powerful advisor to the young King Louis XIII, was made grand master and superintendent of navigation and commerce and became interested in the fur trading company in Québec. He decided to revoke the license of the present company and form a new one made up of 100 associates or investors—all influential merchants and men of rank. He called it the Company of New France and placed himself at the head of it. The Company of New France, or the Hundred Associates, as it was also known, was granted control of all of New France as well as a monopoly of the fur trade — in perpetuity. A monopoly of all other commerce was granted them for 15 years with the exception of the cod and whale fisheries, which were to remain open to all.[31]

In return the company was expected to send two or three hundred tradesmen to the colony in 1628, and by 1643 there were to be 4,000 settlers— men and women — sent to Canada. The company was required to give the settlers houses to live in and food to eat for a period of three years, after which the settlers were to be given cleared land so they could support themselves. Immigrants to New France had to be both French and Catholic.

In 1627, when the Company of the Hundred Associates took control of the colony, what exactly did it consist of? French settlement in Canada had been centered in two areas— Acadia in Nova Scotia and the St. Lawrence. In Acadia, at Port Royal, there was a trading station with a year-round population of about twenty people. In the St. Lawrence, there were only two ports for ships arriving from France. One was at Gaspé, which had no buildings, and the other was at Tadoussac, which could boast of a house with galleries surrounded by a moat. The building was for the use of company employees, but no one ever wintered there. In spite of all the efforts of Champlain to persuade ships to come upriver to land at Québec, he was unsuccessful, and Tadoussac remained the port for the colony.

Some buildings had been constructed on Miscou Island in the Gulf of St. Lawrence, and in 1627 some men had wintered there, but it was unoccupied in 1628. One hundred miles up the St. Lawrence River was Cap Tourmente, the land granted to Guillaume de Caën in 1624. He had established a farm on the Cap in 1626 and sent seven or eight people to look after it and the forty or fifty head of cattle that grazed there. Thirty miles from Cap Tourmente was Québec, consisting of the Habitation, which had been rebuilt of stone, the storehouse from 1608, the house for the priests, which had been built in 1615, and some other small houses. On top of the cliff overlooking the Habitation was Fort St. Louis, which had recently been rebuilt on the site of the 1620 fort and close by the fort was the enclosure belonging to Louis Hébert. Below the fort on either side of the river were the houses of the Jesuit and Récollet priests and about twenty acres of cleared land. In 1626, some 18 years after the founding of Québec, there were only 127 French men, women and children in all of Canada, with only 72 at Québec itself.[32]

This, then, was the situation in Canada when the Company of the Hundred Associates took control. However, under their leadership and with the large amount of money at their disposal, things were bound to improve. In the spring of 1628, the Company outfitted a fleet with provisions, along with 400 new settlers, for the settlement in Québec. Since the colonists were dependent on food from France to sustain them, the provisions were much needed and the addition of 400 new settlers would have been a tremendous boost for the small colony. Unfortunately England and France were at war in the spring of 1628, and the English had sent a fleet under the Kirke brothers to the St. Lawrence to drive the French out of Canada. The French fleet sent by the Hundred Associates reached the mouth of the St. Lawrence in the summer of 1628, only to find the English fleet in possession of it.

Upon arrival at the mouth of the St. Lawrence, the English sent a small boat upriver to Québec to demand its surrender. Champlain and the settlers at Québec were in no position to defend the settlement, as there were only 50 pounds of gunpowder in the magazine and the ramparts of the new fort had not yet been finished. Champlain, hoping that the supply ships from France would arrive soon and drive off the English, refused to surrender, telling the messenger that he was prepared to defend the fort to the end.[33]

The English captured one of the supply ships arriving from France and then sailed to Tadoussac and occupied the harbor there. The rest of the French fleet anchored in Gaspé Bay and, knowing that the English were at Tadoussac, decided to sail up the St. Lawrence, hoping to slip past them in the fog. They did not succeed, and in the ensuing encounter, which lasted until the next afternoon, the French ships were overpowered and forced to surrender. Champlain, when he heard of the capture of the relief fleet, remarked that the actions of the French fleet, which he considered unwise, had left "all the country in ruin, & nearly a hundred men, women & children to die of hunger, and these would be forced, for lack of succor, to abandon the fort & habitation to the first enemy who might come."[34]

Champlain and the settlers at the fort waited for the English to appear, but they never came. They had simply sailed away after burning the farm at Cap Tourmente and the buildings on Miscou Island, not wanting to take the risk of attacking the fort at Québec, which Champlain had indicated he would defend to the last man.

However, the situation in the settlement was grim, for food supplies were low, and as the long Canadian winter set in, the people were forced to dig for roots in the nearby woods to feed themselves. In July 1629, the Kirke brothers with three ships under their command arrived again in the St. Lawrence and sailed up to Québec to demand its surrender. And as Champlain had predicted, the settlers were forced to agree to the English terms.

The Kirke brothers were in partnership with a Scot, Sir William Alexander, who in 1621 had been granted all the land between the St. Croix River to the St. Lawrence by James I of England. He called his new territory Nova Scotia. In 1629 he had captured Port Royal and the twenty some Frenchmen who were still living there, and he was making plans to establish a settlement there with colonists from Scotland.

With the surrender of Québec and the capture of Port Royal, the French no longer had a presence in Canada. Almost a hundred years of exploration and attempts to settle the land in Canada had come to nothing. The French had been singularly unlucky in their colonization efforts, having been driven off the coast of Brazil by the Portuguese, out of Florida by the Spanish and now out of Canada by the English.

It would be different on this occasion, however, for by the time the French surrendered Québec to the Kirke brothers in 1629, the war was over and the two countries had signed a peace treaty. The French immediately demanded that the territory taken by the English in Canada be returned to them. The English king, Charles I, indicated that he was willing to give Québec back to the French but not Acadia, which had long been considered part of the English territory in North America. Negotiations dragged on for years, but finally in 1632 all the land taken by the English in Canada was returned to France and the French were free to re-establish their colony.

There was some feeling in France that the settlement was not worth reclaiming. The Company of New France had lost a considerable amount of money in its colonizing effort, and much more investment would be needed to rebuild the settlement. Was it worthwhile to attempt to re-establish the colony? Some felt it was not. However, most felt that France needed to retain a settlement in the land that her explorers had discovered. The fur trade and the fisheries could turn out to be very profitable, and there was always the possibility of finding gold and silver mines. And if people were needed to live in the area, could not beggars, petty criminals and women from the streets be sent there? Then too, should France not bring the light of the Catholic faith to the thousands of natives living in Canada? The answer to these two questions was an undoubted yes. A new association was formed and the charge of converting the Indians was given to the Jesuits, who had previously had only a small presence in Canada but who would from then on play an important role in the colony.[35]

On July 13, 1632, the French returned to Québec. The 40 people and three Jesuit priests who had made the voyage must have stood at the site of their settlement and looked about them with consternation. Many of the buildings had been burned down, including the Habitation, which now consisted of nothing but "walls of crumbling stone."[36] Most of the other houses were not fit to live in, as the doors and windows were missing or broken and most of the furniture was gone.

On May 23, 1633, Champlain returned to Québec as governor of the colony, bringing with him three ships with provisions, supplies, soldiers and workmen, some with their families. Slowly the colony would start to grow and, with the possibility of owning land held out as lure, the population would increase. In the next 30 years it would swell from 100 to 2,500.[37]

Québec now took on the aspect of a mission and trading post, as the prime supporters of the colony were the fur trading company and the French Jesuits. It was the Jesuits that would take up the mantel of exploration from Champlain and continue his work, going eventually all the way to the mouth of the

Mississippi. In 1634 a permanent settlement was established at Trois Rivières, and in 1642 Montréal was settled.

For about thirty years, the colony came under numerous attacks from the Iroquois, who had obtained guns from Dutch traders on the Hudson River and returned to seek vengeance on the French and their Indian allies. Despite the hardships and the constant threat of Indian attack, many of those who had come to live in the colony remained there. They had land and had worked hard to build a life for themselves; they were not willing to let it go and return to France to live in poverty. In 1663 King Louis XIV took control of the colony, and at last a serious colonization effort was undertaken. The Iroquois were subdued, settlers began to arrive in Canada in large numbers, commerce was regulated and women of marriageable age were sent to encourage family life. Champlain's vision for Canada was on its way to being fulfilled.

However, Champlain did not live to see it happen. On Christmas Day 1635, he died at the age of 68 in Québec. For 27 years he had devoted all his energies to colonizing Canada, for he saw it as a place rich in trade and agriculture. He established the first permanent French settlement in North America and although it remained very small in his lifetime, it would grow and eventually become the capital of the province of Québec.

## *Breakdown of the Colony at Québec*

| | |
|---|---|
| *Nationality of settlement* | French |
| *Sponsored by* | A commercial company headed by Sieur de Monts and merchants from Rouen. |
| *Physical location* | On a flat point of land on the banks of the St. Lawrence River beneath the cliffs of Cape Diamond. |
| *Why that location* | Champlain, after visiting many sites on his voyage in 1603, felt this was the most suitable. |
| *Purpose of settlement* | To plant a permanent settlement, search for the Northwest Passage, barter with the Indians for furs and convert the Indians to the Christian religion. |
| *When settled* | July 3, 1608 |
| *Climatic conditions* | Long cold winters |
| *Relationship with Indians* | The French were successful in convincing the various Indian tribes in the area to unite against their common enemy, the Iroquois, and live in peace with each other and the French. In return, the French aided them in their wars against the Iroquois. The French had a very good relationship with the local Indians but incurred the enmity of the Iroquois, who waged a relentless war against them later in the century. |
| *Internal quarreling* | There was an attempted mutiny soon after the settlers arrived at Québec. The plot was revealed to |

|  |  |
|---|---|
|  | Champlain and he was able to put a stop to it. He hanged one of the ringleaders and sent the other three back to France. There was no more dissension after that. |
| *Number of initial settlers* | There were 28 men. |
| *Makeup of initial settlers* | Gentlemen, workmen, carpenters, sailors, locksmiths, and a surgeon. |
| *Number of additional settlers* | Another 15 men came to the settlement in June 1609. |
| *Percentage that survived* | Of the 28 men who wintered in Québec in 1608–1609, only 8 survived, or about 28 percent. The men died of scurvy and dysentery. |
| *Initial supplies* | Supplies are not listed but must have contained not only food but also tools and seeds for planting. |
| *How often supplies arrived* | Supplies arrived every spring. A supply ship came to Tadoussac every spring with men and supplies for the colony and stayed to trade for furs with the Indians before returning to France in the fall. In the early years of the colony, the settlers had gardens that provided food for them in addition to what they received from France. |
| *Stability of the mother country* | France was at peace with both Spain and England at the time of settlement, but there was periodic instability from 1614 to 1664. |
| *Fate of settlement* | Québec became the capital of the province of Québec and is still the capital today. |

# NINE

# The Failed Settlements

## Beginning of Western Migration: Greenland

Shortly after his return from Fort Caroline in 1565, René Laudonnière wrote an account of his experiences in the New World entitled *Three Voyages.* In the preface to the work he wrote:

> In my opinion there are two reasons which have principally stimulated man to travel to foreign lands, both in the past and in the present. The first has been a normal desire to discover the means for a better life, fully and easily achieved whether by totally quitting the native land to live in a better one, or by making frequent trips of discovery to bring back things greatly desired or required in the homeland. The other reason for people's going to distant lands has been the population explosion which has made it impossible for people to stay in their native lands.[1]

He then went on to cite examples throughout history of how people moved from one place to another to satisfy these needs. In this examination of history, Laudonnière discovered yet another reason for immigration. He wrote: "I find that the Romans added another to these two principal reasons for foreign settlement. They were anxious to establish their laws, customs and religion in the areas which they conquered."[2]

Europeans first ventured out into the Atlantic Ocean to settle new lands in 874, when the Norse left their homeland for Iceland. Later some of these people traveled to Greenland and then some went to Vinland. This migration of people to the west, of course, was just the beginning of a later and much larger migration of Europeans to settle newly discovered lands across the Atlantic. No matter in which century the migration occurred, the purpose was the same: people either went to discover and bring back to their respective countries goods that were needed or desirable there or they went to settle in a place that promised opportunities to better their lives. And — like the Romans — they were "anxious to establish their laws, customs and religion" in the new lands.

When the Norse relocated to Greenland, they created a world there that bore as much resemblance to their European homeland as possible, and for 400 years, the two settlements there survived—and then they disappeared. Why? What happened to cause two large settlements that had existed for four centuries to disappear? The precise answer to this question may never be known, but we do know that a series of events took place that contributed to the decline of the settlements.

Greenland, like later settlements in North America, depended on trade with the mother country not only for essentials that were unavailable locally but also for luxury items. Norwegian merchant ships arrived once or twice a year bringing such diverse items as timber, iron tools, wine, raisins and nuts in exchange for white falcons, polar bear skins and walrus ivory. In the 14th century, however, several circumstances caused the situation to change, ultimately leading to the end of the Greenland settlements. The Black Death raged through Europe during that century and decimated the population in Norway, causing a shortage of workers in all fields, including the maritime industry. The 14th century also saw the rise of the Hanseatic League, a group of German and Scandinavian seafaring merchants, who challenged Norway's dominance of the North Sea trade. The lack of sailors to man merchant ships and dwindling trade opportunities meant that Norwegian ships could no longer bring trade items to Greenland as frequently as they had before.

The merchant ships of the Hanseatic League were not interested in calling in Greenland, as the goods offered by that country were no longer in demand. Elephant ivory from Africa was readily available and took prominence away from walrus ivory, while noblemen in Europe no longer desired white falcons, leaving Greenland with nothing of value to trade except polar bear skins. The ocean crossing to Greenland had become dangerous, and the profit in trade was too small for merchant ships to take the risk of sailing there; thus climate change added another obstacle to maintaining contact with Europe.

The passage from Iceland to Greenland had always been dangerous because of the wind, rough seas and sea ice. Of the 24 boats that carried the first group of settlers from Iceland to Greenland in the summer of 986, only 14 reached their destination; the others were forced to return to port or were lost at sea. The "Little Ice Age," which began in the 13th century, made the passage even more difficult. Gradually over the years, the amount of sea ice between Iceland and Greenland increased, until by 1350 the sea route between the two countries was almost impassable, leaving Greenland, for all practical purposes, isolated.

Lower temperatures caused by the ice age meant shorter summers and thus shorter growing seasons, which seriously affected the ability of the Norse to grow food for themselves and their domestic animals. Food and wood for fuel became scarce, and people and animals were lean and gaunt, huddling together inside the houses for warmth during the long cold winters, trying to conserve as much fuel as possible.

Obviously, the quality of life in Greenland was slowly deteriorating. Greenland was not a place that attracted new settlers or even a place that could keep its present inhabitants. Young people, despairing of their future in this harsh land, must have been anxious to leave to seek a better life elsewhere. Slowly they began to drift away whenever the opportunity arose, leaving behind the people who had neither the energy nor inclination to start over again somewhere else. Archeological evidence indicates that the Norse still continued to live in Greenland until 1480. They were the last, for in 1510, when German merchants visited the region, they found only Inuit living in the ruins of the once prosperous Eastern Settlement.[3]

Whether it was the lack of valuable trade goods, the stiff competition faced by Norwegian merchants or the presence of sea-ice on the route from Iceland to Greenland, regular contact with Norway, the mother country, was lacking. The people in Greenland could not sustain their settlements without that contact. The next wave of Europeans to travel to North America to establish their laws, customs and religion in a new country would also find it difficult to maintain their settlements without regular support from home.

# Spanish, French and English Failures

European efforts to establish a permanent settlement in the unconquered regions of North America began with the Spanish in 1521, when Juan Ponce de León tried to colonize the southwestern coast of Florida. France followed the Spanish lead in 1541 by sending Jacques Cartier to found a colony in Canada, while the English, latecomers to the field, made their first serious attempt at settlement in 1585. Eventually all three countries would be successful in establishing a permanent settlement on the shores of North America, but it took many years and a number of failures before they were able to accomplish this mission. What were the circumstances surrounding the establishment of these early settlements that caused them to fail?

None of the unsuccessful expeditions sent by the Spanish, French and English to colonize North America embarked on this undertaking with the expectation of failure. In fact it was quite the reverse — the sponsors of these voyages had high hopes of success in their ventures and planned and organized them well. The list of supplies for the new settlements is impressive — domestic animals, seeds for planting, medical supplies, portable forges, horses, armaments, munitions, trade goods, tools, and so on. The task of organizing the acquisition of all these articles and then transporting them, especially the animals, two or three thousand miles across the ocean must have been formidable. The sponsors of the expeditions also thought about the kinds of people that should be included in a new settlement. Expeditions to the New World comprised soldiers, gentlemen volunteers, doctors, surgeons, pharmacists, blacksmiths, bricklayers, ministers, priests, coopers, carpenters, barbers, tailors, shipwrights, laborers and, in some cases, African slaves and Mexican servants.

By 1521, the date of Ponce de León's attempt to settle Florida, the Spanish had 27 years of experience in the area. They had established successful colonies in Hispaniola, Puerto Rico, Cuba and Jamaica, with Mexico soon to be added. The Spanish had achieved their conquest of the islands with relative ease, as they had taken the native populations, who had never seen Europeans before, by surprise. It was easy for them to settle the islands—they simply took over existing Indian villages and fields, forcing the conquered Indians to work for them. Although the conquest of Mexico required more effort, the Aztecs were finally subdued, thanks in part to Spanish firearms, armor and horses. The victors then took over an organized civilization with a system of agriculture already established and used the native peoples as their labor force. The Spanish were fortunate in finding gold in their island colonies and even greater riches in Mexico, and hundreds of eager settlers flocked to the new territories.

It was in this triumphant atmosphere that the Spanish undertook the conquest of the rest of North America. Based upon their previous experiences in colonizing the New World, the Spanish made certain assumptions about the new land they were going to settle. They assumed that they would find a land rich in gold, silver and precious stones, with established Indian civilizations capable of producing large amounts of food. They also assumed that they would be able to intimidate the Indians by their mere presence or, if the natives proved hostile, to subdue them with their superior weapons. The conquerors then planned to take over the towns and fields of the vanquished people, enslave them and live in comfort on their labor.

This was the expectation, but the reality was quite different. Europeans categorized all the people they found living in the New World as "Indians" and believed that all Indian societies were the same, when, in fact, the natives of the New World were a diverse people with different languages, customs, religions and cultures.

The Indians in the eastern part of North America were different from the natives the Spanish had previously encountered in the New World. For one thing, they were not confined to a specific area, as the island natives were, nor were they part of a highly developed, populous and opulent civilization, as was found in Mexico. The people in North America inhabited a vast, sparsely populated land, living, for the most part, in scattered villages and towns, hunting, fishing, planting fields and gathering wild plants and berries for food. That is not to say that there were not impressive Indians cultures in North America, especially in the southeast, where there were nations with a decided and developed social order, an abundance of corn and powerful leaders with enough warriors to carry on successful wars if needed, but these cultures were modest compared with those of the Maya, Aztecs and Incas.[4]

In general the Spanish did not find large Indian civilizations with acres of cultivated land when they arrived in North America; instead, they found small, scattered villages and towns whose inhabitants basically produced enough food for their own use. Although some of these people did produce surplus food, the Indians were not in the practice of growing food in great quantities to trade or sell. The Spanish who came to settle North America brought a large amount of food with them, but they expected to augment their supplies with food obtained from the Indians. The fact that they were not always able to acquire enough food in this way caused not only discontent among the members of the expeditions but also friction with the Indians.

The Indians in the Caribbean and Mexico had been caught unawares by the arrival of the Spanish in their land and did not know what to expect from them. In conquering these lands, the Spanish enslaved the native inhabitants and set them to work in the fields and mines. The hard work, harsh treatment and exposure to European diseases decimated native populations and caused the conquerors to raid other islands and coastal areas of North America for more slaves. By the early 1520s whole islands in the Bahamas had been depopulated by slave hunters.

The natives of North America more than likely had casual encounters with Europeans in the early 1500s, as eager explorers sailed the along the coast on their voyages of discovery. Perhaps some of the expeditions came ashore to investigate the land and made contact with the Indians, even trading with them, as Giovanni da Verrazzano had done. Then others, who ostensibly came in friendship, kidnapped people and took them away to sell into slavery, as did Lucas Vásquez de Ayllón's captain. The Indians inhabiting the coastal areas of North America soon learned to be wary of the arrival of European ships on their shores.

Moreover, news of the treatment meted out to native inhabitants by the Spanish was surely spread throughout Florida by Indians who had escaped from the islands. As early as 1513, on his voyage to the western coast of Florida, Ponce de León encountered an Indian who spoke Spanish. This person knew enough about the Spanish and their obsession with gold to trick Ponce de León into remaining in the area by telling him that the local cacique had gold and wanted to trade with him. This familiarity with not only the language but also the mindset of the Spanish had to have been gained by experience in the island colonies.[5]

Whether it was rumors of what life was like under Spanish rule or the harsh reality of negative encounters with them, the Indians in Florida and the southeastern part of North America were more prepared for the Spanish expeditions than their counterparts in the islands and Mexico had been. Perhaps that is why the southeastern Indians proved to be belligerent and uncooperative. Ponce de León found them to be so on his voyage of discovery and on his attempt at colonization. Their hostility was the reason for the abandonment of his colony after just four months.

Ayllón found the Indians uncooperative when he tried to settle on the coast of South Carolina. He and his settlers, dazzled by the tales of Francisco

Chicora, were eager to reach their destination and explore the wondrous land of Chicora. Unfortunately all they found was disappointment. No sooner had they entered the harbor than the flagship sank, the Indian guides—including Chicora—ran away and the men sent to scour the countryside and coastal areas for food could find neither food nor any trace of the towns and harbors so convincingly described by Chicora. There were no Indians available in the area to come to their assistance, and when they moved their settlement to a new area, the Indians there offered no aid either. The memory of the treachery of the Spanish captains five years before was probably still fresh in their minds.

Ayllón and his colonists were not the only ones to come to North America searching for a rich civilization to exploit. Pánfilo de Narváez and Hernando de Soto both landed in Florida with the intention of finding another Aztec or Inca civilization to conquer. Since both these men had made finding the civilization the prime objective of their mission, they spent their time scurrying around the countryside looking for it—always tempted by the hints thrown out by the Indians that what they were searching for was in some other place. Neither man even attempted to establish a settlement, in spite of the fact that to do so was one of their stated goals.

The last Spanish endeavor to colonize Florida, which appeared to have had the best chance at success, was sponsored by the king and meticulously planned. There was no question that colonization, not a search for gold and silver, was the goal of the mission. However, the loss of most of the supplies and the destruction of 10 of the 13 ships in a hurricane was a devastating blow. There was little food to be found in the countryside, as the Indians, no doubt remembering the brutality of de Soto and his men, simply deserted the area, burning their villages and fields. This scorched-earth policy kept the colonists short of food until discontent with the conditions in the settlement precipitated the resignation of Tristan de Luna and the eventual abandonment of the colony.

It had not been the intention of the Spanish crown for the leaders of the colonizing missions to alienate the Indians—they were supposed to be won to friendship by fair means. As we have seen, in the royal grants given to the leaders of the colonies, there were specific instructions as to how the Indians were to be treated. Unfortunately there was always the loophole that if the Indians were hostile, force could be used against them. Whether it was intentional or not, the leaders of some of the expeditions acted in such a way that hostility was guaranteed. The most damning denouncement of the treatment of the Indians came from Peter Martyr, a Spanish historian and chronicler of the Indies. He wrote:

> Nevertheless I think that the sighs and groans of those wretched innocents [the Indians] have provoked Divine wrath, and the many massacres and disorders among these peoples have been punished, the more so because the Spaniards pretended they laboured to propagate religion while influenced by cupidity and avarice.[6]

The Indians of North America were not impressed with the supposed superiority of the Spanish and not afraid to challenge them. The horses, armor and firearms, which the Spanish thought would be such an advantage, did not always assure victory, as the Indians, familiar with the terrain, were able to move swiftly from one area to another, showering arrows at the Spanish and then disappearing into the woods to attack at another point. They proved to be a formidable enemy, and for 44 years they were instrumental in keeping the Spanish out of North America.

\*\*\*

France was the next of the three rival European powers to try to establish a colony in North America. In 1524 the French king, Francis I, sent Verrazzano to explore the coast of North America in hopes of finding the Northwest Passage. Verrazzano began his exploration on the southeastern coast and continued northward, ending his unsuccessful search somewhere in the vicinity of Maine. In 1534 Jacques Cartier took up the search where Verrazzano left off and became the first European to explore the Gulf of St. Lawrence. On his second voyage in 1535–1536 he discovered the St. Lawrence River and opened up a vast new land for French exploration and potential settlement.

It was in this area, on the banks of the St. Lawrence, that the first two French settlements were attempted. The French entered their colonizing venture expecting to have several advantages. They knew the area they were going to settle, as Cartier had spent nine months there in 1535–1536; therefore they thought the severity of the winters would not come as a surprise to them, and they had learned how to treat the inevitable outbreaks of scurvy. Cartier had established a relationship with the Iroquois who lived on the St. Lawrence, whom he described as a friendly and unassuming people. He created great excitement for the colonizing venture by bringing Donnaconna, the chief, and nine of his people to France to tell the king and his court about the fabulous kingdom of Saguenay — a land filled with gold, silver and great rubies. The stories about Saguenay related to the French court by Donnaconna fired the imaginations of all who heard them, especially the king. Francis I, looking for a way to pay for his expensive wars with Spain, was only too willing to believe everything he heard and to discount anything that cast a doubt on the validity of Donnaconna's statements.

This was the background, then, for the first two French attempts at establishing a permanent settlement in North America. The French anticipated that there would be no trouble with the Indians, and they had every expectation of finding a rich Indian civilization to conquer and exploit. However, the constant wars between France and Spain that plagued the early part of the 16th century kept the French from immediately forming an expedition to settle Canada and find Saguenay. It was not until five years later, in 1541, that the expedition was ready to sail, and by that time the Sieur de Roberval had been added as the chief commander over Cartier. It was Cartier who sailed first, though. Arriving in the area in August 1541, he attempted to establish a settlement upriver from the Indian village of Stadacona on the banks of the River Rouge, a tributary of the St. Lawrence.

Things did not turn out as expected. The friendly, unassuming Iroquois did not greet the return of the French to their village with enthusiasm. Perhaps they were still angry that Cartier had explored the upper St. Lawrence on his last visit against their wishes, or they may have remembered that after promising that he would take no unwilling adults back to France, he kidnapped ten people, including the chief Donnaconna. Perhaps it would have helped if Cartier had been able to bring the ten Iroquois back with him, but unfortunately they had all died in France. While he was a "guest" in France, Donnaconna told Jean Alfonce, who was Jean-François de Roberval's chief pilot, that the French made a practice of visiting the Iroquois and stealing their possessions in addition to using their swords on them. It is not surprising that Cartier and his settlers did not receive a warm welcome when they arrived in 1541. There certainly must have been some sign of tension between the two groups, as Cartier decided to build his settlement several miles upriver from the Indian village.

Cartier and his people came to Canada with great expectations of finding the marvelous kingdom of Saguenay — the land so graphically described by Donnaconna. Cartier tried to locate it but was discouraged by the rapids that had to be passed to get there. Disappointed at not achieving what was obviously his primary objective and finding the Indians hostile, Cartier returned to France with what he thought was a valuable cargo of gold and diamonds. Again he was disappointed, as his cargo turned out to be worthless.

Roberval, who was supposed to sail to Canada shortly after Cartier's departure, dallied for a year engaging in acts of piracy before he left for Canada to join Cartier. He arrived in Newfoundland just as Cartier and his settlers were returning to France with their cargo of "gold and diamonds." The king had placed Roberval in command of the expedition, but Roberval could not make Cartier return to Charlesbourg-Royal with him, so he traveled on with his people to start another settlement in the same area. Roberval was not successful in his search for Saguenay either and, citing the lack of profit to be made in the country and the harshness of the climate, he abandoned his settlement and returned to France.

In 1542, France's attention from the settlement of Canada was diverted by the fifth war with Spain. The constant wars carried on by Francis I and his successor, Henri II, drained money, manpower and energy from the venture of exploration and settlement in North America. It would take 20 years for interest for another attempt to mount again.

In 1562, the time appeared to be right for another colonizing effort — this time in the southeastern part of North America. Unfortunately, 1562 also saw the outbreak in France of the first of the religious wars, which would afflict the country into the 17th century. The upheaval and turmoil caused by this religious conflict prevented the colony at Charlesfort from being resupplied, which in turn caused the desperate men there to abandon the fort and embark on a nightmarish voyage back to France in 1563.

In 1564, shortly after the return of the men from Charlesfort, René de Laudonnière set out to try to establish another settlement in roughly the same area. The sponsors of the expedition, Admiral Coligny, the queen mother, Jean Ribault and Laudonnière, wanted to establish a permanent settlement on the southeast coast so that France could lay a formal claim to the land, they also wanted to explore for natural resources and above all to undermine the power of Spain. Whereas the sponsors at court had a grand vision for the colony, the merchants who backed the voyages and the mariners, gentlemen "adventurers" and ordinary men who went to settle the land had a different objective. In their experience there could be only one reason to establish a settlement in that particular area, and that was to attack Spanish shipping. If gold and silver were found there also, so much the better, for in any case they would become rich. When the chance to gain wealth in either of these ways was denied the settlers, many of them mutinied and deserted the colony. Their subsequent actions brought down the wrath of Spain on Fort Caroline.

Two circumstances that hurt the colony more than anything were the actions of the mutineers in attacking Spanish settlements and shipping and the relentless hostility of the Indians. After capturing French privateers operating in the Caribbean and discovering that they had come from a French fort on the Florida coast, nothing more was needed to convince the Spanish that Fort Caroline had been established for the sole purpose of attacking Spanish possessions in the Indies. It made them determined to eliminate it, and they were able to enlist the aid of the local Indians to accomplish their goal.

Laudonnière alienated the local Indians soon after his arrival by going back on his word to help them fight their enemies. The estrangement between the French and the Indians flared into overt hostility later as the French, running short of provisions, began to use extremely harsh measures to obtain food from them. When the Spanish landed at St. Augustine, the Indians revenged themselves on the French by helping Pedro Menéndez de Avilés and his men reach Fort Caroline by land to take the garrison by surprise.

French interest in colonizing North America waned after the capture of Fort Caroline by the Spanish. When it was revived, the French looked to Canada, which had the advantage of being far away from the Spanish settlement at St. Augustine. By 1604, after extensive exploration and several half-hearted attempts at settlement, the French were at last able to embark on a colonizing venture that had every chance of success. Acadia came very close to being the first permanent French settlement in North America and failed only because of a lack of financial support at home.

The French, like the Spanish, had based some of their colonizing efforts on expectations that were not realistic. There were no rich Indian civilizations with copious amounts of gold, silver and precious gems for them to exploit. Nor were there gold and silver mines in great quantities waiting to be discovered, and the friendly, unassuming Indians turned hostile when treated badly and sought revenge. Also, the French had underestimated the determination of the Spanish to keep their rivals from establishing a base from which to attack either the treasure fleet or their possessions in the Caribbean. French efforts to return to the land Cartier had discovered were hampered by instability at home and a lack of adequate financial support. However, the French had learned much from their mistakes and, after the abandonment of Acadia in 1607, were on the brink of success.

***

England was the last of the three major European powers to undertake the mission of establishing a colony in North America. The English, unlike the Spanish and French, had no first-hand experience in the area they were interested in settling, but that does not mean that they had no knowledge of the country and the hazards of colonization. Richard Hakluyt, an Anglican minister and writer, gathered all the information he could about Spanish and French experiences in the New World, along with all the available maps of the areas. He translated Laudonnière's writings into English and published the works of Peter Martyr, the Spanish historian of the Indies. Englishmen interested in starting colonies in North America had plenty of written information readily available to them and had access to men who did have first-hand experience of the New World. Jacques le Moyne, the French historian at Fort Caroline, immigrated to England after his return to France and settled in London. There is some indication that he was a member of the circle of men in London who were interested in promoting settlement in North America — a group that included John White and Sir Walter Raleigh. The English were as prepared as they could be for their venture.

Like the French and Spanish, the English expected to find the land in North America rich in gold, silver and precious gems. Also like their rivals, they assumed that they would be able to augment their food supply with provisions obtained through trade with the Indians. They, like the French, were also interested in attacking Spanish ships. When the English settled Roanoke Island in 1585, they did so with the intention of making it a permanent settlement as well as a base from which they could launch raids against the Spanish.

The Roanoke Island expedition was England's first serious attempt at establishing a foothold in the New World. Unfortunately, Sir Richard Grenville, the commander of the expedition, was not a seaman and not well liked by the mariners who served under him. Grumbling and discontent among the crew was widespread during the voyage. Then, as soon as they arrived at Roanoke Island, one of the ships ran aground, resulting in a loss of some of their provisions, which in turn made it necessary for the settlers to rely on the Indians for food. During the winter, the once friendly relations the English enjoyed with the Indians deteriorated into open hostility.

When Grenville left the settlement in August of 1585, he promised to return by Easter of 1586 with additional colonists and supplies. By June he had not arrived, and the colonists began to doubt that he would return at all. At a time when things seemed most bleak, Sir Francis Drake arrived at Roanoke Island fresh from his expeditions against the Spanish. He was prepared to leave the colonists supplies as well as a ship when a hurricane wreaked havoc on his fleet. In the aftermath, Drake had very little that he could leave with the settlers, and seeing no other option, the men decided to go back to England with him. Grenville did show up shortly after they departed and, leaving 15 men behind with supplies to maintain the settlement, he went home. Since these 15 men either died or were killed before the next attempt at settlement, Grenville's departure for all practical purposes ended the first English attempt at starting a colony in Virginia.

Raleigh had learned some lessons from this first effort and made some changes to ensure success for his second attempt at settlement. First, he made sure that he had enough financial support, which he did by enlisting the help of 19 merchants and 13 gentlemen. Second, he reorganized his approach to the colony, changing it from a military organization to a civilian one with a governor and some men to assist him. Third, he changed the makeup of the colonists to include men, women, and children, with the idea that families would be more apt to stay in the colony instead of abandoning it. The fourth thing Raleigh changed was the leadership. Grenville would not be a part of this second voyage — instead, John White was installed as governor. The last thing that was changed was the location of the settlement. Ralph Lane, the leader of the first group of settlers, had suggested that a place along Chesapeake Bay would be more suitable for a settlement, and Raleigh agreed.

In the summer of 1587, with everything in place, the colonists set sail for Virginia. Simon Fernandez, the pilot, brought the settlers to Roanoke Island, where they were supposed to confer with the 15 men left there by Grenville and then proceed to Chesapeake Bay to establish a settlement. Much to the surprise of White and the others, Fernandez refused to take the group on to Chesapeake Bay, stating that it was too late in the season. So the settlers were forced to remain on Roanoke Island with the intention of moving to a better location later.

Unfortunately they arrived too late in the summer to plant crops, and the Indians had little food to trade, as the area was in the middle of a severe drought that began in 1587 and lasted until 1589. Although some of the Indians were still hostile, the Croatoans remained friendly owing to the efforts of Manteo, a member of that tribe who had gone to England with the first English explorers in 1584.

Since the colony was facing the winter with a shortage of food, White reluctantly agreed to sail back to England to hasten the arrival of the resupply ships. When he got back, he found the country busily preparing to defend itself from the Spanish Armanda. The queen ordered that no ship that could be used to defend England be allowed to leave. It was not until 1590 that White was able to return, only to find the settlement deserted.

One of the many problems facing the Roanoke settlements was the fact that they relied on the financial support of one primary person, Sir Walter Raleigh. Raleigh tried to persuade Queen Elizabeth I to fully back the colony, but she refused, merely granting him the use of a Royal Navy ship and giving him £400 worth of gunpowder. In order to raise more funds, Raleigh was forced to resort to privateering, sending one of his ships out to prey on foreign shipping. This ship was fortunate enough to intercept three ships (two Dutch and one French) whose cargoes were sold to help fund the colony. Raleigh was able to get monetary support from others for the second attempt at colonization in 1587, but the main financial burden still fell on him.

Since the potential for enormous profits from privateering was great, some of the men who were supposed to be helping the colonies put personal gain before the welfare of the settlements and the settlers. This was an interesting situation. Money raised from acts of piracy was needed for the good of the colonies, but at the same time privateering took the focus away from the main goal, which was to establish a permanent settlement.

Grenville, on his way to establish a settlement on Roanoke Island in 1585, paused during his voyage to attack and capture two Spanish ships, and on his return to resupply the colony in 1586, stopped to capture several more ships, which delayed him in reaching the settlement with the needed supplies. Although he sent a small ship with provisions ahead, he had no way of knowing whether it arrived safely or how bad the situation was for the men at Roanoke. Also, when he arrived to find the settlers gone, he left only 15 men to maintain the settlement when he had 400 at his disposal. His motive for this will probably never be known for sure, but reducing the number of men onboard his ships would mean that he would have fewer men for his privateering activities.

Simon Fernandez, the ship's pilot on the expedition headed by John White, also appears to have been more interested in privateering than in the well-being of the colony. His refusal to take the settlers to Chesapeake Bay might have been due to his desire to reach the Azores in time to plunder the Spanish treasure ships that were soon to arrive there. This same problem occurred again in 1588, when White was able to get two small ships loaded with supplies for the colony, but instead of heading directly to the settlement, the captains decided to engage in some privateering, with the result that one of the ships was captured. In 1590 White was able to get passage to Roanoke with a privateer who reluctantly agreed to take him but absolutely refused to take additional colonists and supplies. Obviously the main goal for the privateers was to capture treasure ships, not wasting time with the colony.

The enormous cost to maintain a settlement was obviously not viable for an individual or even a small group. It was therefore decided that the next colonies would be administered by a joint-stock company. Investors could "adventure" as much or as little money as they wanted, the risk to the individual investors would be small and all would share proportionately in the profits. This would prove to be a good way to ensure funding, but it did not always go as planned.

The Plymouth Company, which was a division of the Virginia Company, put its support behind colonizing the southern part of the present-day state of Maine. Even though the settlement was a company venture, it appears that it was the personal project of the man who was the head of the Plymouth Company, Sir John Popham, lord chief justice of England. The venture got off to a bad start in August 1606 when the Spanish captured the *Richard* on her way to Maine. The loss of the ship and the supplies on board was a costly mishap that would prove detrimental to the next attempt to settle the area.

In the summer of 1607 another group of colonists left England for the coast of Maine. They were inadequately supplied owing to the lack of funds caused by the loss of the *Richard*. George Popham was in charge of the colony, but Raleigh Gilbert, the son of Sir Humphrey Gilbert, began to challenge Popham's authority almost from the beginning.

When Sir John Popham died in the summer of 1607, the colony lost its main backer, which hampered attempts to continue it. Also, about half the colonists returned to England in December with mixed reports. The winter was proving to be harsh, and one of the ships was sent back to England to report on the shortage of food. Then George Popham died, leaving Gilbert in charge.

The colonists and investors began to wonder if this was a viable settlement. Gilbert had found no mines that would yield precious minerals, and trading with the Indians produced only a small number of animal pelts. When supply ships finally arrived in the summer of 1608, they brought news that Raleigh Gilbert's brother had died and that he was now heir to the family estate. Raleigh decided to return to England, and so did the remaining colonists, putting an end to the settlement.

A series of lawsuits came about after the failure of the colony. They show that when Sir John Popham died, not enough funds had been invested in the Plymouth Company to allow sufficient time to see if the settlement could succeed, even as a trading post. Despite the fact that this was a company-sponsored colony, the heavy involvement of just one person proved to be one of the main factors leading to the abandonment of the settlement.

The English had failed in three attempts to establish a colony in North America. However, they had learned from their failures. They knew that the financial burden of colonization was too heavy to rest with one man or a small group of men and that raising money by privateering should not be allowed to override the goal of establishing a settlement. In the year 1608, the Popham colony was abandoned, but there was still an English colony left in North America.

# TEN

# The Three Settlements That Survived

## St. Augustine

For 44 years the Spanish had tried to establish a permanent settlement in Florida and, in five attempts, had failed. There had always been a need to have a base on the Florida coast to protect the treasure fleet and provide assistance to shipwrecked Spaniards, but in the last half of the 16th century there arose another reason for a settlement. The Spanish were a slave-holding society and as such had brought slavery to their colonies in the New World. At first they relied on the conquered Indians as slaves, but when the number of enslaved Indians fell drastically, they imported Africans to work in the fields and mines of their new territories. By the 1560s the number of African slaves had grown to the point that they outnumbered their Spanish masters. Pedro Menéndez de Avilés pointed out the danger to Philip II in a letter:

> In the Island of Puerto Rico there are above 15,000 Negroes and less than 500 Spaniards, and in all of the Island of Hispaniola there may be 2,000 Spaniards and there are over 30,000 negroes.... The same is the case in the island of Cuba ... and with the lapse of time they will increase to a great many more.
>
> In France no Negro is a slave, neither can he become one by law of the realm. Were France to arm three or four thousand men they would be masters of all these islands ... and by freeing the negroes ... so that they be no longer slaves, they would kill their own masters, and put all their faith in the French, because the French had made them free.[1]

There was good reason for the Spanish to establish a stronghold in Florida and keep the English and especially the French from settling it.

However, in 44 years, neither France nor England had even tried to establish a base there. Tristán de Luna's expedition had been spurred on by rumors of possible French activity on the South Carolina coast, but the rumors proved false and no Frenchmen came to settle the region. Therefore when de Luna's settlement failed, Philip II decided it was not worthwhile to try to establish a base in Florida, since there appeared to be no urgent need to do so. Then came the establishment of Fort Caroline—a genuine threat to Spanish interests in the area.

It was clear to Philip II that he must not only remove the French from Florida but also establish a permanent Spanish settlement there to keep them and, indeed, anyone else out of it. Menéndez was chosen to accomplish this mission and he did it well, for St. Augustine would survive mutinies, shortages of food and supplies, attacks by Indians and pirates and still go on to become the first permanent European settlement in North America.

Menéndez faced enormous problems right from the beginning. He had been forced by the urgency of his mission to sail without his full complement of ships and provisions. He was then forced to land his men, artillery, ammunition and other supplies near an Indian village in the harbor at St. Augustine and fortify the area against a possible French attack as quickly as he could. His two largest ships could not enter the harbor because of the presence of a sand bar, and after unloading all the artillery and ammunition on board, he sent the ships to a safe port in Santo Domingo to keep them from falling into the hands of the French. Aboard these ships were all the provisions that Menéndez had not had time to unload. He was therefore short of provisions and tools and had approximately one hundred noncombatants to protect. He had the friendship of the Indians, though, and he was determined to keep it by not taking food from them. It was a daunting task.

After the successful attack on Fort Caroline, Menéndez left most of his men at the captured fort, renamed San Mateo, to rest and enjoy the provisions they found there. He then returned to St. Augustine with a small group of men. With the food supplies they had captured at Fort Caroline and the provisions he had been able to offload from his ships, Menéndez had reasonable expectations of being able to feed his people with no difficulty. Then disaster struck—a fire broke out at Fort San Mateo, destroying not only the fort but also all the provisions. Menéndez had to share the food at St. Augustine with the men at San Mateo.

In November Menéndez sailed to Cuba to try to gather together the rest of his fleet and see to acquiring provisions for St. Augustine and San Mateo. According to the grant issued to him by the king, Menéndez was responsible for providing most of the provisions for the new settlement while the king paid the expenses for a certain number of soldiers. He had decrees from the king commanding the governor at Cuba to give him "one armed ship, forty soldiers and twenty horses, with pay for four months, and all the help and favor that he might ask."[2] When Menéndez arrived in Havana, he found some of the ships from his fleet in the harbor, and he went immediately to visit the governor and ask for his assistance. He did not need the armed ship or the soldiers right away, but he did need provisions for the two forts he had established.

The governor of Cuba proved to be extremely uncooperative and refused to give Menéndez the supplies he asked for or any assistance at all, even refusing to allow him credit or to use the cargo of a Portuguese caravel that one of his ships had captured. In his grant, the king had given Menéndez the right to attack pirate ships operating in the Caribbean and to keep whatever cargo the ships carried. Menéndez took this to mean that he had the sole right to search for and attack pirate ships in the area, effectively cutting out all other ships from a share of this profitable business. This may have been one of the reasons Menéndez found the governor so uncooperative. The cooperation of the officials in the island did not improve and Menéndez complained to the king and the council for the Indies in Spain at great length about it.

Menéndez had the king's favor, but he tended to be haughty and impatient with rules and regulations, which he often ignored. During his career he had annoyed officials both in Seville and in the Indies, so that they offered him little assistance. In 1567 Menéndez returned to Spain to give an account of his accomplishments to the king, who was pleased with the report and rewarded him generously. The problem of uncooperative officials in Cuba was solved, for in September of 1567 Menéndez was given:

> twelve armed ships fitted with galleys, two thousand infantrymen, and two hundred thousand ducats as part of the cost, to protect the Indies trade route from the corsairs. Because in his opinion it seemed important that the island of Cuba be under the Adelantado's [Menéndez] command the better to assure the Florida enterprise, the King also made Menéndez governor of that island.[3]

However, the colony at St. Augustine was continually short of food and was kept alive only by the arrival of supply ships from Mexico, the islands and Spain. The king provided supplies for the soldiers and Menéndez poured his personal fortune into providing the rest. The food supplies were slow in coming and the people constantly complained about the lack of provisions. Once the supplies arrived, there was a problem of spoilage from the heat and dampness—even the biscuit was said to spoil and the corn had to be ground daily, for it would not keep otherwise.

The soil around the fort was sandy and not much could be grown there, but the settlers planted their gardens and raised some corn and pumpkins. The best land for agriculture was farther inland and held by the Indians. To take the land from them would be difficult if not impossible, and the fort needed to be on the coast to protect the treasure fleets. Eventually, when the Indians were pacified, they paid taxes to the governor at St. Augustine in the form of food and labor. Their contribution helped the food supply but was never enough to make the settlement self-sufficient.

The people raised chickens, and there were some cattle and hogs foraging for food on one of the islands—but according to one report, the cattle and hogs were for use only by the governor and other high officials. Fish made up a large part of the diet of the people at St. Augustine, as did palmetto stalks and berries. The lack of food was a serious problem for the colony, and it led to increasing discontent among the soldiers, which in turn led to another major problem: mutinies and desertions.

Many of the soldiers who came to Florida had expectations of profiting from it by gaining access to gold and silver, either by trade with the Indians or by exploring for mines. The Spanish had found gold, silver and precious gems in Fort Caroline when they took it from the French, and they could see that the Indians in the area wore gold and silver ornaments. Despite the evidence of its existence, it did not take the men long to realize that there was very little chance of their having an opportunity to obtain any of it. This disappointment, along with the lack of food and the harsh living conditions, not to mention the chance of being killed by the Indians, led many men to mutiny in order to escape. Gonzalo Solís de Merás described the situation in St. Augustine and San Mateo:

> there were few soldiers in the forts, and most of them were ill and misused and very discontented, owing to the great hardships and dangers they had had and were having every day; that there had been mutinies and double-dealing among some of the captains, wherefore more than 400 soldiers had gone from these two forts; that there were more than 500 in that island of Cuba, not only of those who had set out from the forts as rebels, but also of those who came from Spain to Florida ... had landed on that island and had remained there, without desiring to go to Florida.[4]

Once deserters reached one of the islands, they were generally safe, and to get to the islands they needed a boat. The officials at the settlement had only to make sure that no boats were available. As one report stated: "they [the soldiers] have been wanting to mutiny because of the hunger and lack of clothing that they suffer, but since there is nowhere they can go by land, and they have no boat in which to leave by sea, they have not done so."[5] Eventually a system was worked out that allowed people who wanted to leave an opportunity to buy their way out of Florida — the money going into the pocket of the governor.

The last major problem facing the settlement was the relationship with the Indians. St. Augustine was originally established near an Indian village, and Menéndez had taken great care to build a good relationship with the inhabitants, vowing that he would not risk alienating them by taking food from them. Unfortunately Menéndez was not often in St. Augustine to see that his orders were obeyed, and as the food supply in both St. Augustine and San Mateo dwindled, the soldiers took food from the Indians by force. The good feeling that had existed at first deteriorated into open hostility in a matter of months.

In his explorations along the coast, Menéndez established friendly relations with a number of Indian tribes and placed soldiers in the villages to learn the language and teach the Indians about Christianity. He boasted of these friendships in his letters to the king, but the Spanish would discover, as the Jamestown settlers did later, that it was the Indians living closest to the settlement that would prove the most difficult. The Indians between St. Augustine and San Mateo had declared war on the Spanish and were inflicting damage both on the fort and its inhabitants.

Menéndez sought a solution to the problem by moving the fort to an island near the entrance to the harbor. The island was to be kept free of Indians, and this was to be "enforced by letting dogs loose on the island, so that whenever a native was found he would be hounded to death."[6] The Indians would be forced to stay away and would not be able to cross the water at night to kill the cattle that foraged there. The dogs would be tied up during the day and roam only at night, and would be trained principally to hunt Indians.

For protection during the day, Menéndez ordered two blockhouses to be built on an island close to the Mantanzas inlet a few miles south of the fort. They were built on high ground and commanded a view not only of the land around the fort but also of the sea and any approaching ships. The blockhouses were to be manned and constant communication kept up with the fort at St. Augustine. Another blockhouse was built on the mainland near the site of the first fort, two more at San Mateo and one at San Felipe on Santa Elena. The blockhouses were built "to overawe the unfriendly Indians who had never desired alliance with the Christians."[7]

Menéndez tried to punish Indians who attacked his men or who attacked other Indians who were friendly to the Spanish. He attempted to capture Satouriona, but failed; however, he did manage to kill 20 of his braves. After 1567 Menéndez spent little time administering his settlement in Florida, as Philip II had other missions for him. St. Augustine was left to the management of a series of governors. The Indian situation was tenuous, with periods of calm and peace followed by sporadic uprisings.

In 1573 the situation at Santa Elena was becoming tense and the people there complained bitterly, but to no avail. In 1576 Hernando Miranda was sent to St. Augustine as governor and, on visiting Santa Elena in February set off an uprising by insisting that pressure be put on the Indians to stop killing the settlers' cattle and that they be forced to supply the settlement with corn. The Indians revolted and laid siege to the fort, keeping the settlers penned up inside the fort until they were rescued by Miranda. The settlement was then abandoned. The revolt spread southward and threatened St. Augustine. Miranda lacked the will to meet the threat and instead took 6,000 ducats—the soldiers' pay—from the treasury and left the country. The king then decided to take the colony under his control and appointed Pedro Menéndez Marqués governor.

In 1577, when Marqués came as governor, he found all the Indians on the coast in rebellion and allied with the Indians of Santa Elena and Guale. He brought soldiers with him to augment the force at St. Augustine and successfully rebuilt the fort at Santa Elena. Then he tackled the problem of the Indians. He wrote:

> I should much like to break the spirit of those Indians, because, although they have greatly felt the strength of Santa Elena, yet they are much on their mettle, as they see that I have not enough men to go and hunt them in their houses. And even though it be but for one year, I intend to drive them from their lands, burn their

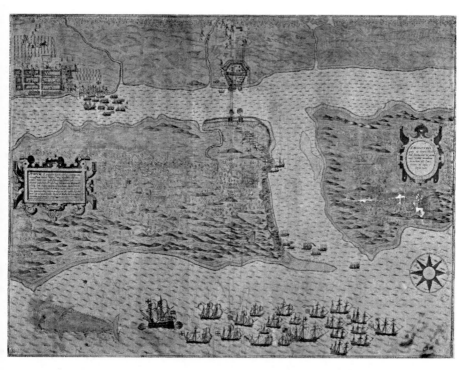

Baptista Boazio was an Italian artist who worked in London, making maps depicting English expeditions. This map, one in a series illustrating Sir Francis Drake's campaign in the West Indies, shows how Drake captured and burned the Spanish settlement at St. Augustine in May of 1586 (State Archives of Florida).

villages, and teach them that we are going after them; this would put a curb on them for their entire lives.[8]

By 1579 Marqués had managed to savagely subdue the Guale Indians and to move against the Coosa at Santa Elena. He burned 19 villages, killing some of the Indians and destroying their "maize and other supplies."[9] The Indians soon came to sue for peace, bringing with them some Frenchmen who had been living in their villages and giving them up to the Spanish, who promptly executed them. In a report on his suppression of the Indians, Marqués wrote:

In this province of San Agustín the people are peaceful, and although they were previously, they are much more so now since they have seen the war I made on the other Indians. May it please our Lord that they many some time become good and Christian, for at present there is no discussing that. They say flatly that they do not wish to become so, especially the adult men and women, who say that their fathers and ancestors had that religion; that they must preserve it; that, if the young people wish to become Christian, they may; that they will not give up their faith. But if we come to ask them for their children in order to teach them the doctrine, they will not give them up.[10]

St. Augustine had been in existence for 20 years in 1585 and, thanks to Marqués, the Indians had been pacified, a town had grown up near the fort, fruit trees planted and some plans made to try to attract merchants to the area. In 1586, in response to reports that the English were trying to establish a settlement north of St. Augustine, Marqués was assembling a force to go there and destroy it. On June 6, 1586, Sir Francis Drake and a fleet of 42 ships appeared at the entrance to the harbor at St. Augustine. Marqués in a letter to the Casa de Contratación wrote:

> At dawn on the 7th he landed 500 men and with seven large pinnaces sought me forthwith in the fort. With 80 men I had in the fort I resisted him until nearly midday. In view of my resistance he sent to the ships which lay outside the bar for reinforcements, and in nine vessels landed some 2,000 men and planted four pieces of artillery among certain sand dunes near the fort, with which he began to batter it. I retired as best I could, to protect my women and children (more than 200 persons).
>
> Having occupied the fort, the enemy took and sacked the town and burned the Church with its images and crosses, and cut down the fruit trees, which were numerous and good. He burned the fort and carried off the artillery and munitions and food supplies.
>
> We are all left with the clothes we stood in, and in the open country with a little munition which was hidden. We are without food of any sort except six hogs-heads of flour which will last twenty days at half a pound per head.[11]

The situation was desperate, and Marqués recalled the garrison from the fort at Santa Elena with all its artillery, munitions and provisions to St. Augustine. The settlement at Santa Elena was never occupied again. Aid came from both Cuba and Spain, and according to the royal officials in a letter to the king:

> General Pedro Menéndez Marqués built a new fort at the harbour mouth, at the bar, at the end of the channel, to protect the entrance. There he placed all the artillery and munitions. Considering how quickly it was done and by how few people, and with what scanty materials, the fort was very effective and well situated.[12]

St. Augustine was rebuilt and was to continue despite this setback and despite calls from various people that it should be abandoned because it was expensive to maintain and was of dubious benefit to the country. It survived because it was important to the viceroy in Mexico and the Council of the Indies in Spain that the treasure fleet be protected on its journey home, and a permanent settlement ensured that no other country would occupy the land to prey on Spanish shipping or the island colonies. St. Augustine was established as a result of the French settlement at Fort Caroline, and it owed its continuance to the fact that there were commodities in New Spain that were desirable and needed at home. The purpose of St. Augustine was to protect their passage.

# Jamestown

The settlement at Jamestown was the fourth attempt by the English to establish a permanent settlement in North America. The colony had a number of problems in its early years—a high death rate for its settlers, dissension among the governing council, shortages of food, trouble with the Indians and, as far as the London Company was concerned, a disappointing return on its investment. However, these problems were eventually overcome; the settlement survived and grew into the large and prosperous colony of Virginia.

The first summer in Virginia was a devastating experience for the settlers, as only 38 of them survived until the fall; unfortunately, this experience was repeated in the summers that followed. The heat and humidity of summer in southeastern Virginia came as a shock to new arrivals from England, who had just endured a long and exhausting voyage to the colony. Passengers in those days were housed in the tween-deck of a ship — an area between the hold and the main deck. In larger ships this area was about six feet in height, but in the smaller ones it could be only four to four and a half feet. In this space the passengers were crowded together with all their belongings for the length of the voyage — anywhere from nine to twelve weeks— and were only occasionally allowed on deck, a few at a time, to get some fresh air and a modicum of exercise.

The voyage took them through the West Indies, and the heat in the tween-deck must have been intense. If you add to that the sanitary conditions and the poor diet aboard ship, it is no wonder that some of the passengers died on the way. Once in the colony, the stress of dealing with the climatic conditions would have aggravated any ills the settlers might have contracted on their voyage.

This situation caused great concern to the Royal Council in England, and they sought ways to combat it. First they commissioned Captain Argall to find a shorter, more northerly route to Virginia, one that avoided the tropics, where there was a danger of contracting a fever known as *calenture*. The council hoped that this shorter voyage would ensure that settlers arrived in better health and would be able to cope with the heat and humidity of summer in Virginia. And then Governor de la Ware ordered two forts to be built, "upon a pleasant hill and near a little rivulet ... in which forts it is resolved that all those that come out of England shall be at their first landing quartered, that the wearisomeness of the sea may be refreshed in this pleasing part of the country."[13]

Jamestown itself was held to be an unhealthy site, and Thomas Dale built a new settlement called Henricus at the falls of the river, which he intended to be the principal seat of the colony. Somehow that never happened, because despite its unhealthy location, Jamestown continued to be the seat of government. Then Henricus was destroyed during the Indian uprising in 1622 and never rebuilt. There were numerous suggestions during the years to move the seat of government to another location, but no action was ever taken until 1699. Jamestown was never a place with a high number of inhabitants, as most people lived on plantations scattered over the countryside. The only time people came to Jamestown was when the General Assembly was sitting or the General Court was in session. The rest of the time, people who ran taverns and ordinaries (places to eat) made up the population of the town.

When land was distributed to settlers and they moved away from Jamestown to their own plantations, there was an improvement in their health, and as their children matured and began to raise families, a native-born population was established that was acclimated to the conditions and therefore healthier. However, the heat and humidity of summer would continue to take their toll on new arrivals, and potential settlers to Virginia were warned to arrive in the fall, so that they could have several months to "season" before the summer's heat brought the inevitable sickness and disease.

Another major concern of the Royal Council in England was the dissension among the members of the council and the factions that had developed in its wake. The constant bickering and arguing over what course of action to follow led to indecision and inaction and was the cause, the Royal Council felt, of many of the problems besetting the colony. They realized that the form of government for the new settlement was ineffective, as the president had no real authority or power. All decisions were made by majority vote of the council, and even though the president had two votes to cast, he was often outvoted by the council.

The Royal Council therefore decided to improve the situation by creating the position of governor and captain general and giving that person absolute authority to govern the colony. To assist the new governor, a council of men in Virginia was appointed to advise him — but the governor had the final word on any action taken. It is interesting to note that when Sir Thomas Gates came to Virginia as lieutenant governor in 1609, he brought with him a company of soldiers who had fought with him in the Netherlands. The new governor had not only the written authority to rule the colony but also the physical power to do so. Gates and Dale, the two men who were to rule the colony after the departure of Lord de la Ware, were veteran soldiers who had fought in the Netherlands, and they embellished the martial laws set down by de la Ware. Their regime was harsh, and while grumblings were heard and some colonists attempted to run away to live with the Indians, there were no mutinies. Thus order was brought to the settlement, and with it progress.

The next serious matter to command the attention of the council in England was the shortage of food in the colony. The council felt that the settlers relied too heavily on the Indians for food, and it was true that without the provisions provided by the Indians, the settlers would have starved. Why was this so? Part of the problem was the amount of food sent from England and the lack of accountability in its distribution. The amount of provisions sent by the company was never enough for the number of people in the colony, especially since the crews of the supply ships had to be fed out of the supply for the length of their stay in Virginia and then to be provisioned for the return voyage.

The food and equipment sent to the colony by the London Company was kept in a common storehouse, but there did not appear to be any account kept of what arrived or how it was distributed among the settlers. Stealing of tools was commonplace, as settlers took the tools from the storehouse and traded them on the sly to the Indians, receiving furs and other commodities in exchange. These commodities were then traded to the sailors aboard ship for butter, cheese, beef, pork, aqua vitae, beer, biscuit, oatmeal, and oil, which the settlers would then pretend had been sent to them from friends and family at home.

The London Company also sent men to the colony to make glass, perfume and other things that the company thought would make a profit. These men were not available to help grow food, defend the fort or help repair it and had to be fed from the common store. The settlers begged the company not to send any more "till more necessary things be provided. For in overtoiling our weak and unskillful bodies to satisfy this desire of present profit, we can scarce ever recover ourselves from one supply to another."[14]

The settlers made a determined effort to grow food from the very beginning, but the task of clearing the land for planting was very difficult for them. Smith reported that in the spring of 1608, some 50 men worked to clear land for planting, and during his term as president, thirty or forty acres of land were cleared. The harvest from their fields, however, was never enough to feed the settlers from one year to the next.

The drought may have played an important role in the small amount of grain the settlers were able to grow and might account for the Indians complaining to Smith that they had little food to trade, as their harvest was bad. Smith reported that the Youghtanund and Mattapanient Indians "imparted what little they had with such complaints and tears from the eyes of women and children"[15] that Smith said he was moved to compassion. One Indian chief repeatedly sent Smith many gifts and asked him "to pray to his god for rain or his corn would perish, for his gods were angry."[16]

The settlers had brought domestic animals with them, and by the fall of 1609 there were "sixty and odd"[17] hogs happily foraging for food on Hog Island across from Jamestown and nearly five hundred chickens. As for supplementing the food supply with hunting and fishing, Smith wrote, "Though there be fish in the sea, fouls in the air, and beasts in the woods, their bounds are so large, they so wild, and we so weak and ignorant, we cannot much trouble them."[18]

Hunting and fishing, except for commercial ocean fishing, were privileges enjoyed by "gentlemen" in England and were conducted for sport and pleasure, not to put food on the table. The only people in Virginia who would have even known how to fire a gun, much less be capable of hunting, were the gentlemen and the musketeers—soldiers.

However, the reports that reached England from people in Virginia finally convinced the council that the settlers were not completely to blame for the lack of food and that changes needed to be made. Ratcliffe, in a letter to Lord Salisbury dated October 4, 1609, wrote:

Also we have been bold to make stay of a small ship for discovery and to procure us victuals, whereof we have exceeding much need, for the country people [Indians] set no more that sufficeth each family a year. And the wood is yet so thick as the labor to prepare so much ground as would be to any purpose is more than we can afford, our number being so necessarily dispersed — so that, if I might be held worthy to advise the direction of this business, I hold it fit that there should be a sufficient supply of victuals for one year, and then to be sparing. It would less hinder the colony.[19]

Evidently the council agreed, for they proposed to send enough provisions with new settlers to last them for a whole year. They wanted the new arrivals to have "a seed time and a harvest before them."[20]

However, there still remained the problem of seeing that the provisions were actually received in the colony without pilfering by the mariners. William Strachey in his *A True Reportory* mentioned that the mariners had "never yet in any voyage hither but have made a prey of our poor people."[21] Lord de la Ware, according to Strachey, sought a "speedy redress of this"[22] and advised the council in England that a strict account of all the provisions sent from England on every voyage should be kept by a commissary general. The items to be transported were to be delivered to the ship and the captain made to sign for them. In Virginia the treasurer of the store would receive the goods and if any were found missing, the ship's captain would be obliged to replace them from his own supply.

The problem of growing food to feed the settlers was solved by the plan instigated by Dale in 1613. There were two significant aspects to this plan. One was the incentive offered to the farmers which involved being able to profit from their labors. In June 1614 Ralph Hamor wrote:

For formerly, when our people were fed out of the common store and labored jointly in the manuring of the ground and planting corn, glad was that man that could slip from his labor. Nay, the most honest of them in a general business would not take so much faithful and true pains in a week as now he will do in a day. Neither cared they for the increase, presuming that howsoever their harvest prospered, the general store must maintain them; by which means we reaped not so much corn from the labors of 30 men as three men have done for themselves.[23]

The second significant feature was the fact that the men were relieved of other duties in order to devote their time to farming. In the past the men at the fort had been called upon to carry out many different kinds of missions— they had to participate in military training exercises, for many of the men had no military experience at all, to repair the fort and the buildings, to clear and plant land, to stand guard at the fort, to go on expeditions to look for gold and silver or the Northwest Passage, to travel to Indian villages trading for food, to cut clapboard or to gather other things that might bring a profit to the Virginia Company. Then, too, a number of settlers were set to work on specific things, such as making glass, potash, refining the gold and silver found in the colony, and so on. In addition to all that, there was the drought and the physical weakness of the settlers due to inadequate diets, the weather and sickness. It is not surprising that they did not produce a great quantity of food.

The type of person sent to the colony also came under scrutiny. There was much criticism of the men in Virginia—from the "gentlemen" to the lowest worker. The council decided to be more selective in the future and came up with a list of "men of most use and necessity to the foundation of a commonwealth."[24] The list included ministers, surgeons, druggists, ironworkers, armorers, gun founders, blacksmiths, sawyers, carpenters, shipwrights, gardeners, turners, brickmakers, fishermen, fowlers, salt makers, coopers, vine dressers, soap-ash men, pitch boilers, mineral men, planters of sugar cane, silk dressers, pearl drillers, bakers, brewers, and colliers. Lord de la Ware advised the Royal Council in London that gentlemen should not be excluded from the list of potential settlers, "For he amongst us that cannot dig, use the square, nor practice the ax and chisel, yet he shall find how to employ the force of knowledge, the exercise of council and the operation and power of his best breeding and quality."[25]

A major problem facing the settlement was their relationship with the Indians. It had always been tenuous, but after the departure of John Smith in the fall of 1609, it had become overtly hostile. Upon his arrival in the colony, Lord de la Ware sent messengers to Powhatan, asking him to punish the people who had assaulted the blockhouse at Jamestown and killed some of the men and demanding that he return the weapons that belonged to the English as well as the men belonging to the fort that he had detained. When all this had been done, Lord de la Ware said, Powhatan could be assured of his friendship. Strachey reported Powhatan's response in his *A True Reportory*:

> unto all Powhatan returned no other answer but that either we should depart his country or confine ourselves to James Town only, without searching further up into his land or rivers, or otherwise he would give in command to his people to kill us, and do unto us all the mischief which they at their pleasure could and we feared.[26]

The ensuing hostilities with the Powhatan Indians drained energy, resources and manpower from the colony. The council in England had criticized Smith for his harsh treatment of the Indians, but the actions of the new government in Virginia were far more brutal than any measures Smith had ever undertaken. Villages and cornfields were burned and all inhabitants—men, women and children—killed. In an attempt to bring Powhatan to talk peace, Argall kidnapped Pocahontas. This ploy did not succeed, but the conversion of Pocahontas to Christianity and her eventual marriage to John Rolfe did bring peace between the two people.

Eight years of peace and apparent harmony between the Indians and the English ensued. Trade between the two cultures flourished, and when the colonists began to settle on their own land, contact with the Powhatans was maintained, as the Indians brought wild game and furs to trade with the English on their plantations. On the surface relations seemed cordial between the two peoples, and the Powhatans moved freely among the settlements and were often invited to stay and share a meal with the English.

The Virginia Company, always anxious to promote the conversion of the Indians to the Christian faith, put forth a plan to build a college near Henricus for Indian youths and in 1621 sent George Thorpe to Virginia to oversee the project.

However, close contact does not always foster friendship and respect between two different cultures. It did not take Thorpe long to realize that the English settlers did not share the Virginia Company's vision of a biracial community living in friendship and harmony. He wrote: "There is scarce any man amongst us that doth soe much as afforde them [the Indians] a good thought in his hart and most men with their mouthes give them nothinge but maledictions and bitter execrations."[27]

The English were to discover, as the Spanish had discovered in Florida, that the Indians were not interested in adopting European customs and decidedly not interested in changing their religion. The Powhatans bitterly resented the intrusion of the English into their country and disliked the fact that the land the English were taking for their plantations was land that belonged to them. And there seemed to the Powhatans to be no end to the influx of these people into their territory.

In 1618 Powhatan died and was eventually succeeded by his younger brother Opechancanough, who harbored a bitter hatred of the English. He bided his time, and on March 22, 1622, he struck. His plan was well thought out and designed to catch the English off guard. He asked the warriors of the tribes living on the James River to visit their English neighbors as usual, and when the sun reached a certain point in the sky, he ordered them to take up any weapon at hand and kill all the English in sight. The attack was so unexpected that in a few hours almost three hundred fifty settlers were killed. Jamestown itself was spared. A young Indian boy named Chanco, who was living with an English family across the river from the fort, told Richard Pace, his master, about the proposed attack, and Pace rowed across the river to warn the people at Jamestown.

The English retaliated with a vengeance, destroying villages and cornfields, and when the inhabitants returned and rebuilt, destroying them all over again. They had decided that total extermination of the Powhatans was the only way to ensure the safety of the colony. However, after 2½ years of intense warfare, the colonists began to realize that total extermination would be a costly and time-consuming enterprise. Constant warfare was hindering the development of the colony and the planting of tobacco.

The official end of the Anglo-Powhatan war did not come until 1632, but after 1625 fewer raids were carried out. The colonists slowly resettled areas that had been wiped out by the uprising in 1622, but this time they erected palisades around their property. The English had tried living in close contact with the Indians and found it unworkable. They had tried to exterminate the Indians and were forced to relinquish that idea. They now turned to a defensive arrangement — one that would allow the colony to grow and develop while at the same time offering the settlers protection from the Indians. In the mid 1630s a palisade four miles in length was built across the area between Queen's Creek, which empties into the York River, and College Creek, which empties into the James River. This barrier between the English and the Powhatans was reflective of the new policy with regard to the Indians: that of avoiding all contact with them. The barrier effectively opened up 300,000 acres of secure land for English settlement along the York River south of the palisade.[28]

After several years of growing prosperity and peace, interaction between the Indians and the English was slowly restored, and soon English settlers were taking Indian children into their homes to convert to Christianity, Indian servants began to seek work on English plantations and trade began again between the two peoples. The increased contact and the continuing encroachment of the English onto Indian lands caused frustration and anger and resulted in a second Indian uprising led by Opechancanough in 1644.

The attack, which came on April 17, 1644, was unexpected and well planned. It lasted two days and caused the deaths of approximately four hundred settlers. The English retaliation was immediate and harsh, as the colonists resorted to the tactic of destroying Indian villages and burning their fields. The war lasted for 2½ years. Opechancanough was captured and imprisoned at the fort, where he was shot in the back by one of the soldiers. As a result of the war and Opechancanough's death, the tribes were so subdued that the General Assembly reported the Indians were "so routed and dispersed that they are no longer a nation, and we now suffer only from robbery by a few starved outlaws."[29]

The terms of the Treaty of 1646 stipulated that the Powhatans accept the sovereignty of the king of England over them, and in return the governor and General Assembly of the colony promised to protect them from their enemies. In acknowledgement of this arrangement, the chief and his successors were to pay a tribute to the governor "in the number of twenty beaver skins att the goeing away of the Geese yearely."[30]

The treaty restricted the Powhatans to the territory north of the York River while the English were to have the land south of it. The Indians were not to be permitted to enter English territory unless on official business, and then they were to wear a "coat of striped stuffe"[31] to distinguish them. Any Powhatan who was caught in the prohibited area without the "coat" was liable to be shot.

Although the Powhatans were prohibited from entering English lands, the English settlers were allowed to enter Indian lands to cut timber or gather sedge if they obtained a warrant from the governor first. They were also allowed to settle in Powhatan territory if the governor and council of government thought it "fitt"[32] and informed the Powhatans of it beforehand.

There were troubles with Indians outside the Powhatan chiefdom in 1675, which resulted in Bacon's Rebellion. In 1677, after the rebellion was put down, a new treaty was drawn up with the Powhatan Indians. The treaty confirmed the right of the Powhatans to their tribal lands and granted more land to those tribes whose territory was lacking. The yearly tribute was to be paid to the governor every March — three arrows and 20 beaver skins. After this date the Indians were no longer a threat to English settlements.[33]

The last major concern of the London Company was the lack of profitable commodities coming from Virginia. The search for the Northwest Passage proved futile, as did the search for gold and silver. Timber, potash, pitch and tar and sassafras root did not bring great wealth to the company, neither did the glass that was manufactured there. John Rolfe's tobacco was the only commodity that proved of value. At this time, Spain held a monopoly on the tobacco trade in Europe and as Spain and England were allies, Spain provided all the tobacco sold in England. The London Company, under the leadership of Sir Edwin Sandys, worked tirelessly to procure part of the tobacco trade in Europe for Virginia tobacco, and soon Virginia planters were trading their tobacco to English and Dutch merchants.

The Virginia Company was not successful in a business sense, as it was bankrupt in 1624, when the king dissolved its charter and put the colony under his control. However, the company was successful in establishing a permanent settlement in Virginia and establishing a form of government in the colony that is the basis of our government today. In spite of the many problems the colony faced in its early years, it was fortunate that its sponsor, the London Company, had both the resources through its stockholders to support the settlement until the problems could be solved and a belief in the colony that gave its leaders the determination and courage to see it through until it was successful. In justification for their continued efforts in supporting Jamestown, the Virginia Council published a "True Declaration." In it they said:

> The admiral of France, among all the fears and discouragements of civil wars, never once gave over the project of plantation in Florida. Black envy and pale fear being not able to produce any arguments why that should be lawful for France which is in us unlawful [or] that which to others is honourable and profitable in us should be traduced as incommodious, base, and contemptible.[34]

# Québec

For over sixty years the French had been unsuccessful in their attempts to establish a permanent settlement either in Canada or on the southeastern coast of North America. Then, in 1603, the task of establishing a colony in Canada was given to Pierre du Gua, Sieur de Monts. The first settlement he founded in Acadia lasted for three years but had to be abandoned when the king revoked his monopoly on the fur trade.

In spite of their disappointments, the French were not discouraged in their attempt to plant a colony in Canada. They had gained an enormous amount of knowledge from their expeditions to the area, had a friendly relationship with the Indians, were in the process of setting up a profitable trade network with them and knew how to deal with the Canadian winters. They were ready and anxious to try again, and under the leadership of Samuel de Champlain, Québec, the first permanent French settlement in North America, was founded in 1608. Why, after all the previous attempts, was this particular one a success?

When de Monts named Champlain his lieutenant in New France, he could not have chosen a better representative. By 1608, when he embarked on the expedition to plant a permanent settlement in Canada, Champlain had considerable experience in the region. He had explored the St. Lawrence all the way to the Lachine rapids with Gravé in 1603 and had been part of the Acadia settlement of 1604, spending three winters in the colony before it was abandoned. He had used his time well, analyzing his observations and coming to some definite conclusions on how a colony should be established. Champlain had great determination, but he was flexible, and no matter how many obstacles he encountered in trying to reach his goals, he was willing to work around them in order to achieve success. No European colony ever had a leader who had a better grasp of what was needed to ensure success than the French colony at Québec.

Champlain, realizing that the former monopoly granted to de Monts was too large to be effectively monitored, persuaded him to petition the king for a short-term monopoly on just the St. Lawrence. He then proposed to establish a settlement upriver from Tadoussac to dominate the furs coming from the west and cut out the competitors who operated downriver. As the fur trade was to be the financial base for the settlement, the Indians became an integral part of the process, for without the furs they brought to the trading center each spring there would be no money to finance the colony. Therefore their cooperation was vital to the success of the project, but French traders had not always treated the Indians well, using such methods to obtain furs that the Indians held "the French name odious and deserving of contempt."[35] Some of the traders even went to the extreme of robbing Indian graves to get the "Beaver skins that these poor folk put over their dead as a last act of kindness upon burial."[36]

Champlain set about to change the negative perception that the conduct of the traders had created among the Indians. He had begun this process as early as 1603, during his voyage up the St. Lawrence, when he had made an effort to establish a friendly relationship with the Indians he encountered. He had even promised to give them his assistance in their fight against their common enemy and, unlike Laudonnière, he kept his word, winning their friendship and trust.

When the Indians complained about the cruelty and dishonesty of the independent fur traders, Champlain decided to bring some order and control to the fur trade. He went to France and acquired the patronage of a powerful nobleman, who assumed nominal charge of a new company which included as many rival merchants as could be persuaded to join. Thus the Company of Canada was formed and, although the independent traders were not entirely removed from the area, their numbers were reduced and the Indians were once more willing and active participants in the fur trade.

Champlain also showed tact and restraint in dealing with the Indians. His greatest wish was to explore the land and discover the Northwest Passage, but in 1610 the Indians showed some reluctance to take him to the interior of the country as he wished. The Indians did not want the French to visit tribes in the north and west for fear that their role as middlemen in the fur trade would be in jeopardy. Champlain did not set off on his own, as Cartier had done, thereby offending the Indians, but instead devised an alternate plan. He convinced the Indians to take a young Frenchman back with them to learn something about the countryside and also to learn their language. In this way he was able to gain knowledge of the area without alienating the Indians.

This system was so successful that it was continued, and from 1610 onward the French made a practice of placing a few of their men as interpreters among the Indians. The job of these interpreters was to see that the Indians came to French trading centers each spring with the beaver pelts they had either trapped themselves or gathered in trade with nations living in the distant northern and western regions of Canada. In this manner an unlimited trade area was opened for the French — an area that no other European power was able to penetrate. The French had also established a good relationship with the Indians during their stay at Port Royal in Acadia, and in the future this relationship would gain the French access to trade in the area of the St. John River as well as the St. Croix, the Pentagouët and Kennebec Rivers.[37] The fur trade network was one of France's greatest achievements in the New World.

The fur trade was going well for the French, and the terrible death rate of their first winter in Québec was not repeated. They also had good relations with the Indians in the area. Then, why after 20 years, had the colony not grown and developed? In 1628 the French population in Canada was only 107. At the same time, to the south, the English colony in Virginia could boast of 2,000 inhabitants, with more coming every year. The French had only two settlements in Canada — Port Royal and Québec — while the English had established four — one in Virginia, two more in New England and there were 100 English colonists at a settlement in Newfoundland. The Dutch had also entered the scene in North America with their colony in the Hudson River valley, and in 1625 there were 200 people living there.[38]

It seemed that in 20 years the fur trade had grown but the colony had not. The Company of Canada had been granted a fur monopoly, and in return they were supposed to use the profits to support the colony, to encourage settlers and — the grant stipulated — to establish agricultural settlements. Although the company had supported the colony by shipping food and other supplies to Québec each spring, there was little attempt to attract settlers to the area and no effort to encourage agriculture.

Champlain had proved that grain and vegetables grew very well in Québec and alleged that if people were sent to the colony to clear the land and plant crops, the colony would soon be self-sufficient. This would be a great advantage both to the company, for it would not have to send food to Québec each spring, and to the settlers, for they would no longer live in fear of starvation if the supply ships did not arrive. The fur company, however, lived from year to year, with its income depending on the quantity of furs obtained each summer. Sometimes the trading was good and at other times the Indians, for one reason or another, did not show up in great numbers at the trading centers and the resultant trade was poor. Since they never knew from one year to the next the extent of their profit, they were reluctant to put out money to send people to the colony to establish agricultural settlements; indeed, they tried to cut their costs as much as possible.

Settlers who wanted to come to the colony were offered very little in the way of incentives. In 1617 the apothecary Louis Hébert came to Québec with his wife and three children. He was an employee of the fur company and his two-year contract with the company stipulated that he was to perform whatever tasks were required, for which he would be paid a salary, but he was also expected to minister to the sick during his free time. Land had been cleared at Québec and was available for the cultivation of grain and vegetables. Hébert had permission to use this land if he wished, but everything he grew would be the property of the company. When the two years were over, he could remain and continue with his garden; however, he would be able to sell his produce only to the company, and he was forbidden to participate in trade with the Indians.

Understandably, there were not many families willing to immigrate to Canada with so little to gain; therefore, the colony was made up of employees of the company who worked there for a few years and then returned to France. In 1627, out of the 107 French people in Canada, there were only 20 or so who were permanent residents in the colony.[39] In fact, the company did not want a large number of permanent settlers in Canada. Settlers might decide to interfere in the fur trade by dealing with the Indians themselves and then selling the furs to the company, becoming middlemen and thereby reducing the company's profits.

The lack of commitment on the part of the Company of Canada for establishing settlers in the colony was a major problem for those who wanted to see Québec grow and prosper. Champlain and de Monts, who was still a member of the Company of Canada and still interested in the colony, strove to find a solution to the problem by convincing the company to increase their involvement in the settlement. In 1617 De Monts thought he had persuaded his associates to agree to a number of articles that would have meant major improvements for the colony, but as Champlain wrote, "all went up in smoke, by I know not what misfortunes."[40]

Champlain then tried to get the French Chamber of Commerce to back a large colonization effort, listing all the commodities that were available in the country, which he estimated would bring in 6,400,000 livres a year. He also pointed out the possibility that he would find "that shortened road to China by way of the St. Lawrence River."[41] Champlain asked that 300 families and 300 soldiers be sent to Québec and voiced the fear that if it were not done, the Dutch and English might seize control of the St. Lawrence.[42] The Chamber of Commerce was interested, but not enough to sponsor it, referring him instead to the king.

The young King Louis XIII approved the plan and sent the merchants of the Company of Canada a letter in which he stated his approval. Champlain was encouraged by the letter to implement his proposed plan, but he was not given any means of accomplishing it. The king told the merchants that they should participate in the plan but placed no stipulations on them. It all came to nothing.[43]

There were people in France other than Champlain who were supportive of the colony and wished to see it grow and prosper. The colony's reputation had suffered over the years, but some tried to restore it by writing letters and publishing various accounts of the beauty and fertility of the country. Champlain, the Jesuit priest Biard and Marc Lescarbot, one of the colonists at Port Royal, all wrote glowingly of Canada. It was Lescarbot who penned the best summation of all the appeals: "In a New France, all of Old France may one day rejoice, with profit, honor and glory."[44] However, the letters written by Father Biard and the accounts published by Champlain and Lescarbot were read, for the most part, by people who already supported the colony—few new converts were gained and little progress was made. It appeared that Québec would remain nothing but "a storehouse for the skins of dead beasts."[45]

If the fur company whose task it was to encourage settlement and agriculture in the colony was not doing its job properly, were there not people in positions of authority who could compel the company into compliance? What of the viceroy of Canada and the king and his ministers—the very people who had the most to gain from a robust and populous colony? As important as it was for the French to establish a permanent settlement in Canada, there were other more pressing matters closer to home that demanded the attention of those in authority. European wars as well as political and religious upheaval at home had created a very unstable atmosphere in France—an atmosphere that had drained energy and resources from more than one colonizing effort in the past and was to do so again.

At the beginning of the 17th century, France was in the best position she had been for years. The religious wars had ended with a union of Catholics and

Protestants under King Henri IV, and the new king had vanquished the Spanish threat to his kingdom, had brought powerful nobles under his control and led France to take her place as one of the economic powers in Europe. It was during this period of tranquility that the colony of Québec was founded.

However, only two years later, in 1610, the colony suffered a blow — the assassination of Henri IV. The king, who had been interested in colonization and given his support to the establishment of Québec, was dead, leaving the throne to his son, a young boy only nine years old. The new king, Louis XIII was, of course, too young to reign and a regent was appointed to rule in his place — the queen mother, Marie de Médici. Once again France was thrown into turmoil as the nobles, who had been brought under control by Henri IV, formed opposing factions in the court, with the queen regent and her favorites on one side and a party led by Prince de Condé, the viceroy of Canada, on another, while the young king and his ministers struggled to gain control of both.

When Champlain arrived in France in 1617, he found that Prince de Condé, his patron, had been arrested and taken to the Bastille. The merchant associates then saw an opportunity to rid themselves of Champlain and worked to have him removed as commander of the Habitation. The ploy did not succeed, and Champlain retained his post. In was in this atmosphere that Champlain presented his plan for improving the colony to the Chamber of Commerce and then to the king. It is not surprising that Louis XIII gave it only nominal support — he had more pressing matters to consider.

In 1620 the new viceroy, Montmorency, wrote to Champlain that he had revoked the fur monopoly of the Company of Canada and in their place, he wrote, "I have chosen the Sieurs de Caën, uncle and nephew, and their associates; the one is a good merchant, and the other a good sea captain."[46] The new company was required to bring six families consisting of at least three people each to Québec during a 15-year period and to feed and maintain them, to build one house at least 25 yards wide every three years and to be responsible for all administrative costs. These goals, while not providing Canada with a sizable increase in population, were at least achievable, and there was hope that some progress would at last be made.

The new company headed by the de Caëns got off to a very slow start. The associates of the old company complained bitterly about the loss of the fur monopoly, and the legal battle between the two companies dragged on for 16 months. The legal battle was waged in France, while a strident vocal battle was carried on in the colony, where employees of both companies were in residence. In fact, the verbal exchange between the employees of the rival companies became so heated that blows were actually struck. The Council of State finally settled the issue and the de Caëns kept the fur monopoly — with one setback. Religious disputes between Huguenot and Catholic had once again erupted in France and the Council of State had decided that Huguenots were not to be allowed to go to Canada. Guillaume de Caën, one of the partners of the new company, was a Protestant and had already made several voyages to Canada. He was hereafter barred from the country.

The year 1622 saw the end of the dispute between the two fur companies, and the attention of the de Caëns could now be focused on the colony. In 1623 land was granted for the first time in Canada, as Louis Hébert was granted the land he had lived on in perpetuity. Viceroy Montmorency also initiated the system of seigneury in the colony by granting lands in fief to Guillaume de Caën, Since he was not allowed to come to Québec, his lands were looked after for him by Champlain and, in 1626, with Champlain's help, he established a farm on his land at Cap Tourmente. Some forty or fifty head of cattle were kept there so the inhabitants of Québec would have fresh meat to eat during the winter. Unfortunately his farm was burned by the English in 1628 and all but four or five head of cattle slaughtered.

The young King Louis XIII had managed, by 1622, to subdue the warring factions at court and had taken the reins of government into his own hands. The king was surrounded by a few dedicated and trusted ministers and in 1624 Cardinal Richelieu, the most influential and powerful of these ministers, rose to a prominent position as adviser to the king. Richelieu, along with several other ministers, had decided that it was time for France to take her rightful place among the countries of Europe. Spain, Portugal, England and the Netherlands all had colonial empires in the New World and were becoming wealthy and powerful as a result. So far France had only a small colony in Canada that was basically a permanent fur-trading center. It was time to implement changes in the colony in order to reap the benefits outlined in 1617 by Champlain in his appeal to the Chamber of Commerce.

In 1626 Richelieu was appointed grand master and superintendent general of the navigation and commerce of France, and he turned his attention to the situation in the colony of Québec. Richelieu decided to revoke the license of the present company and form a company of his own called the Company of New France. In return for having control of all of New France and monopolies on the fur trade and other commodities, the company was required to send a certain number of tradesmen to the colony immediately, and by 1643 a total of 4,000 men and women were to have been sent as settlers. Under the new company, for the first time, settlers in Canada were to be allowed to trade with the Indians with the stipulation that the beaver pelts they gathered would be sold only to the company.

The king did his best for the success of the Company of New France by making some important changes in the existing laws. Previously, noblemen and men of the church had not been allowed, without losing their rank, to participate in commercial ventures. This was changed and noblemen and clergy were now able to become shareholders in a business venture without losing their rank and privileges. The king also promised to confer titles on 12 of the commoners who had invested in the company. For the first time in France, commerce became a steppingstone to political and social advancement. To encourage immigration and industry in Canada, the king ordered that the title of master craftsman be conferred on any tradesman who had practiced his trade in the colony for six years. If the tradesman decided to return to France after six years, he would be able to hold "open shop" and would be recognized for his skill — a recognition that otherwise would be difficult to acquire. Last, the king promised that all children born to French settlers in Canada would automatically become citizens of France; if they immigrated to France, they would have the same privileges as if they had been born in that country.[47]

The company was sometimes called the Company of the Hundred Associates, but in actuality there were 107 members; 26 were merchants and businessmen and the remainder were upper-level members of the government. Since most of these men were situated in Paris, the center of the colonizing enterprise shifted from Normandy and Brittany to Paris. The associates raised a large amount of money. Very quickly, they outfitted a fleet with provisions and supplies for the colony and recruited 400 settlers to go to Québec.

Just when it seemed that the colony was a last going to receive the help it needed to grow and develop into a viable asset for France, the volatility that so often plagued the country flared up once again. Religious tensions had risen again in France and Huguenots and Catholics were at war once more. England, trying to come to the aid of the besieged Huguenot town of La Rochelle, was drawn into a war with France and consequently sent a fleet to drive the French out of Canada. The fleet carrying the first group of 400 settlers plus provisions and supplies for the colony reached Canada in 1628, only to be attacked by the English. The ships were either sunk or captured.

The loss of these ships was a financial blow to the associates, but nevertheless they sent more ships the following spring, only to find the English in possession of Québec. Some of these ships returned to France, but others were lost at sea with all their cargo— another financial setback. Add to that the fact that for two summers the company had not been able to trade for furs and so had no income; therefore it is not surprising to learn that by the time the English had restored Canada to the French in 1632, the Company of New France was bankrupt.

Being unable to attract investors, the company decided to lease its commercial rights. The new owners were able to make a profit from the fur trade, but these profits were not enough to allow them to fulfill the requirement set forth in the charter: to settle at the minimum two to three hundred settlers a year. To solve this problem, they issued seigneuries, tracts of land, to members of the nobility, who were then required to send settlers to the colony. In this way, the obligation of the company to provide settlers was satisfied. The first grant was issued in 1634, and 70 more would be granted, both to individuals and to the Church, in the next 30 years. In 1640 there were a total of 356 people living in the colony —158 men, 116 women, 29 Jesuits, and 53 soldiers.[48]

The land was offered to potential settlers on good terms, as they would be housed and fed by the company for three years and then given cleared land so they might support themselves. Many in France were interested in taking advantage of the offer. The opportunity to own land was a powerful attraction, as the English had found in Virginia. And just as the English faced great hardships to keep their land, so would the people in Canada. For they were about to encounter a ferocious enemy determined to destroy them — the Iroquois, the traditional enemy of the Indians affiliated with the French.

The Iroquois had long nourished a hatred of the French for joining their enemies in attacking them. Now they had guns obtained in trade from the Dutch on the Hudson River and they came to Canada to wage a savage war against their Indian enemies and their allies, the French. For 30 years they attacked, burned, killed and took prisoners, and there were some settlers who gave up and went home. But others stayed, unwilling to leave the land they had worked hard to develop and return to penury in France.

The colony was hard pressed to defend itself and appealed to the government for aid. Unfortunately the French government was not in a position to send help, having serious matters to contend with in Europe. The Thirty Years' War that at one time or another had involved all the European powers was finally over in 1648. The French King Louis XIV was only ten years old in 1648, and the actions of his ministers had angered the nobility to the point of armed rebellion. No sooner had peace been declared than a civil war between the nobility and the crown broke out. The first uprising lasted from 1648 to 1649 and then another rebellion occurred in 1650. Also during the 1650s Spain and France were at war again. The affairs of the far-off colony in Canada received little attention.

The situation in the colony was so dire at the end of the 1650s that the fur trade was brought to a virtual standstill. In 1663 the new governor asked for troops to fight the Iroquois and sent an emissary to Paris to appeal to the king for assistance. The timing was right. In 1659 the war with Spain had ended, and in 1661 Louis XIV had taken control of his kingdom and was ruling in his own right. He became interested in the fate of his colony in Canada. The wars of the last decades had been expensive, the French treasury was low and there was wealth in Canada if it could be properly managed.

Therefore Louis XIV decided to make the colony a royal province. From now on he would be responsible for the government, defense and financing of the colony. In 1665 he named Jean-Baptiste Colbert comptroller general of France and turned the task of reorganizing the colony over to him. Colbert was a firm believer in mercantilism — an economic theory that sought to keep imports of manufactured goods and raw materials down and to encourage exports. Colonies were essential to mercantilism, as the English had proved to the south. Raw materials from her North American colonies flowed into England, to be turned into manufactured goods that were in turn bought by the people in the colonies. Colbert wanted to emulate this success in Canada for his country.

Under Colbert the first real effort was made to settle Canada. The colony took on the status of a province and was to be governed in the future by two directors—one to exercise military authority and the other to administer civil affairs. A sovereign council would serve the colony as a court and legislative council, and Québec was made a city ruled by a mayor and aldermen.[49] Settlers began to pour into the colony, shiploads of marriageable women were sent, commerce was regulated and the Iroquois, at last, were silenced.

In 1665 the king sent the Carignan Salières regiment to Canada to deal with the Iroquois. These soldiers were veterans of the Turkish wars and were successful in subduing the Indians; thereafter, for 27 years, there was peace in Canada. The next outbreak of trouble with the Iroquois came in 1687, and Louis de Buade de Frontenac, a former governor, was sent to take care of the situation. According to George Stewart, Jr.:

> Frontenac divined the Indian nature well, he knew when to bully and when to conciliate, when to apply blandishments and when to be stern.
> True to his allies he would not make peace with the ferocious Iroquois unless the treaty included the Indians friendly to the French. He would never abandon his friends to save himself and gained a reputation as a man of fair dealing.[50]

Frontenac, using all his diplomatic skills, managed to make peace with the Iroquois, and there was no more trouble with the Indians.

In establishing their colony at Québec, the French did not encounter the same problems that the English had at Jamestown or the Spanish at St. Augustine. For 30 years they had no great trouble with the Indians; they had so much experience in the area that the weather presented few problems for them, and they were not plagued with sickness. However, unlike Jamestown and St. Augustine, the colony did not receive much support or encouragement from its backers and remained very small for over fifty years. Until it was made a royal province, the colony survived because there was something of value in the country—beaver pelts—which people in Europe wanted. When land was offered to settlers in 1634, another incentive was added: the colony offered a chance for a better life. All that was lacking at that point was sufficient support and guidance from the government, and when that happened, the colony grew and prospered. When Frontenac first saw Québec, he wrote: "I never saw anything more superb than the position of this town. It could not be better situated as the future capital of a great empire."[51]

# Eleven

# Conclusion

The Rev. Alexander Whitaker came to Virginia as a missionary in March 1611; in July 1612 he wrote a paper entitled "Good News from Virginia," which he sent to the Council in England. He began his paper by writing "The noblest attempts have always had the most doubtful beginnings, most dangerous enemies."[1]

Whitaker was, of course, referring to the colony in Virginia, but this statement could just as well have been applied to all the European colonies in North America. All their attempts, whether noble or otherwise, had "the most doubtful beginnings," none more so than the successful settlements at St. Augustine, Jamestown and Québec. In fact, at one time all three of these colonies faced abandonment, as many people at home doubted the feasibility of continuing them. Yet in spite of all the tribulations encountered in the founding of these settlements, they managed to survive when others failed. Why? What was different about these settlements that allowed them to succeed?

In order to discover why these three colonies were successful, perhaps we should start by looking at why the others failed. All the colonies had basically the same goals— to establish a permanent settlement, to look for gold and silver, to search for the Northwest Passage and to bring their brand of Christianity to the Indians. In most of the failed colonies there seems to have been an overemphasis on the search for riches and more enthusiasm displayed for the discovery of gold, silver and precious gems than for colonizing. There was also eagerness on the part of the French and Spanish to search for fabulous native civilizations that would rival the richness of Mexico and Peru, and at times the French and the English seemed more interested in privateering than founding permanent settlements. When the opulent civilization and the gold and silver could not be found, interest in maintaining the colony waned, and when the good of the colony interfered with privateering, the interests of the colony were put aside.

All the colonies had sponsors who were responsible not only for providing adequate supplies for the colony but also for recruiting new settlers, promoting the settlement and maintaining contact between the colony and the homeland. In at least half the failed colonies this responsibility fell on the shoulders of one man, and when that man died, as five of the six one-man sponsors did, there was no one to replace him and the settlements were abandoned. Even having the king or a high government official as a sponsor of a colony did not guarantee success, for European wars, civil unrest and political infighting were apt to distract attention from the welfare of tiny settlements thousands of miles across the Atlantic. The settlers of more than one European colony watched in vain for a relief fleet from home to arrive, wondering what was happening in their country and why they had been forgotten.

The settlers in all the colonies faced many problems as they tried to adjust to life in a new land. They suffered from lack of food, from the weather, from sickness and disease and from the hostility of the Indians. What they needed was time — time to find a way to solve all these problems. However, none of the unsuccessful colonies lasted long enough to even begin this process. Of the 13 failed settlements studied, only four survived for longer than one year. This does not include de Soto's expedition which spent four years looking for a suitable place to establish a settlement and never finding it.

What was needed was strong, determined leaders in the colony who could be depended upon not to abandon it and a sponsor that had the resources to support the settlement until a solution to the problems confronting it could be found. These essentials were missing from the 13 colonies that failed; for whether it was disappointment at not finding great wealth, the inability of the sponsors to adequately support it or a lack of leadership in the colony itself, the settlers in all the unsuccessful colonies abandoned their settlements after a relatively short period of time.

These, then, were the major stumbling blocks to success in the thirteen failed colonies studied here. How did the circumstances surrounding the establishment of St. Augustine, Jamestown and Québec differ from those of the unsuccessful colonies? All 16 of the colonies shared the same goals, but there was a slight difference in priorities in the three successful colonies. There had always been powerful national incentives for the Spanish, French and English to establish permanent settlements in North America in addition to the search for riches, and these incentives took on a new importance in the last half of the 16th century.

Once the French had founded Fort Caroline on the Florida coast, the Spanish were galvanized into action. It became a matter of extreme importance to them that the settlement at St. Augustine be a success — the search for gold and silver became a low priority. Likewise, the founding of St. Augustine made it a matter of national pride and renewed self-interest for the French and English to establish their own colonies in North America. After being driven out of Florida by the Spanish, the French were anxious to claim Canada as theirs and had been frustrated by the failure of several attempts to settle there. The English had failed twice to plant a colony at Roanoke and were doubly interested in achieving success elsewhere. Although the desire to find great wealth in North

America or a water passage to the East was still present, the French and English were equally interested in planting a permanent settlement in order to claim territory in North America.

In order to achieve their goal of founding a permanent settlement, each country needed a steady, reliable sponsor for their ventures—for a solid backer was essential for success. It was the responsibility of the sponsor to see that adequate supplies were sent with the colonists and that they had regular contact with the mother country. It was extremely important that ships arrive in the colonies on a regular basis, bringing the things the colonists needed and could not find in their new homes: clothing, shoes, tools, household goods and food items such as olive oil, wine, sugar and spices. The ships also brought something else that was vital to the colonists, and that was news of what was happening in the outside world. The three successful colonies never lost contact with home. Even though the settlers at St. Augustine thought the supply ships were slow in coming, they did come. The London Company was very diligent in sending relief ships to Virginia, and we have seen that ships arrived from France every spring to resupply the settlement at Québec.

Under the leadership of Pedro Menéndez de Avilés, St. Augustine was established as a permanent settlement in 1565 (State Archives of Florida).

The three colonies had different methods of financing their efforts. St. Augustine had one man—Menéndez—as its sponsor, but he was assisted by the king, as it was important not only to him but also to the viceroy in Mexico and the officials of the island colonies to keep the fort at St. Augustine as an outpost on the Florida coast. The English used a joint-stock company as the backer for the Jamestown colony, and it was very effective. The company was able to raise money for the colony through the sale of its stock, and many of its investors were wealthy merchants or members of government, most of whom were staunch supporters of the colony. It was a fur trading company that sponsored the settlement at Québec, and it was the fur trade that kept the settlement in existence in its early years. It cannot be said that the backers of these three colonies profited much from their sponsorship, for in spite of the assistance of the king, Pedro Menéndez de Avilés poured his personal fortune into the settlement and died a poor man, and both the Virginia Company and the various fur trading companies in Canada went bankrupt. Eventually all three colonies were made royal colonies under the protection of their respective kings.

The last component needed for success was good strong leadership in the colony, for without someone who could direct affairs in the colony with decision and vigor, there could be little chance of success. When Philip II gave the task of establishing a settlement on the Florida coast to Menéndez, he made an excellent choice. Menéndez, a 46-year-old nobleman from Asturias, had considerable naval experience, especially in the Indies, and had served his king faithfully and well for many years. Menéndez was not only the sponsor of the colony in Florida but also the governor of the territory and as such had complete control of affairs there. On his shoulders rested the responsibility for the success or failure of the enterprise.

Menéndez has been described as bold, courageous, resourceful, intolerant, ruthless and arrogant, but his loyalty to the king was never questioned. He saw his goals clearly; and if bending the rules a little would help him achieve those goals more quickly, he was very willing to do so. This attitude, plus his rather domineering manner, made enemies for him among Spanish officials, but he never lost the confidence of his king.

Menéndez was promised a salary for serving as governor of Florida, but his salary was to be paid out of the profits found in the country. If no profits were found, he would receive no pay for his work. A different kind of man would have lost no time in trying to find the resources needed to ensure his salary, but Menéndez made his primary goal the establishment of a permanent settlement in Florida.

He had a grand vision for the colony, which, unfortunately, was not shared by the king or his ministers and was therefore never realized. Nevertheless, he worked tirelessly and proved to be a capable administrator as well as an able military commander, and he managed to establish St. Augustine in spite of countless problems. After his death, the governorship went to his heirs, who proved to be unfit for the post, and it was then that Philip II assumed control of the colony. The governors he appointed proved to be very capable and effective.

The settlement in Virginia was organized in a different way than the settlement at St. Augustine. The men with the vision for the colony and the money to support it were in London and remained there, not caring to "adventure their person" by actually going to Jamestown. It was the Council in England that controlled and directed the business of colonization, and the men who went to Virginia were there to carry out its directives.

The Council in England chose the seven men who were to be members of the Council in Virginia — the men who were to direct the affairs of the colony on site. As we have seen, the council was torn by factions and dissension and could never agree on the course of action to follow. As a result, little action was taken and nothing much was accomplished. The first two presidents were deposed, and at last a new president took over — one who proved to be a strong leader. He was Captain John Smith.

Smith was 27 years old when he arrived in Virginia, but he had already had much experience as a soldier of fortune, having fought in the Netherlands, France, Turkey and Transylvania. He had seen much of the world, traveling throughout Europe and even venturing to Morocco looking for work as a soldier. He came from yeoman[2] stock and was not a member of the nobility, but his military experiences in faraway places undoubtedly rendered him a valuable member of the council. In Virginia he served as a soldier, explorer, cartographer, writer and the main negotiator for food with the Indians.

By the time Smith was elected president, some of the original members of the council had died and others had returned to England. Smith decided not to replace them and governed the colony, for all practical purposes, alone without the advice or consent of the few remaining members of the council. For this action and for his high opinion of his own worth, he was highly criticized by some of his fellow colonists. However, in taking the reins of government into his own hands, Smith was only doing what the Council in England was preparing to do, and that was to put a governor with absolute authority in charge of the colony. Smith, like Menéndez, was willing to bend or ignore rules if he thought the situation warranted it and, like Menéndez, he made enemies both in the colony and in England. However, as the sole authority in Virginia he saw to it that progress was made at Jamestown during his term as president.

Smith left Virginia in the fall of 1609 and never returned. Fortunately, Sir Thomas Gates arrived with the survivors of *Sea Venture* in May 1610. As a young man, Gates had been part of Drake's expedition to the Caribbean and had taken part in the attack on St. Augustine in June 1586. He was also with the fleet that brought Grenville's men off Roanoke Island during that same month. Whether this adventure to the New World inspired him with an absorbing interest in the area or not, he became a strong advocate for English colonization and was one of the first men to petition James I for a charter to settle Virginia. Gates was a professional soldier fighting in the Netherlands when the charter of 1609 was granted, and he obtained a leave of absence from his post in order to sail to Jamestown aboard *Sea Venture* as the governor and lieutenant general of Virginia.

In November 1619, at a meeting of the Virginia Company, Sir Edwin Sandys, the treasurer of the company said that

Sir Thomas Gates had the honor to all posterity of being the first named in His Majesty's patent and grant of Virginia, and was also the first that, by his wisdom, industry, and valor, accompanied with exceeding pains and patience in the midst of many difficulties, had laid the foundation of the present prosperous state of the colony.[3]

Gates remained in Virginia as governor until April 1614, and upon his return to England continued to be involved with colonization in Virginia. In 1620 he was appointed to the council overseeing the establishment of a colony in New England.

Thomas West, Lord de la Ware, a former soldier who had fought in the Netherlands, spent the last ten years of his life working to establish English colonies in North America. He was on the Council for Virginia in England in 1609 and under the charter of 1609 was named governor and captain general of the colony for life. He came to Virginia to take up his duties in June 1610 but was forced by illness to return to England a year later. He worked tirelessly to promote the colony in England and was on his return voyage to the colony in 1618 when he died.

John Smith was in the colony of Virginia for only two years and served as president of the Council from 1608 to 1609. His leadership held the struggling colony together and helped it to survive (The Library of Virginia).

These two men, Sir Thomas Gates and Lord de la Ware, were staunch supporters of the settlement, and it is mostly due to their belief in the future of Virginia that the Council in England did not call for the abandonment of the colony — Lord de la Ware even going so far as to say if the company were to abandon Jamestown, he would pledge his own fortune to continuing it. The Virginia Company continued supporting the settlement in spite of financial difficulties until the colony was taken over by the king in 1624.

Although the colony in Virginia had many supporters at home and many determined settlers in the colony, the settlement at Québec had an entirely different situation. It was a French nobleman by the name of Pierre du Gua, Sieur de Monts, who was the prime motivator behind the settlement. Joined with him in the enterprise was Samuel Champlain. These two men would successfully establish Québec as a permanent French colony in Canada — de Monts would remain in France and use the profits from his fur trading company to finance the colony and Champlain would serve as his lieutenant in Canada and direct the day-to-day operations there. It was a most fortunate combination.

Champlain was 41 years old in 1608, when he founded Québec. He was born in Brouage, France, where he learned seamanship and navigation before serving in the army. In 1599 he was the commander of one of a fleet of ships just embarking on an expedition to the West Indies and spent almost three

Sir Thomas Gates, a professional soldier and a staunch supporter of colonization, was one of the first men to petition James I for a charter to settle Virginia. Under his leadership as governor and lieutenant general of Virginia from 1610 to 1614, the colony became stable (The Library of Virginia).

years in the Caribbean observing the Spanish colonies there. He wrote an account of his journey with thoughtful comments on the colonizing methods employed by the Spanish. He presented this work to the king on his return to France.

The king was impressed and offered him a place on the expedition de Monts was planning to send to Canada to gather information for his proposed colony. His task on the voyage was to explore the St. Lawrence, write a full account of the expedition, note suitable sites for settlement and make maps of the area. He also established friendly relations with the Indians who were essential to the success of the fur trade, which was to pay for the new settlement. When de Monts decided to send his first settlers to Acadia instead of the St. Lawrence, Champlain was a member of the expedition. The knowledge he gained from these experiences was valuable to him when he established the colony at Québec. Indeed, the French colony had fewer problems dealing with life in Canada than the English had in Virginia or the Spanish in Florida.

Both de Monts and Champlain placed great emphasis on the establishment of a permanent

*Left:* Thomas West, baron Delaware, was named governor and captain general of the colony of Virginia in 1609. Because of his poor health, he did not spend much time in the colony but worked to support it in England. It was his belief in the future of the colony that kept the London Company from abandoning it (The Library of Virginia). *Right:* Samuel de Champlain's leadership, vision and determination were responsible for the founding of the French colony at Québec. This is the image most associated with Champlain, as no authentic portrait of him is known to exist. It was used in an exhibition celebrating the 400th anniversary of the founding of Québec City in 2008 (Print Collection, Rare Books and Special Collections, McGill University Library).

settlement as their main goal and saw the fur trade as a means of supporting it, not as a source of profit to themselves. Champlain in particular was a man of vision who saw more to Canada than immediate riches and wanted to colonize the country as the English had done to the south. Unfortunately he could not convince the king or his ministers that it was in the best interests of France to do so.

Of the three successful colonies, Québec suffered the most from the disinterestedness of people in the homeland, and it was due to the efforts of Champlain that the colony survived, as he was not only its governor but also its chief promoter. He saw that the great wealth of Canada was not in the gold and silver that might be found there but in its potential for agriculture and trade. Thirty years after his death, the young King Louis XIV took over the colony, and his minister Colbert saw the same potential and recognized the advantages of colonizing Canada. It was then that Champlain's dream became reality.

Our three successful colonies, then, owed their success to the fact that their founders placed the goal of establishing a permanent settlement on a par with the goal of finding the Northwest Passage or deposits of gold, silver and precious gems. The sponsors of each colony were able to find ways to support the colony financially and were at times willing to sacrifice their own profits for the good of the colony. Finally, they were fortunate in that they had strong leaders in the colony to direct and govern it. It had not been an easy task for any of them, but as John Smith once wrote that "Everything of worth is found full of difficulties, but nothing so difficult as to establish a commonwealth so far remote from men and means."[4]

In 1521 Juan Ponce de León attempted to plant a settlement on the west coast of Florida, and thus began the long struggle by the Spanish, French and English to colonize North America. By 1621, one hundred years later, the struggle was over. Spain was firmly entrenched on the east coast of Florida, with its mission system spread throughout the country; the English had established colonies in Virginia, Bermuda, Newfoundland and Massachusetts; and the French had laid claim to Canada by establishing a permanent settlement in Québec.

St. Augustine, Jamestown and Québec symbolize the end of the long struggle by Europeans to colonize North America and the end of the dream of finding another Mexico or Peru on its shores or great mines of gold and silver and precious gems in its mountains. Sadly for the native people of North America, these settlements also symbolize the gradual end of their way of life. But for every end there is also a beginning; therefore, the three permanent settlements also symbolize a beginning — the beginning of the colonial era, which would see the migration of thousands of Europeans to this new land across the Atlantic drawn by the lure not of gold and silver but of the land itself. For the real wealth of North America was the land — a rich, fertile land capable of producing great quantities of grain, fruits and vegetables, with large tracts of forest full of valuable timber and great rivers teeming with fish. It was a place that promised a chance for a better life.

# Chapter Notes

## Introduction

1. For more information about Greenland and Vinland, see Morison, *The European Discovery of America: The Northern Voyages,* 32–80.

## Chapter One

1. Morison, *The European Discovery of America: The Northern Voyages,* 104.
2. Hoffman, "Diplomacy and the Papal Donation," 152.
3. Davenport, *Treaties,* I:77–78.
4. Hoffman, "Diplomacy and the Papal Donation," 151.
5. Ibid., 179, 183.
6. Quadra to Chantonnay, November 23, 1561, as cited in Hoffman, "Diplomacy and the Papal Donation," 176.
7. Morison, *The European Discovery of America: The Northern Voyages,* 211.
8. Ibid., 215.
9. Ibid., 225.
10. Morison, *The European Discovery of America: The Southern Voyages,* 587–588.
11. Hoffman, "Diplomacy and the Papal Donation," 157.
12. Bonvallot to Charles V, n.d. [November 8–10, 1540?], as cited in Hoffman, "Diplomacy and the Papal Donation," 161.
13. Bonvallot to Charles V, December 1540, as cited in Hoffman, "Diplomacy and the Papal Donation."
14. Ibid.

## Chapter Two

1. February 23, 1512. Capitulations between King Ferdinand and Juan Ponce de León for a voyage to discover and colonize the Island of Bimini. Printed in *Colección de documentos inéditos de Indias,* XXII:26–32; translated in T. F. Davis, "History of Juan Ponce de León's voy-

ages to Florida. Source Records," *Florida Historical Quarterly,* XIV (1935):9–14.
2. Ibid.
3. September 26 (or 27), 1514. Capitulations by King Ferdinand with Juan Ponce de León for the continuation of the discovery of Florida. Translated in Davis, "History of Juan Ponce de León's voyages to Florida. Source Records," *Florida Historical Quarterly,* XIV (1935):53–56.
4. Ibid.
5. Ibid.
6. February 10, 1521. Letters of Juan Ponce de León to the Cardinal of Tortosa and to King Charles I (the Emperor Charles V) before leaving for Florida. Printed in Colección de documentos inéditos de Indias, XL (1883), 47–49; facsimiles printed in V. Murya Sanz, *Juan Ponce de León,* 240, 248; translated.
7. September 27, 1514. Queen Juana to Juan Ponce de León. Printed in Sanz, *Juan Ponce de León,* 300–303; translated.
8. Oviedo, *Historia general y natural de las Indias,* (1535), bk. xvi, chap. xii; translated in T. F Davis, "History of Juan Ponce de León's voyages to Florida. Source Records," *Florida Historical Quarterly,* XIV (1935):59–61.
9. Antonio de Herrera y Tordesillas, *Historia general de los hechos de los Castellanos en las isles i tierra firme del mar oceano,* 8 vols. (Madrid, 1601–1615), II (1601):30–31; translated in Davis, "History of Juan Ponce de León's voyages to Florida. Source Records," *Florida Historical Quarterly,* XIV (1935):62.
10. Morison, *The European Discovery of America: The Southern Voyages,* 515.
11. Oviedo, *Historia general y natural de las Indias,* (1535), bk. xvi, chap. xii; translated in T. F. Davis, "History of Juan Ponce de León's voyages to Florida. Source Records," *Florida Historical Quarterly,* XIV (1935):59–61.
12. Ibid.
13. Ibid.
14. There is some disagreement over the

number of Indians lured aboard the ships. Lowery says 150 (see Lowery, *The Spanish Settlements Within the Present Limits of the United States 1513–1561*, 156) and Morison says 70 (see Morison, *The European Discovery of North America: The Northern Voyages*, 332). In June 1526, Pedro de Quexos, the commander of the ship owned by Matienzo, testified in the lawsuit brought by Matienzo against Ayllón, that "they captured about sixty-odd people and brought them on board the ships." (See June 2, 1526. Replies by Pedro de Quijos [Quexos] to interrogatories administered on behalf of Matienzo in Shea Papers, Georgetown University Library.)

15. Peter Martyr on the voyages of Ayllón and on the supposed customs of the North American Indians in Martyr, *De orbe novo decades* (1530), Dec. VII, lib. ii–iv; *Peter Martyr, De Orbe Novo*, edited and translated by F. A. MacNutt, II:254–271.

16. Ibid.

17. Ibid.

18. June 1523. Asiento and capitulations from Charles V to Lucas Vásquez de Ayllón, with extension of time granted in 1524. Charter of June 12, 1523, as translated in Paul Quattlebaum, *The Land Called Chicora*, 135–141.

19. Ibid.

20. Ibid.

21. Ibid.

22. Ibid.

23. Oviedo, *Historia general y natural de las Indias*, 5 vols., IV:325–330, translated.

24. March 5, 1526. Statement by Lucas Vásquez de Ayllón to the king, made available to the inquiry at Santo Domingo, transcribed by John Gilmary Shea in Shea Papers, Georgetown University Library.

25. For more information on the location of San Miguel, see Morison, *The European Discovery of North America: The Northern Voyages*, 337.

26. Oviedo, *Historia general y natural de las Indias*, 5 vols., IV:325–330.

27. Ibid.

28. Ibid.

29. Ibid.

30. Quinn, *New American World: A Documentary History of North America to 1612*, 5 vols., II:3. According to Quinn, there is some confusion as to the exact location of the Rio de las Palmas.

31. December 11, 1526. Capitulations between Charles V and Pánfilo de Narváez for the conquest of the land between the Rio de las Palmas and Florida, printed in *Colección de documentos inéditos de Indias*, 1874; XXII:224–245, translated.

32. Lowery, *The Spanish Settlements Within the Present Limits of the United States 1513–1561*, 173.

33. December 11, 1526. Capitulations between Charles V and Pánfilo de Narváez for the conquest of the land between the Rio de las Palmas and Florida, printed in *Colección de documentos inéditos de Indias*, 1874; XXII:224–245, translated.

34. Ibid.

35. Alvar Núñez Cabeza de Vaca published *La relación que dio Alvar Núñez de Vaca* in 1542. It was translated into Italian in 1555, and this version was eventually translated into English in 1851. This translation was used by Hodge and Lewis in *Spanish Explorers in the Southern United States 1528–1543*, 12–126.

36. Ibid.

37. Ibid.

38. Ibid.

39. Ibid. (Pánuco was in reality a long distance away on the eastern coast of Mexico.)

40. Ibid.

41. Ibid.

42. Lowery, *The Spanish Settlements Within the Present Limits of the United States 1513–1561*, 182.

43. Vaca, *La relación que dio Alvar Núñez de Vaca* in 1542, *La relación que dio Alvar Núñez de Vaca*, translated in Hodge and Lewis, *Spanish Explorers in the Southern United States 1528–1543*, 12–126.

44. April 20, 1537. Capitulations between Charles V and Hernando de Soto in Bourne, *Narratives of the Career of Hernando de Soto*, 2 vols., I:3–223.

45. Ibid.

46. Ibid.

47. Lowery, *The Spanish Settlements Within the Present Limits of the United States 1513–1561*, 217–218.

48. May 18, 1539. The officials of Hernando de Soto's army to Charles V, translated in Bourne *Narratives of the Career of Hernando de Soto*, 2 vols. I:3–223.

49. 1539–1541. The official narrative of the expedition of Hernando de Soto by Rodrigo Rangel, his secretary, as rendered by Gonzalo Fernández de Oviedo and cited in Lowery, *The Spanish Settlement Within the Present Limits of the United States 1513–1561*, 219.

50. Ibid., 223.

51. Among the relics there they discovered Biscayan iron axes, glass beads, and rosaries with crosses. Ibid., 229–230.

52. The location of Cufitatchiqui is thought to have been on the Savannah River at Silverbluff, about twenty miles below Augusta, Georgia. The Spanish assumed that the Savannah River was the Santa Elena River and that at its mouth was the Punta de Santa Elena — or the site of Ayllón's settlement. The presence of pearls in the river, the Spanish relics and the testimony of the Indians was enough to convince them.

53. 1539–1541. The official narrative of the expedition of Hernando de Soto, by Rodrigo Rangel, his secretary, as rendered by Gonzalo Fernández de Oviedo in Bourne, *Narratives of the Career of Hernando de Soto*, 2 vols., II:49–149.

54. The name Santa Elena in connection with Ayllón's colony appeared in the works of Oviedo, *Historia general y natural de las Indias*, 5 vols., IV:325–330. He wrote: "The land of Gualdape, and also down the river of Santa Elena to the west, is all flat land." Francisco López de Gómera, who wrote about the 1521 voyage sponsored by Ayllón in his *Historia general de las Indias*, published in 1553, also uses the name. According to Gómera, Gordillo and Quexos were looking for slaves and, not having found any, decided to travel north to see if they would have better luck there. He wrote: "They reached a land named Chicora and Gualdape, which is in 32 degrees of latitude, and what is now called the Cape of Santa Elena and the River Jordan." Gómera, *Historia general de las Indias*, 2 vols., 89–90.

55. December 29, 1557. Phillip II to Luis de Velasco on the Luna expedition, translated in Priestley, *Luna Papers*, I:47–53.

56. Ibid.

57. Ibid.

58. Ibid., II:333–337.

59. September 30, 1558. Luis de Velasco, viceroy of Mexico, to Philip II in Priestley, *Luna Papers*, II:257–261.

60. May 1, 1559. Tristán de Luna to Philip II in Priestley, *Luna Papers*, II:211–213.

61. May 25, 1559. Luis de Velasco to Philip II in Priestley, *Luna Papers*, II:221–231.

62. June 17, 1560. Petition of the married soldiers of the expedition to Luna in Priestley, *Luna Papers*, I:139–143.

63. Ibid.

64. The opinion of Jorge Cerón, Maestre de Campo, in Priestley, *Luna Papers*, I:199–219.

65. June 19, 1560. Representation of the six captains to Luna, in Priestley, *Luna Papers*, I:159–165.

66. Ibid.

67. August 1, 1560. Fray Domingo de la Anunciación and others to Tristán de Luna in Priestley, *Luna Papers*, I:223–233.

68. August 11, 1561. Testimony of Alonso de Montalván, in Priestley, *Luna Papers*, II:281–311.

## Chapter Three

1. Wroth, *The Voyages of Giovanni da Verrazzano*, 133–143.

2. Ibid.

3. Trudel, *The Beginnings of New France 1524–1663*, 4.

4. Ibid.

5. Ibid., 5.

6. Wroth, *The Voyages of Giovanni da Verrazzano*, 133–143.

7. Ibid.

8. Jacques Cartier's First Account of the New Land, Called New France, Discovered in the Year 1534. Printed in Biggar, *The Voyages of Jacques Cartier*, 10–81.

9. Ibid.

10. 1535–1536. Jacques Cartier's voyage to the Gulf and River of St. Lawrence and the first French settlement established on the site of Québec. Printed in Biggar, *The Voyages of Jacques Cartier*, 83–246.

11. The two Indian boys used the word *Canada* when they were speaking to Cartier about their home. In their language the word meant "village" or "settlement," and they used it in reference to Stadacona, which was the name of their village on the St. Lawrence. Cartier used the word to refer not only to the village of Stadacona but also to all the territory ruled by Donnaconna — roughly the area from the Isle Aux Courdres in the St. Lawrence to a point some distance to the west from present-day Québec City. By 1547 the word *Canada* referred to all the land north of the St. Lawrence.

12. 1535–1536. Jacques Cartier's voyage to the Gulf and River of St. Lawrence and the first French settlement established on the site of Québec. Printed in Biggar, *The Voyages of Jacques Cartier*, 83–246.

13. Ibid.

14. Ibid.

15. Ibid.

16. Ibid.

17. Ibid.

18. Cartier, *Brief recit, & succincte narration, de la navigation faicte es ysles de Canada, Hochelage & Seguenay & autres...*, translated in Hakluyt, *A Shorte and Briefe Narration*, and cited in Morison, *The European Discovery of North America: The Northern Voyages*, 418.

19. 1535–1536. Jacques Cartier's voyage to the Gulf and River of St. Lawrence and the first French settlement established on the site of Québec. Printed in Biggar, *The Voyages of Jacques Cartier*, 83–246.

20. January 22 [1539 or 1540]. A Portuguese report on Cartier's preparations. Translated in Biggar, *A Collection of Documents Relating to Jacques Cartier and the Sieur de Roberval*, 75–81.

21. Ibid.

22. Ibid., 70–74.

23. Ibid., 190.

24. Parkman, *France and England in North America*, I:166.

25. 1541–1542. Jacques Cartier's voyage to the St. Lawrence River and his second settle-

ment upstream from Québec. Hakluyt, *Principal Navigations*, III:232–237.

26. Ibid.

27. Ibid.

28. Biggar, *A Collection of Documents Relating to Jacques Cartier and the Sieur de Roberval*, 275–278.

29. 1541–1542. Jacques Cartier's voyage to the St. Lawrence River and his second settlement upstream from Québec. Hakluyt, *Principal Navigations*, III:232–237.

30. Ibid.

31. Ibid.

32. Ibid.

33. Ibid.

34. Ibid.

35. Ibid.

36. Ibid.

37. Ibid.

38. Ibid.

39. September 23, 1542. A report on the Cartier-Roberval meeting at Newfoundland based on the deposition of Martin de Actalecu of Fuenterrabia. Translated and printed in Biggar, *A Collection of Documents Relating to Jacques Cartier and the Sieur de Roberval*, 454–459.

40. 1542–1543. The voyage of Jean François de la Rocque, Sieur de Roberval, to the St. Lawrence and his settlement upstream from Québec. Taken from Hakluyt, *Principal Navigations*, III:240–242.

41. Morison, *The European Discovery of North America: The Northern Voyages*, 441.

42. September 23, 1542. A report on the Cartier-Roberval meeting at Newfoundland based on the deposition of Martin de Actalecu of Fuenterrabia. Translated and printed in Biggar, *A Collection of Documents Relating to Jacques Cartier and the Sieur de Roberval*, 454–459.

43. 1542–1543. The voyage of Jean François de la Rocque, Sieur de Roberval, to the St. Lawrence and his settlement up stream from Québec. Taken from Hakluyt, *Principal Navigations*, III:240–242.

44. 1541–1542. Jacques Cartier's voyage to the St. Lawrence River and his second settlement upstream from Québec. Taken from Hakluyt, *Principal Navigations*, III:232–237.

45. November 12, 1541. An early report of Cartier's third voyage. Copy of a letter written from Nantes to the ambassador of the king of Portugal at the court of France. Taken from Biggar, *A Collection of Documents Relating to Cartier and Roberval*, 406–411.

46. 1542–1543. The voyage of Jean François de La Rocque, Sieur de Roberval, to the St. Lawrence and his settlement upstream from Québec. Taken from Hakluyt, *Principal Navigations*, III:240–242 and Biggar, *The Voyages of Jacques Cartier*, 262–270.

47. April 1541. The Spanish spy's report of the Cartier–Roberval fleet taken from Biggar, *A Collection of Documents Relating to Cartier and Roberval*, 275–278.

48. 1542–1543. The voyage of Jean François de La Rocque, Sieur de Roberval, to the St. Lawrence and his settlement upstream from Québec. Taken from Hakluyt, *Principal Navigations*, III:240–242 and Biggar, *The Voyages of Jacques Cartier*, 262–270.

49. Ibid.

50. Roberval would not use Cartier's name for the settlement or the river.

51. 1542–1543. The voyage of Jean François de La Rocque, Sieur de Roberval, to the St. Lawrence and his settlement upstream from Québec. Taken from Hakluyt, *Principal Navigations*, III:240–242 and Biggar, *The Voyages of Jacques Cartier*, 262–270.

52. Ibid.

53. Ibid.

54. Ibid.

55. Ibid.

56. Morison, *The European Discovery of North America: The Northern Voyages*, 450.

57. 1542–1543. The voyage of Jean François de La Rocque, Sieur de Roberval, to the St. Lawrence and his settlement upstream from Québec. Taken from Hakluyt, *Principal Navigations*, III:240–242 and Biggar, *The Voyages of Jacques Cartier*, 262–270.

58. Ibid.

59. For more information on the Desceliers map, see Morison, *The European Discovery of North America: The Northern Voyages*, 462.

60. In those days the admiral of France was responsible for the defense of the coastline of the country and was not a naval commander. His duties were generally confined to land defense. It is doubtful that Coligny had ever been to sea.

61. McGrath, *The French in Early Florida: In the Eye of the Hurricane*, 66.

62. May–June 1564. The testimony of Guillaume Rouffin, taken from Rojas, Manrique de Rojas's report on the French settlement in Florida 1564, translated by Lucy L. Wenhold in *Florida Historical Quarterly*, 1959; XXXVIII: 45–62.

63. Ibid.

64. Ibid.

65. Laudonnière, *Three Voyages*, 17.

66. Ibid., 18.

67. Ibid.

68. Ibid.

69. Ibid., 22.

70. Ibid., 23.

71. Ibid., 30.

72. In his account of the expedition, Ribault said there were 30 men who remained, Laudonnière reported 28 and Guillaume Rouffin said 26.

73. May–June 1564. The testimony of Guillaume Rouffin, taken from Rojas, Manrique de Rojas's report on the French settlement in Florida 1564, translated by Lucy L. Wenhold in *Florida Historical Quarterly*, 1959; XXXVIII: 45–62.
74. Laudonnière, *Three Voyages*, 34. The French were on Parris Island in South Carolina.
75. Ibid., 35. According to Charles E. Bennett in his translation of Laudonnière's *Three Voyages*, a toise equals 6.396 U.S. feet. Therefore the fort measured 102.336 by 83.148 feet. (From notes, page 220.)
76. Ibid.
77. May–June 1564. The testimony of Guillaume Rouffin, taken from Rojas, Manrique de Rojas's report on the French settlement in Florida 1564, translated by Lucy L. Wenhold in *Florida Historical Quarterly*, 1959; XXXVIII: 45–62.
78. Laudonnière, *Three Voyages*, 44.
79. Ibid., 47.
80. McGrath, *The French in Early Florida: In the Eye of the Hurricane*, 84–91.
81. Le Moyne's narrative as translated in Bennett, *Settlement of Florida — Le Moyne's Narrative and Drawings*, 91.
82. Ibid., 92.
83. Ibid., 93.
84. Laudonnière, *Three Voyages*, 66.
85. The French mistakenly thought that Thimogona was the name of the Indian tribe, but actually it was the word for "enemy" in the language of Satouriona's people.
86. Laudonnière, *Three Voyages*, 66.
87. Ibid., 68.
88. Ibid.
89. Ibid., 70.
90. Ibid., 72–73.
91. Le Moyne's narrative as translated in Bennett, *Settlement of Florida — Le Moyne's Narrative and Drawings*, 92.
92. Laudonnière, *Three Voyages*, 82.
93. Le Moyne's narrative as translated in Bennett, *Settlement of Florida — Le Moyne's Narrative and Drawings*, 95.
94. The area is present-day northern Georgia and southwestern North Carolina. In fact, prior to the discovery of gold in California in 1849, this area was the main source of domestic gold in the United States. There is a state park in North Carolina, Reed Gold Mine, where today a person can experience the thrill of panning for gold or looking for emeralds and sapphires. For more information, see notes in Bennett, *Fort Caroline and Its Leader*, 60.
95. Le Moyne's narrative as translated in Bennett, *Settlement of Florida — Le Moyne's Narrative and Drawings*, 101–102.
96. Ibid., 95.
97. Ibid., 96–97.
98. Laudonnière, *Three Voyages*, 93.
99. Le Moyne's narrative as translated in Bennett, *Settlement of Florida — Le Moyne's Narrative and Drawings*, 99.
100. Laudonnière, *Three Voyages*, 106.
101. Le Moyne's narrative as translated in Bennett, *Settlement of Florida — Le Moyne's Narrative and Drawings*, 110.
102. Laudonnière, *Three Voyages*, 142.
103. July 1565. John Sparke's report on Florida. Taken from Hakluyt, *Principal Navigations*, 537–543.
104. Ibid.
105. McGrath, *The French in Early Florida: In the Eye of the Hurricane*, 126.
106. 1566. Nicholas Le Challeux, *Discours de l'histoire de la Floride*, English translation (London: Henry Denham for Thomas Hackett, 1566).
107. September 11, 1565. Pedro Menéndez de Avilés to Philip II. Translated by Ware, "Letters of Pedro Menéndez de Avilés," in Massachusetts Historical Society Proceedings, second series, 1894; VIII:419–425.
108. Le Moyne's narrative as translated in Bennett, *Settlement of Florida — Le Moyne's Narrative and Drawings*, 113.
109. Ibid.
110. Ibid.
111. McGrath, *The French in Early Florida: In the Eye of the Hurricane*, 147.
112. Ibid., 127.
113. February 18, 1566. Fourquevaux to Charles IX cited in McGrath, *The French in Early Florida: In the Eye of the Hurricane*, 158.
114. October 15, 1565. Pedro Menéndez de Avilés to Philip II. Translated by Ware, "Letters of Pedro Menéndez de Avilés," in Massachusetts Historical Society Proceedings, second series, 1894; VIII:419–425. In his letter, Menéndez reported that there were four Germans in the group he captured on the sandbar.
115. Gourgues, *Histoire memorable de Dominique de Gourgues de la reprinse de l'isle de la Floride, faict par François*, 1568, and included in Hakluyt, *Principal Navigations*, III:357–361.

## Chapter Four

1. March 20, 1565. Capitulations and Asiento between Philip II and Pedro Menéndez de Avilés regarding the conquest of Florida. Translated in Connor, *Pedro Menéndez de Avilés*, "Memorial [Memoir] by Gonzalo Solís de Merás," 259–270.
2. Ibid.
3. Ibid.
4. Ibid.
5. Ibid.
6. Ibid.
7. Ibid.

8. September 11, 1565. Pedro Menéndez de Avilés to Philip II. Translated by Ware, "Letters of Pedro Menéndez de Avilés," in Massachusetts Historical Society Proceedings, second series, VIII:419–425.

9. Ibid.

10. Ibid.

11. Ibid.

12. October 15, 1565. Pedro Menéndez de Avilés to Philip II, in Massachusetts Historical Society Proceedings, second series, VIII:425–439.

13. Gonzalo Solís de Merás's account of Pedro Menéndez de Avilés's attack on the French fort in Florida. Translated in Connor, Pedro Menéndez de Avilés, "Memorial [Memoir] by Gonzalo Solís de Merás," 64–137.

14. Zacatecas was located in northern Mexico and Menéndez mistakenly thought Mexico was much closer that it actually is. He wrote that Santa Elena was "the land of the Indians who are in Mexico"; therefore he assumed that the Appalachian Mountains were part of a mountain chain located in northern Mexico. See October 15, 1565, Pedro Menéndez de Avilés to Philip II. Translated by Ware, "Letters of Pedro Menéndez de Avilés," in Massachusetts Historical Society Proceedings, second series, VIII:425–439.

15. Ibid.

16. Ibid.

17. Ibid.

18. Quinn, New American World: A Documentary History of North America to 1612, 5 vols., II:475.

19. Gonzalo Solís de Merás's account of Pedro Menéndez de Avilés's attack on the French fort in Florida. Translated in Connor, Pedro Menéndez de Avilés, "Memorial [Memoir] by Gonzalo Solís de Merás," 64–137.

20. Ibid.

21. 1566–1567. Gonzalo Solís de Merás's account of the achievements of Pedro Menéndez de Avilés in Florida. Translated in Connor, Pedro Menéndez de Avilés, "Memorial [Memoir] by Gonzalo Solís de Merás," 138–245.

22. Ibid.

23. 1565. Gonzalo Solís de Merás's account of Pedro Menéndez de Avilás's attack on the French fort in Florida. Translated in Connor, Pedro Menéndez de Avilés, "Memorial [Memoir] by Gonzalo Solís de Merás," 64–137.

24. In June 1996 archeologists from the University of South Carolina announced that they had found the remains of Charlesfort at the edge of a golf course on the Marine Corps training base at Parris Island. The fort had lain undiscovered because the Spanish had burned it and built Fort San Felipe and a town, Santa Elena, over the ruins.

25. 1566–1567. Gonzalo Solís de Merás on the achievements of Menéndez de Avilás in Florida. Translated in Connor, Pedro Menéndez de Avilés. Memorial [Memoir] by Gonzalo Solís de Merás. 138–245.

26. Ibid.

27. Ibid.

28. Ibid.

29. Ibid.

30. Ibid.

31. Ibid.

32. Ibid.

33. July 11, 1567. A report by Francisco Martinez, a soldier who accompanied Juan Pardo on his journey into the interior printed in Caravia, La Florida, 2 vols., II:477–480, translated.

34. Captain Juan Pardo's account of his expeditions into the interiors in 1565 and 1566 printed in Caravia, La Florida, 2 vols., II:465–473, translated. Secondary sources on Juan Pardo's expedition are Lowery, The Spanish Settlements Within the Present Limits of the United States 1562–1577, 275–276 and Quinn, North America from First Discovery to Early Settlements, 271–274.

35. 1566–1567. Gonzalo Solís de Merás on the achievements of Menéndez de Avilás in Florida. Translated in Connor, Pedro Menéndez de Avilés, "Memorial [Memoir] by Gonzalo Solís de Merás," 138–245.

36. November 30, 1567. News of Juan Pardo reaches France. Le Prêtre, usher of the Privy Chamber of Charles IX, from Dépêches de M. de Fourquevaux, edited by Douais, I:304–305 translated.

37. Quinn, New American World: A Documentary History of North America to 1612, 5 vols., II:475–477.

38. Circa 1572. A critical report on Florida from an official in Cuba. Wright, The Early History of Cuba, 273–290.

39. Ibid.

40. Ibid.

41. Ibid.

42. Ibid.

43. Ibid.

## Chapter Five

1. March 5, 1496. Letters Patent to John Cabot from King Henry VII, documents in English Archives and cited in Morison, The European Discovery of North America: the Northern Voyages, 159.

2. Ibid.

3. From the household books of Henry VII, cited in Morison, The European Discovery of North America: the Northern Voyages, 219.

4. Letter from John Rut as cited in Morison, The European Discovery of North America: the Northern Voyages, 234.

5. Frobisher Bay, as it is now called, is land-

locked. The real Northwest Passage is located through Baffin's Bay. Roald Amundsen, a Norwegian explorer, was the first to successfully sail through the passage to the Pacific Ocean in 1903.

6. Letters-patent issued to Sir Humfrey Gilbert from Queen Elizabeth I, cited in Morison, *The European Discovery of North America: the Northern Voyages*, 566.

7. Charter in Favor of Sir Walter Raleigh, Knight, for the Discovery and Planting of New Lands in America, March 25, 1584, and cited in Parker, *North Carolina Charters and Constitutions 1578–1698*, 7.

8. Letter written by Edward Hayes, captain of the *Golden Hind*, printed in Hakluyt, *Principal Navigations*, and cited in Morison, *The European Discovery of North America: the Northern Voyages*, 573.

9. Arthur Barlowe's Discourse of the First Voyage, in Hakluyt, *Principall Navigations (1589)*, 728–733.

10. Quinn, *The Roanoke Voyages 1584–1590*, I:159.

11. Ibid., 162.

12. A small 17th-century ship having two or three masts and a flat stern, used in northern Europe as a warship and merchant ship as well as an auxiliary ship to a larger one.

13. In those days the ship that carried the admiral, commander of a fleet of ships, was called the "admiral."

14. Journal of the *Tiger*. In Hakluyt, *Principall Navigations (1589)*, 728–733.

15. Ibid.

16. Letter from Ralph Lane to Richard Hakluyt the Elder and Master H— of the Middle Temple, in Hakluyt, *Principall Navigations (1589)*, 728–733. This is the earliest mention of a fort at Roanoke.

17. Ralph Lane's Discourse on the First Colony. In Hakluyt, *Principall Navigations (1589)*.

18. John White's Narrative of His Voyage, in Hakluyt, *Principall Navigations (1589)*, 764–770.

19. A flyboat was a light European warship of between 70 and 200 tons. It generally had two or three masts and was small, inexpensive and maneuverable — ideal for privateering in coastal waters.

20. John White's Narrative of His Voyage, in Hakluyt, *Principall Navigations (1589)*, 764–770.

21. Ibid.

22. Ibid.

23. Ibid.

24. Ibid.

25. Ibid.

26. Quinn, *The Roanoke Voyages 1584–1590*, II:523.

27. John White's Narrative of His Voyage, in Hakluyt, *Principall Navigations (1589)*, 764–770.

28. Ibid.

29. David W. Stahle et al., "The Lost Colony and Jamestown Droughts," *Science* Vol. 280, no. 5363 (24 April 1998):564–567.

30. John White's Account of the Abortive Voyage of the *Brave* and the *Roe*, in Hakluyt, *Prinicipall Navigations (1589)*, 771–773.

31. John White's Narrative of the 1590 Voyage to Virginia, in Hakluyt, *Principall Navigations (1600)*, 288–295.

32. February 4, 1593. Letter from John White to Richard Hakluyt, in Hakluyt, *Principall Navigations (1589)*, 287–288.

33 According to www.eh.net, the purchasing power in 2005 of £40,000 in 1589 is £6,396,567.21 or approximately $11,817,711.

34. Rosier, *A true relation of the most prosperous voyage made in this present yeere 1605 by Captaine George Waymouth*, originally printed in London in 1605 and later included in Purchas, *Hakluyt Posthumus or Purchas His Pilgrimes, containing a history of the World in Sea Voyages and Lande Travells by Englishmen and Others*, 20 vols., IV:1659–1667.

35. Ibid.

36. Ibid.

37. Ibid.

38. Brown, *Genesis of the United States*, I:46.

39. November, 1606. Relation of John Stoneman on the voyage of the *Richard* and the fate of her men printed in Purchas, *His Pilgrims*, IV:1833–1836.

40. Smith, *The General Historie of Virginia, New England, and the Summer Isles*, 203–204.

41. Brain, *Fort St. George Archaeological Investigations of the 1607–1608 Popham Colony*.

42. 1607–1608. "The relation of the Whole Voyage to Virginia." The author is unknown, but Purchas attributed it to James Davies in the 1614 and following editions of his *Pilgrimage*. Parts of it appeared in Strachey, *The Historie of Travaile into Virginia Britannia*, published in 1612, and can be found in Wright and Freund, eds., *The Historie of Travell into Virginia Britania*, 170–173.

43. Smith, *The General Historie of Virginia, New England and the Summer Isles*, 203–204.

44. December 1, 1607. Sir Ferdinando Gorges reports the first news of the Sagadahoc colony to Lord Salisbury printed in Baxter, *Sir Ferdinand Gorges and His Province of Maine*, 3 vols., III:154–156.

45. December 3, 1607. Gorges reports further to Salisbury on the Sagadahoc colony, printed in Baxter, *Sir Ferdinand Gorges and His Province of Maine*, 3 vols., III:154–156.

46. Ibid.

47. December 1, 1607, Sir Ferdinando Gorges reports the first news of the Sagadahoc colony

to Lord Salisbury, printed in Baxter, *Sir Ferdinand Gorges and His Province of Maine*, 3 vols., III:154–156.

48. February 7, 1608. Gorges reports the return of a further ship from the Sagadahoc colony, printed in Baxter, *Sir Ferdinand Gorges and His Province of Maine*, III:161–164.

49. December 1, 1607. Sir Ferdinando Gorges reports the latest news of the Sagadahoc colony to Lord Salisbury, printed in Baxter, *Sir Ferdinand Gorges and His Province of Maine*, 3 vols., III:154–156.

50. February 7, 1608. Gorges reports the return of a further ship from the Sagadahoc colony, printed in Baxter, *Sir Ferdinand Gorges and His Province of Maine*, 3 vols., III:161–164.

51. Ibid.

52. 1607–1608. "The relation of the Whole Voyage to Virginia," printed in Wright and Freund, eds., *The Historie of Travell into Virginia Britania*, 170–173.

53. Ibid.

54. Quinn, *New American World: A Documentary History of North America to 1612*, 5 vols., III:426.

## Chapter Six

1. Smith, *The General History of Virginia, New England, and the Summer Isles*, bk. 3, ch. 1. Printed in Barbour, *The Complete Works of Captain John Smith (1580–1631)*, 3 vols., II: 140–142.

2. Orders in Council — written by his Majesty's Council for Virginia. Brown, *The Genesis of the United States*, 2 vols., I:80.

3. Ibid.

4. Ibid., 81. They were referring, of course, to the Spanish attack on Fort Caroline and then the French attack by Gourgues on San Mateo.

5. Ibid., 84.

6. In England the word *corn* simply meant small grains; however, the settlers also used the word to denote the maize that the Indians grew. Indian corn or maize was not grown or used in England at this time.

7. Orders in Council — written by his Majesty's Council for Virginia. Brown, *The Genesis of the United States*, 2 vols., I:82.

8. Ibid., 83.

9. Ibid., 84.

10. Ibid.

11. Percy, *Observations gathered out of a discourse of the plantation of the southern colony in Virginia by the English, 1606. Written by that honorable gentleman, Master George Percy*. First published in Purchas, *Hakluyt Posthumus or Purchas His Pilgrimes, containing a history of the World in Sea Voyages and Lande Travells by Englishmen and others*, 20 vols. in 1625, IV;

reprinted in Brown, *The Genesis of the United States*, 2 vols., I:156.

12. Ibid.

13. Ibid., 158.

14. Ibid., 161.

15. It was a good defensive site, as it was fortified and used during the Anglo-Dutch wars in the 1660s and 1670s, during the French and Indian Wars and the Revolution. Kelso and his team of archeologists found the original fort under part of an earthen fort built by the Confederates during the Civil War. For more information on the archeology at Jamestown, visit the Jamestown Rediscovery website at www.apva.org/rediscovery.

16. The Council in Virginia. Letter to the Council of Virginia, June 22, 1607, in the Northumberland Papers: Alnwick mss., vol. 7, and reprinted in Brown, *The Genesis of the United States*, 2 vols., I:107.

17. Smith, *A True Relation of such occurrences and accidents of note as hath hap'ned in Virginia since the first planting of that colony which is now resident in the south part thereof, till the last return from thence. Written by Captain Smith, one of the said colony, to a worshipful friend of his in England*. Published in London in 1608 and reprinted in Barbour, *The Complete Works of Captain John Smith (1591–1631)*, 3 vols., I:29.

18. Smith, *The General History of Virginia, New England, and the Summer Isles*, bk. 3 ch. 1, printed in Barbour, *The Complete Works of Captain John Smith (1580–1631)* 3 vols., II:138.

19. Ibid.

20. August 12, 1607. Sir Walter Cope to the Earl of Salisbury, printed in Barbour, *The Jamestown Voyages under the First Charter*, 2 vols., I:108.

21. Percy, *Observations gathered out of a discourse of the plantation of the southern colony in Virginia by the English, 1606. Written by that honorable gentleman, Master George Percy*. First published in Purchas, *Hakluyt Posthumus or Purchas His Pilgrimes, containing a history of the World in Sea Voyages and Lande Travells by Englishmen and others*, 20 vols. in 1625, IV, and reprinted in Brown, *The Genesis of the United States*, 2 vols., I:165.

22. The Council in Virginia. Letter to the Council of Virginia, June 22, 1607, found in the Northumberland Papers: Alnwick mss., vol. 7, and printed in Barbour, *The Jamestown Voyages under the First Charter*, 2 vols., 78.

23. Ibid.

24. Smith, *The General History of Virginia, New England and the Summer Isles*, bk. 3, ch. 1, printed in Barbour, *The Complete Works of Captain John Smith (1580–1631)*, 3 vols., II:139.

25. Smith, *A True Relation of such occurrences and accidents of note as hath hap'ned in*

*Virginia since the first planting of that colony which is now resident in the south part thereof, till the last return from thence. Written by Captain Smith, one of the said colony, to a worshipful friend of his in England.* Published in London in 1608 and reprinted in Barbour, *The Complete Works of Captain John Smith (1581–1631),* 3 vols., I:33.

26. Percy, *Observations gathered out of a discourse of the plantation of the southern colony in Virginia by the English, 1606. Written by that honorable gentleman, Master George Percy.* First published in Purchas, *Hakluyt Posthumus or Purchas His Pilgrimes, containing a history of the World in Sea Voyages and Lande Travells by Englishmen and others,* 20 vols. in 1625, IV, and reprinted in Brown, *The Genesis of the United States,* 2 vols., I:167.

27. Ibid.

28. Wingfield, *A Discourse of Virginia per Edward Maria Wingfilld,* printed in Barbour, *The Jamestown Voyages under the First Charter,* 2 vols., I:216.

29. Smith, *A True Relation of such occurrences and accidents of note as hath hap'ned in Virginia since the first planting of that colony which is now resident in the south part thereof, till the last return from thence. Written by Captain Smith, one of the said colony, to a worshipful friend of his in England.* Published in London in 1608 and reprinted in Brown, *The Genesis of the United States,* 2 vols., I:35.

30. Ibid., 41.

31. Wingfield, *A Discourse of Virginia per Edward Maria Wingfilld,* printed in Barbour, *The Jamestown Voyages under the First Charter,* 2 vols., I:225.

32. Haile, ed., *Jamestown Narratives Eyewitness Accounts of the Virginia Colony,* 49.

33. Maguel, *Report of what Franciso Maguel, an Irishman, learned in the state of Virginia during the eight months that he was there, July 1, 1610,* translated from Spanish by Maximilian Schele de Vere and printed in Brown, *The Genesis of the United States,* 2 vols., I:393.

34. Ibid., 399.

35. Smith, *A True Relation of such occurrences and accidents of note as hath hap'ned in Virginia since the first planting of that colony which is now resident in the south part thereof, till the last return from thence. Written by Captain Smith, one of the said colony, to a worshipful friend of his in England.* Published in London in 1608 and reprinted in Brown, *The Genesis of the United States,* 2 vols., I:53.

36. Smith, *The General History of Virginia, New England and the Summer Isles,* bk. 3, ch. 3, printed in Barbour, *The Complete Works of Captain John Smith (1580–1631),* 3 vols., II:154.

37. Ibid, 157.

38. Smith, *A True Relation of such occur-*

*rences and accidents of note as hath hap'ned in Virginia since the first planting of that colony which is now resident in the south part thereof, till the last return from thence. Written by Captain Smith, one of the said colony, to a worshipful friend of his in England.* Published in London in 1608 and reprinted in Brown, *The Genesis of the United States,* 2 vols., I:93.

39. Francis Perkins, Letter from Jamestown to a Friend, March 28, 1608, printed in Brown, *The Genesis of the United States,* 2 vols., I:173.

40. Smith, *The General History of Virginia, New England and the Summer Isles,* bk. 3, ch. 5, printed in Barbour, *The Complete Works of Captain John Smith (1580–1631),* 3 vols., II:168.

41. Ibid., 169.

42. Ibid.

43. Ibid.

44. Ibid., ch. 7, 180–181.

45. Ibid., ch. 11, 215.

46. Ibid., ch. 7, 181.

47. Ibid., ch. 8, 194.

48. Ibid., ch. 10, 210.

49. Ibid., 211.

50. Ibid., 208.

51. Ibid., 209.

52. Ibid., ch. 11, 212.

53. Ibid.

54. Ibid., 216.

55. Ibid., 217.

56. The Council of Virginia, *A True and Sincere Declaration of the purposes and ends of the plantation begun in Virginia, of the degrees which it hath received, and means by which it hath been advanced, and the resolution and conclusion of His Majesty's council of that colony for the constant and patient prosecution thereof, until by the mercies of GOD it shall retribute a fruitful harvest to the Kingdom of Heaven and this commonwealth. Set forth by the authority of the governors and councilors established for that plantation,* circulated in England circa 1609 and printed in Brown, *The Genesis of the United States,* 2 vols., I:342.

57. Ibid.

58. Bemiss: *The Three Charters of the Virginia Company of London.* vii.

59. Percy, *A True Relation of the proceedings and occurrents of moment which have hap'ned in Virginia from the time Sir Thomas Gates was shipwrack'd upon the Bermudes, anno 1609, until my departure out of the country, which was in anno Domini 1612,* Elkins 106, Free Library of Philadelphia mss., *Tyler's Quarterly Magazine* 1922; 3:259.

60. Ibid.

61. Ibid.

62. Ibid.

63. Ibid.

64. The Governor and Council in Virginia. Letter to the Virginia Company of London, July

7, 1610, printed in Brown, *The Genesis of the United States*, 2 vols., 405.

65. Strachey, *A True Reportory of the wrack and redemption of Sir Thomas Gates, knight, upon and from the Islands of the Bermudas; his coming to Virginia, and the estate of that colony then, and after under the government of the Lord La Warre. July 15, 1610*, part 4, published in Purchas, *Hakluyt Posthumus or Purchas His Pilgrimes, containing a history of the World in Sea Voyages and Lande Travells by Englishmen and others*, 20 vols., 1734. The "Reportory" was written in the form of a letter to an unknown lady and it somehow managed to fall into the hands of William Shakespeare, who used the story of the shipwreck as the inspiration for his play *The Tempest*.

66. The Council of Virginia, *A True Declaration of the estate of the colony in Virginia, with a confutation of such scandalous reports as have tended to the disgrace of so worthy an enterprise*. Published by advice and direction of the Council of Virginia. Printed in Force, *Tracts and Other Papers, relating principally to the Origin, Settlement, and Progress of the Colonies in North America, from the Discovery of the Country to the Year 1776*, 4 vols., III:21.

67. Ibid., 22.
68. Ibid., 16.
69. David W. Stahle et al., "The Lost Colony and Jamestown Droughts," *Science* Vol. 280, no. 5363 (24 April 1998): 564–567.
70. Morgan, *American Slavery — American Freedom*, 153–154.

## Chapter Seven

1. May 20, 1598. The Parlement of Normandy authorizes the transportation of 250 persons to Canada. Rouen, Archives de la Seine-Inférieure, Parlement de Normandie, Archives Secrètes, 20 Mai 1598, fol. 189v., printed and translated in Morse, *Acadiensia Nova*, 2 vols., II:34–35.
2. Quinn, *North America From Earliest Discovery to First Settlement*, 472.
3. Ibid., 473.
4. March to September 1603. The expedition of François Gravé du Pont and Samuel de Champlain to the St. Lawrence in Champlain, *Des Sauvages, ou voyage de Samuel Champlain, de Brouage, faict en la France l'an mil six cent trois*, edited and translated by Biggar, *The Works of Samuel de Champlain*, 91–189 and cited in Trudel, *The Beginnings of New France*, translated by Patricia Claxton, 67.
5. Cited in Trudel, *The Beginnings of New France*, 69.
6. Cited in ibid., 74.
7. Cited in ibid., 79.
8. Cited in ibid., 81.

9. November 8, 1603. Patent granting a monopoly of trade and settlement to Pierre du Gua, Sieur de Monts translated in Purchas, *Pilgrimes*, IV:1621–1622.
10. Territories over which a nobleman holds jurisdiction. Lands in seigneury can be divided into subfiefs, which can then be given out to individuals. An annual fee is paid to the holder of the seigneury as rent for the land.
11. November 6, 1603. The propositions of the Sieur de Monts to Henry IV for his settlement of Acadia and Henry IV's replies. Morse, *Pierre du Gua, Sieur de Monts*, 6–8, translated.
12. Ibid.
13. April to August, 1604. Voyage to Acadia and the establishment of the settlement on Ste Croix in Champlain, *Les Voyages*, bk. 1, ch. 2–4, translated in Biggar, *The Works of Samuel Champlain*, 233–280.
14. Ibid.
15. Ibid.
16. Ibid.
17. Ibid.
18. Ibid.
19. Ibid.
20. Ibid.
21. Ibid.
22. Ibid.
23. Ibid.
24. Ibid.
25. Trudel, *The Beginnings of New France*, 86.
26. October 1604 to June 1605. The winter experience of the settlers at Ste. Croix, Champlain, *Les Voyages*, ch. 6, translated in Biggar, *The Works of Samuel de Champlain*, 301–311.
27. Ibid.
28. Ibid.
29. Ibid.
30. Ibid.
31. Ibid.
32. June 1605. The establishment of the settlement at Port Royal, Champlain, *Les Voyages*, ch. 10–12, translated in Biggar, *The Works of Samuel de Champlain*, 367–391.
33. Ibid.
34. Ibid.
35. Cited in Trudel, *The Beginnings of New France*, 88.
36. June 1605. The establishment of the settlement at Port Royal, Champlain, *Les Voyages*, ch. 10–12, translated in Biggar, *The Works of Samuel de Champlain*, 367–391.
37. Cited in Trudel, *The Beginnings of New France*, 88.
38. June 1605. The establishment of the settlement at Port Royal, Champlain, *Les Voyages*, , ch. 10–12, translated in Biggar, *The Works of Samuel de Champlain*, 367–391.
39. Ibid.
40. Ibid.

41. Ibid.

42. 1606–1607. Marc Lescarbot's experiences at Port Royal. Lescarbot, *Histoire de la Novelle France*, published in Paris 1609 and translated as *Nova Francia* by Pierre Erondelle in London in 1609 and included in Levermore, *Forerunners and Competitors of the Pilgrims and Puritans*, 2 vols., I: 250–296.

43. Ibid.

44. Ibid.

45. 1606–1607. The second winter at Port Royal and its abandonment in August 1607, Champlain, *Les Voyages*, ch. 16–17, translated in Biggar, *The Works of Samuel de Champlain*, 438–469.

46. 1606–1607. Marc Lescarbot's experiences at Port Royal. Lescarbot, *Histoire de la Novelle France*, published in Paris 1609 and translated as *Nova Francia* by Pierre Erondelle in London in 1609 and included in Levermore, *Forerunners and Competitors of the Pilgrims and Puritans*, 2 vols., I:250–296.

47. Ibid.

48. Ibid.

49. Trudel, *The Beginnings of New France*, 91.

## Chapter Eight

1. 1608. Commission to the Sieur de Monts from Henry IV. Champlain, *Les Voyages*, bk. 2, ch. 1, translated in Biggar, *The Works of Samuel Champlain*, II:3–4.

2. Cited in Trudel, *The Beginnings of New France*, 93.

3. 1608. Champlain's voyage to Canada and his establishment of Québec. Champlain, *Les Voyages*, bk. 2, ch. 1–3, translated in Biggar, *The Works of Samuel de Champlain*, II:3–34.

4. Trudel, *The Beginnings of New France*, 94.

5. Québec is an Algonquin word for "place where the river narrows."

6. 1608. Champlain's voyage to Canada and his establishment of Québec. Champlain, *Les Voyages*, bk. 2, ch. 1–3, translated in Biggar, *The Works of Samuel de Champlain*, II:3–34.

7. Ibid.

8. Ibid.

9. Ibid.

10. Ibid.

11. Ibid.

12. Trudel, *The Beginnings of New France*, 95. Champlain gave the general name *Iroquois* to the traditional enemy of the Algonquins, Montagnais and Hurons when in fact it was only the Mohawk branch of the Iroquois nation that was the enemy.

13. July to October 1609. Champlain's voyage up the St. Lawrence and Richelieu rivers and his return to France. Champlain, *Les Voy-*

*ages*, bk. 2, ch. 9–11, translated in Biggar, *The Works of Samuel Champlain*, II:82–112.

14. Ibid.

15. March 7 to September 25, 1610. Return of Champlain to Canada and his St. Lawrence River expedition in Champlain, *Les Voyages*, bk. 3, ch. 1, translated in Biggar, *The Works of Samuel Champlain*, II:115–154.

16. Ibid.

17. Ibid.

18. If Champlain had been able to go on this expedition in the summer of 1610, the French would have reached Hudson's Bay several weeks before the English, who arrived there on August 3.

19. Quinn, *New American World: A Documentary History of North America to 1612*, 5 vols., IV:316.

20. March 7 to September 25, 1610. Return of Champlain to Canada and his St. Lawrence River expedition. Champlain, *Les Voyages*, bk. 3, ch. 2, translated in Biggar, *The Works of Samuel Champlain*, II:115–154.

21. Ibid.

22. Ibid.

23. March to September 1611. Champlain trades with the Indians of the interior in the vicinity of Montréal in Champlain, *Les Voyages*, bk. 4, ch. 1, translated in Biggar, *The Works of Samuel Champlain*, II:157–214.

24. Ibid.

25. Ibid., ch. 2.

26. Ibid.

27. Ibid. ch. 3.

28. Cited in Trudel, *The Beginnings of New France*, 102.

29. Cited in Trudel, *The Beginnings of New France*, 106.

30. Ibid., 133–134.

31. Parkman, *France and England in North America*, I:313–314.

32. Trudel, *The Beginnings of New France*, 164–165.

33. Parkman, *France and England in North America*, I:318.

34. Cited in Trudel, *The Beginnings of New France*, 173.

35. Parkman, *France and England in North America*, I:325–326.

36. Cited in Trudel, *The Beginnings of New France*, 181.

37. Eccles, *The French in North America, 1500–1783*, 36.

## Chapter Nine

1. Laudonnière, *Three Voyages*, translated by Charles Bennett, 3.

2. Ibid., 4.

3. For more information on the Norse in Greenland, see Dale Mackenzie Brown's article

at www.archaeology.org/online/features/green land/. For climate change, see www.mnh.si. edu/vikings/voyage/subset/greenland/history. html.

4. Quinn, *North America from Earliest Discovery to First Settlements*, 3.

5. Lowery, *The Spanish Settlements Within the Present Limits of the United States, 1513–1561*, 144–145.

6. 1521–1526. Peter Martyr on the voyages of Ayllón and on the supposed customs of the North American Indians. Martyr, *De Orbe Novo*, Dec. VII. lib. ii–iv, edited and translated by MacNutt, 2 vols., II:254–271.

## Chapter Ten

1. Pedro Menéndez de Avilés to Philip II in Caravia, *La Florida*, 2 vols., II:322.

2. 1565. Gonzalo Solís de Merás's account of Pedro Menéndez de Avilés's attack on the French fort in Florida, translated in Connor, *Pedro Menéndez de Avilés*, "Memorial [Memoir] by Gonzalo Solís de Merás," 64–137.

3. 1566. Some episodes on Pedro Menéndez de Avilés by Bartolomé Barrientos, translated in Kerrigan, *Pedro Menéndez de Avilés, Founder of Florida by Bartolomé Barrientos*, 138–142.

4. 1566–1567. Gonzalo Solís de Merás on the achievements of Menéndez de Avilés in Florida, translated in Connor, *Pedro Menéndez de Avilés*, "Memorial [Memoir] by Gonzalo Solís de Merás," 138–245.

5. Circa 1572. A critical report on Florida from an official in Cuba. Wright, *The Early History of Cuba*, 273–290.

6. 1566–1567. Gonzalo Solís de Merás on the achievements of Menéndez de Avilés in Florida, translated in Connor, *Pedro Menéndez de Avilés*, "Memorial [Memoir] by Gonzalo Solís de Merás," 138–245.

7. Ibid.

8. June 15, 1578. Pedro Menéndez Marqués reports on his dealings with the Indians in Florida, printed and translated in Connor, *Colonial Records of Spanish Florida*, 2 vols., II:78–91.

9. April 2, 1579. Pedro Menéndez Marqués reports on his suppression of the Guale Indians, printed and translated in Connor, *Colonial Records of Spanish Florida*, II:224–227.

10. Ibid.

11. June 17, 1586. Pedro Menéndez Marqués to the president of the Casa de Contratación, translated in Wright, *The Early History of Cuba*, 163–164.

12. June 17, 1686. The royal officials of Florida to the Crown, translated in Wright, *The Early History of Cuba*, 164–165.

13. The Council of Virginia, *A True Decla-*

*ration of the estate of the colony in Virginia, with a confutation of such scandalous reports as have tended to the disgrace of so worthy an enterprise.* Published by advice and direction of the Council of Virginia. Printed in Force, *Tracts and Other Papers, relating principally to the Origin, Settlement, and Progress of the Colonies in North America, from the Discovery of the Country to the Year 1776*, 4 vols., III:21.

14. Smith, *The General History of Virginia, New England and the Summer Isles*, bk. 3, ch. 7, printed in Barbour, *The Complete Works of Captain John Smith (1580–1631)*, 3 vols., II:190.

15. Ibid., ch. 9, 205.

16. Ibid., ch. 11, 215.

17. Ibid., 212.

18. The copy of a letter sent to the Treasurer and Councell of Virginia from Captaine John Smith, then President in Virginia in Barbour, *The Complete Works of Captain John Smith (1580–1631)*, ch. 7, 189.

19. John Ratcliffe, alias Sicklemore. Letter to Salisbury, October 4, 1609, printed in Brown, *The Genesis of the United States*, 2 vols., I:335.

20. The Council of Virginia. *A True and Sincere Declaration of the purposes and ends of the plantation begun in Virginia, of the degrees which it hath received, and means by which it hath been advanced, and the resolution and conclusion of His Majesty's council of that colony for the constant and patient prosecution thereof, until by the mercies of GOD it shall retribute a fruitful harvest to the Kingdom of Heaven and this commonwealth. Set forth by the authority of the governors and councilors established for that plantation*, circulated in England circa 1609, printed in Brown, *The Genesis of the United States*, 2 vols., I:339.

21. Strachey, *A True Reportory of the wrack and redemption of Sir Thomas Gates, knight, upon and from the Islands of the Bermudas; his coming to Virginia, and the estate of that colony then, and after under the government of the Lord La Warre. July 15, 1610*, part 3, published in Purchas, *Hakluyt Posthumus or Purchas His Pilgrimes, containing a history of the World in Sea Voyages and Lande Travells by Englishmen and others*, 20 vols., 1734.

22. Ibid.

23. Hamor, *A True Discourse of the present estate of Virginia*, published in England 1615, reprinted in 1860 and 1957 and included in Haile, ed., *Jamestown Narratives, Eyewitness Accounts of the Virginia Colony, The First Decade: 1607–1617*, 814.

24. The Council of Virginia. *A True and Sincere Declaration of the purposes and ends of the plantation begun in Virginia, of the degrees which it hath received, and means by which it hath been advanced, and the resolution and*

conclusion of His Majesty's council of that colony for the constant and patient prosecution thereof, until by the mercies of GOD it shall retribute a fruitful harvest to the Kingdom of Heaven and this commonwealth. Set forth by the authority of the governors and councilors established for that plantation, circulated in England circa 1609, printed in Brown, *The Genesis of the United States*, 2 vols., I:339.

25. The Governor and Council in Virginia. Letter to the Virginia Company of London, July 7, 1610 and printed in Brown, *The Genesis of the United States*, 2 vols., I:412.

26. Strachey, *A True Reportory of the wrack and redemption of Sir Thomas Gates, knight, upon and from the Islands of the Bermudas; his coming to Virginia, and the estate of that colony then, and after under the government of the Lord La Warre, July 15, 1610*, part 4, published in Purchas, *Hakluyt Posthumus or Purchas His Pilgrimes, containing a history of the World in Sea Voyages and Lande Travells by Englishmen and others*, 20 vols., 1734.

27. Records of the Virginia Company, III: 446.

28. Fausz, *The Powhatan Uprising of 1622: A Historical Study of Ethnocentrism and Cultural Conflict*, 514–515.

29. McCary, *Indians in 17th-Century Virginia*, 80.

30. Henings, ed., *The Statutes at Large; Being a Collection of all the Laws of Virginia, from the First Session of the Legislature in the Year 1619*, 13 vols., I:323.

31. Ibid., 324.

32. Ibid.

33. McCary, *Indians in 17th-Century Virginia*, 83.

34. The Council of Virginia, *A True Declaration of the estate of the colony in Virginia, with a confutation of such scandalous reports as have tended to the disgrace of so worthy an enterprise.* Published by advice and direction of the Council of Virginia, 1610, reprinted in Force, ed. *Tracts and Other Papers, relating principally to the Origin, Settlement and Progress of the Colonies in North America, from the Discovery of the Country to the Year 1776.* 4 vols., III:3–4.

35. 1606–1607. Marc Lescarbot's experi-

ences at Port Royal. Lescarbot, *Histoire de la Novelle France*, published in Paris 1609, translated as *Nova Francia* by Pierre Erondelle in London in 1609, and included in Levermore, *Forerunners and Competitors of the Pilgrims and Puritans*, 2 vols. I:250–296.

36. Ibid.

37. Trudel, *The Beginnings of New France*, 167.

38. Ibid., 163–165.

39. Ibid., 165.

40. Cited in ibid., 125.

41. Cited in ibid., 126.

42. Eccles, *The French in North America, 1500–1783*, 26.

43. Trudel, *The Beginnings of New France*, 126–127.

44. Cited in ibid., 125.

45. Cited in ibid., 181.

46. Cited in ibid., 129.

47. Ibid., 170–171.

48. Eccles, *The French in North America, 1500–1783*, 37.

49. Trudel, *The Beginnings of New France*, 279.

50. Winston, *Narrative and Critical History of America*, 326.

51. Ibid., 319.

## Chapter Eleven

1. July 28, 1612. Letter to Sir Thomas Smith, Knight, Treasurer of the English Colony in Virginia from Alexander Whitaker. Whitaker, *Good News From Virginia sent to the Council and Company of Virginia resident in England from Alexander Whitaker. The Minister of Henrico in Virginia*, published in London in 1613, printed in Brown, *The Genesis of the United States*, 2 vols., II:578.

2. Yeoman was the name given to a class of small freeholding farmers in England.

3. Brown, *The Genesis of the United States*, 2 vols., II:895.

4. Smith, The General History of Virginia, New England and the Summer Isles, Bk. 3, Ch. 2, printed in Barbour, *The Complete Works of Captain John Smith (1580–1631)*, 3 vols., II: 144.

# Bibliography

Barbour, Philip L. *The Complete Works of Captain John Smith (1580–1631)*, 3 vols. Chapel Hill: University of North Carolina Press, 1986.

_____. *The Jamestown Voyages Under the First Charter, 1606–1609*, 2 vols., 2nd series, no. CXXXVI. Cambridge, UK: Hakluyt Society, 1969.

Baxter, James P. *Sir Ferdinando Gorges and His Province of Maine*, 3 vols. Boston: Prince Society, 1890.

Bemiss, Samuel M., ed. *The Three Charters of the Virginia Company of London, with Seven Related Documents, 1606–1621.* Williamsburg, VA: 350th Anniversary Celebration Corporation, 1957.

Bennett, Charles E., compiler. *The Settlement of Florida — Le Moyne's Narratives and Drawings.* Gainesville: University of Florida Press, 1968.

Biggar, H. P. *A Collection of Documents Relating to Jacques Cartier and the Sieur de Roberval.* Ottawa: Public Archives of Canada, 1930.

_____. *The Voyages of Jacques Cartier,* Ottawa: Public Archives of Canada, 1924.

_____. *The Works of Samuel de Champlain.* Toronto: Champlain Society, 1922.

Bourne, Edward. *Narratives of the Career of Hernando de Soto*, 2 vols. New York: A. S. Barnes, 1904.

Brain, Jeffrey. *Fort St. George Archaeological Investigations of the 1607–1608 Popham Colony.* Augusta: Maine State Museum and the Maine Historic Preservation Commission, 2007.

Brown, Alexander. *The First Republic in America.* New York: Houghton, Mifflin, 1898.

_____. *The Genesis of the United States,* 2 vols. Boston. 1890. Reprinted New York: Russell & Russell, 1964.

Cartier, Jacques. *Brief recit, & succincte narration de la nagivation faicte es ysles de Canada, Hochelage & Sequenay & autres...* Paris, 1545.

Cole, Robert. *A Traveller's History of France.* New York: Interlink Books, 1995.

Connor, J. T. "Memorial [Memoir] by Gonzalo Solís de Merás." *Pedro Menéndez de Avilés.* Deland: Florida State Historical Society, 1923.

_____, ed. *Colonial Records of Spanish Florida.* Deland: Florida State Historical Society, 1925.

Davenport, Frances Gardiner, ed. *European Treaties Bearing on the History of the United States and Its Dependencies,* vol. I. Washington, D.C.: Carnegie Institution, 1917–1937.

Davis, T. F. "History of Juan Ponce de León's voyages to Florida. Source Records," *Florida Historical Quarterly,* 1935; XIV:53–56.

Dor-Ner, Zvi. *Columbus and the Age of Discovery.* New York: William Morrow, 1991.

Douais, Célestin, ed. *Dépêches de M. de Fourquevaux,* 3 vols. Paris, 1896–1904.

Eccles, W. J. *The French in North America, 1500—1783.* East Lansing: Michigan State University Press, 1998

Fausz, John Frederick. *The Powhatan Uprising of 1622: A Historical Study of Ethnocentrism and Cultural Conflict.* Williamsburg: College of William and Mary in Virginia, 1977.

Force, Peter, ed. *Tracts and Other Papers, relating principally to the Origin, Settlement, and Progress of the Colonies in North America, from the Discovery of the Country to the Year 1776,* 4 vols. Washington: Peter Force, 1836.

Gómera, Francisco López. *Historia general de las Indias,* 2 vols. Madrid, 1932.

Haile, Edward Wright, ed. *Jamestown Narratives, Eyewitness Accounts of the Virginia Colony, The First Decade: 1607–1617.* Champlain, VA: Roundhouse, 1998.

Hakluyt, Richard. *Principal Navigations, 1589.* London: George Bishop, Ralph Newberie and Robert Barker, 1589

_____. *Principal Navigations, III.* London: George Bishop, Ralph Newberie and Robert Barker, 1600.

_____. *A Shorte and Briefe Narration.* London, 1580.

Hening, William Waller, ed. *The Statutes at Large: Being a Collection of all the Laws of Virginia, From the First Session of the Legislature, in the Year 1619.* 13 vols. Charlottesville: Facsimile edition 1809–1823, reprint for the Jamestown Foundation of the Commonwealth of Virginia, 1969.

Herrera y Tordesillas, Antonio de. *Historia general de los hechos de los Castellanos en las isles i tierra firme del mar oceano,* 8 vols. Madrid, 1601.

Hodge, F. W., and T. H. Lewis. *Spanish Explorers in the Southern United States, 1528–1543.* New York, 1906. Reprinted in Denton, Texas, by the Texas State Historical Association, 1990.

Hoffman, Paul E. "Diplomacy and the Papal Donation, 1493–1585." *The Americas,* October 1973; 30(no. 2):151–183.

Kerrigan, Anthony. *Pedro Menéndez de Avilés, Founder of Florida, written by Bartolomé Barrientos.* Gainesville: University Press of Florida, 1965.

Kingsbury, Susan Myra, ed. *The Records of the Virginia Company of London.* 4 vols. Washington, D.C., 1906–1935.

Laudonnière, René. *Three Voyages.* Translated by Charles E. Bennett. Tuscaloosa: University of Alabama Press, 2001.

Le Challeux. *Discours de l'histoire de la Floride.* Dieppe, France: J. Le Sellier, 1566.

Le Moyne de Morgue, Jacques. *Brevis Narratio eorum quae in Florida Americae Provincial Gallis acciderunt, secunda illam Navigationem duce Renato de Laudonniere classis praefecto anno MDLXIIII.* Frankfurt, Germany: Theodore de Bry, 1591.

Lescarbot, Marc. *Histoire de la Nouvelle France, contenant les navigations, découvertes Et habitations faites par les François en les Indes, Occidentales et Nouvelle France.* 3rd ed. Paris: A. Perier, 1618.

Levermore, Charles L. *Forerunners and Competitors of the Pilgrims and Puritans,* 2 vols. Brooklyn, NY: New England Society of Brooklyn, 1912.

Lowery, Woodbury. *The Spanish Settlements Within the Present Limits of the United States 1513–1561.* New York: Russell & Russell, 1959.

_____. *The Spanish Settlements Within the Present Limits of the United States 1562–1577.* New York: Russell & Russell, 1959.

Martyr, Peter. *De Orbe Novo.* Edited and translated by F. A. MacNutt. 2 vols. New York, 1912.

McCarly, Ben C. *Indians in 17th Century Virginia.* Charlottesville: University Press of Virginia, 1957. Jamestown 350th Anniversary Historical Booklet #18.

McGrath, John T. *The French in Early Florida: In the Eye of the Hurricane.* Gainesville: University Press of Florida, 2000.

Morgan, Edmund S. *American Slavery — American Freedom*. New York: W.W. Norton, 1975.

Morison, Samuel Elliot. *The European Discovery of America: The Northern Voyages*. New York: Oxford University Press, 1971.

_____. *The European Discovery of America: The Southern Voyages*. New York: Oxford University Press, 1974.

Morse, W. I. *Acadiensia Nova*, 2 vols. London: Bernard Quaritch, 1935.

_____. *Pierre du Gua, Sieur de Monts*. London: Bernard Quaritch, 1939.

Oviedo, Gonzalo Fernández de. *Historia general y natural de las Indias*, 5 vols. Reprinted in Madrid, 1959.

Parker, Mattie Erma Edwards. *North Carolina Charters and Constitutions 1578–1698*. Raleigh, North Carolina, Charter Tercentenary, 1963.

Parkman, Francis. *France and England in North America*, vol. I. New York: Library of America, 1983.

Purchas, Samuel. *Hakluyt Posthumus or Purchas His Pilgrimes, containing a history of the World in Sea Voyages and Lande Travells by Englishmen and others*, 20 vols. Edinburgh, 1625.

Priestley, Herbert I., ed. *The Luna Papers*, 2 vols. Deland: Florida State Historical Society, 1928.

Quattlebaum, Paul. *The Land Called Chicora*. Gainesville: University Press of Florida, 1956.

Quinn, David B. *New American World: A Documentary History of North America to 1612*, 5 vols. New York: Arno Press and Hector Bye, 1979.

_____. *North America From Earliest Discovery to First Settlements*. New York: Harper & Row, 1977.

_____. *The Roanoke Voyages 1584–1590*. New York: Dover Publications, 1991.

Rojas, Hernando Manrique de. "Manrique de Rojas's report on French settlement in Florida," translated by Lucy L. Wenhold. *Florida Historical Quarterly*, 1959; XXXVIII.

Ruídíaz y Caravia, Eugenio. *La Florida: Su conquista y colonizacíon por Pedro Menéndez de Avilés*, 2 vols. Madrid: Real Academia de la Historia, 1843.

Sanz, Murga Vincente. *Juan Ponce de León*. San Juan, PR, 1959.

Shea, John Gilmary. "Shea Papers." Washington, D.C.: Georgetown University Library, n.d.

Simmons, R. C. *The American Colonies From Settlement to Independence*. New York: W. W. Norton, 1976.

Smith, Captain John. *The General History of Virginia*. London: John Dawson and John Haviland, 1624.

_____. *A True Relation, etc.* London: John Tappe, 1608.

Solís de Merás, Gonzalo. *Pedro Menéndez de Avilés, Adelantado, Governor and Captain-General of Florida: Memorial*, edited and translated by Jeannette Thurber Connor. Deland: Florida State Historical Society, 1923.

Stahle, David W., et al. "The Lost Colony and Jamestown Droughts." *Science* Vol. 280, no. 5363 (24 April 1998):564–567.

Stick, David. *Roanoke Island: The Beginnings of English America*. Chapel Hill: University of North Carolina Press, 1983.

Trudel, Marcel. *The Beginnings of New France 1524–1663*, translated by Patricia Claxton. The Canadian Centenary Series. Toronto: McClelland and Stewart, 1973.

Tyler, Lyon G. "A Trewe Relacyon — Virginia from 1609 to 1612." *Tyler's Quarterly Magazine*, 1922; 3:259–282.

Ware, Henry. "Letters of Pedro Menéndez de Avilés." *Massachusetts Historical Society Proceedings, second series*, 1894.

Winston, Justin. *Narrative and Critical History of America*, vol. IV. New York: Houghton Mifflin, 1884.
Wood, Michael. *Conquistadors*. Berkeley: University of California Press, 2000.
Wright, Irene A. *The Early History of Cuba*. Havana, 1916.
Wright, Louis B., and Virginia Freund, eds. *The Historie of Travell into Virginia Britania (1612) by William Strachey, gent*. 2nd series, no. CIII. London: Hakluyt Society, 1953.
Wroth, Lawrence C. *The Voyages of Giovanni da Verrazzano*, translated by Susan Tarrow. New Haven, CT: Yale University Press, 1970.

# Index

Numbers in **bold italics** indicate pages with illustrations.

LaVergne, TN USA
02 February 2011
214852LV00005B/1/P